THE TIMING OF GUILTY PLEAS

While guilty pleas are the primary mode of criminal case dispositions across different legal jurisdictions, this topic remains an understudied area. The assumption is that defendants are 'playing the system' and that a sliding scale of sentence discounts is necessary to encourage early guilty pleas, which offer utilitarian benefits of efficiency. These assumptions lack a solid empirical foundation. This book offers a comprehensive investigation of how the timing of guilty pleas affects various facets of the criminal process, from the factors that affect this timing, to the effects that the sliding scale of sentence discounts have on sentences and public opinions about them. It also draws comparisons between Western and Asian legal systems, specifically those of England and Wales and Hong Kong. This book is addressed to scholars, legal practitioners, policy-makers, and those interested in criminal justice, socio-legal studies, and empirical legal research.

KEVIN KWOK-YIN CHENG is Associate Professor and Assistant Dean (Research) in the Faculty of Law, The Chinese University of Hong Kong. He has published widely about guilty pleas, plea bargaining, procedural justice, and sentencing. He is co-author of *The Hong Kong Legal System*, 2nd ed. (Cambridge University Press, 2020).

THE TIMING OF GUILTY PLEAS

Lessons from Common Law Jurisdictions

KEVIN KWOK-YIN CHENG
The Chinese University of Hong Kong

CAMBRIDGE
UNIVERSITY PRESS

CAMBRIDGE
UNIVERSITY PRESS

Shaftesbury Road, Cambridge CB2 8EA, United Kingdom

One Liberty Plaza, 20th Floor, New York, NY 10006, USA

477 Williamstown Road, Port Melbourne, VIC 3207, Australia

314–321, 3rd Floor, Plot 3, Splendor Forum, Jasola District Centre, New Delhi – 110025, India

103 Penang Road, #05-06/07, Visioncrest Commercial, Singapore 238467

Cambridge University Press is part of Cambridge University Press & Assessment, a department of the University of Cambridge.

We share the University's mission to contribute to society through the pursuit of education, learning and research at the highest international levels of excellence.

www.cambridge.org
Information on this title: www.cambridge.org/9781009158602

DOI: 10.1017/9781009158626

First published 2023

A catalogue record for this publication is available from the British Library.

Library of Congress Cataloging-in-Publication Data
Names: Cheng, Kevin Kwok-yin, 1985–, author.
Title: The timing of guilty pleas : lessons from common law jurisdictions / Kevin Cheng, The Chinese University of Hong Kong.
Description: Cambridge, United Kingdom ; New York, NY : Cambridge University Press, 2022. | Includes bibliographical references and index.
Identifiers: LCCN 2022032040 (print) | LCCN 2022032041 (ebook) | ISBN 9781009158602 (hardback) | ISBN 9781009158619 (paperback) | ISBN 9781009158626 (epub)
Subjects: LCSH: Pleas of guilty–China–Hong Kong. | Pleas of guilty–England.
Classification: LCC K5458 .C44 2022 (print) | LCC K5458 (ebook) | DDC 345/.072–dc23/eng/20221031
LC record available at https://lccn.loc.gov/2022032040
LC ebook record available at https://lccn.loc.gov/2022032041

ISBN 978-1-009-15860-2 Hardback

To Carol and Owen

CONTENTS

FIGURES

TABLES

PREFACE AND ACKNOWLEDGEMENTS

The topic of guilty pleas has fascinated me for a long time. Most criminal cases across different jurisdictions are disposed by way of guilty pleas, replacing our popular imagination of the adversarial trial. Yet guilty pleas are rather mysterious. Plea bargaining, for instance, is meant to be a secretive affair. When a defendant pleads guilty in court, we are not told of the reasons for why he or she has pleaded guilty, and we quickly move onto the next case. But the guilty plea is pivotal. Not only does it have profound implications for the now convicted defendant, but we are consistently told that without the system of guilty pleas, our criminal justice system would collapse under its own weight. This does not stop us, however, from holding a lot of assumptions about why defendants plead guilty (which will be extensively discussed in this book).

My interest about guilty pleas started from my PhD studies. Prior to the start of my dissertation, I came across the preface of an edition of *Archbold Hong Kong*, where the general editor surprisingly remarked that the high rate of convictions in Hong Kong was 'probably approaching that of North Korea'. What was less surprising was the swift rebuke of this statement by the Hong Kong Judiciary and Department of Justice. One of the main rebuttals to this controversial statement was that the high rate of convictions reflected the combined rates of both guilty pleas and convictions after trial. If the guilty plea rates were removed, then the conviction rates would be more respectable and would be more akin to other common law jurisdictions. What was missing in this whole episode was the question of why then so many people pleaded guilty. This question, and the use of statistics to answer legal questions, planted the seed for my interest in this topic. The question nowadays has increasingly become not just about *whether* the defendant pleads guilty but about *when* the defendant pleads guilty. Sentencing guidelines have been reformed to reflect this. Therefore, this book is about the timing of guilty pleas and the sliding scale of sentence discounts for guilty pleas that has manifested to implement this enhanced shift towards timing.

This book draws on my background in law and in criminology. While the main study focuses on the Crown Court Sentencing Survey (CCSS) and the original dataset of the Hong Kong District Court, this book is informed by my various studies about guilty pleas, plea bargaining, and related topics over the years. It is hoped that this book will be of interest to readers across various disciplines.

This project is generously supported by a General Research Fund (GRF) by the Research Grants Council of Hong Kong, University Grants Committee (Project No. 14609918). I would like to thank Professor Wing Hong Chui, Professor Simon Young, and Dr Rebecca Ong for their support in this endeavor. Special thanks go to Sayaka Ri for her excellent research assistance and to Zenith Lai, Sunny Li, Mona Zhou, and Natasha Pushkarna for their help in coding the Hong Kong dataset. I am also grateful to my acquisitions editor, Joe Ng, for guiding me through the publication process. I would also like to thank John Tai and his team at the Treatise Craftsmen for proofreading the book. The usual disclaimer applies: any remaining errors are my own. I am blessed to have the unwavering support of my wife, Carol, and our son, Owen. It is to them I dedicate this book.

TABLE OF CASES

Attorney General *v.* Lam Ping-chun [1989] 1 HKLR 161; [1989] HKCU 358
Attorney General *v.* Lo Ching-fai [1996] 2 HKCLR 19
Cameron *v.* R (2002) 187 ALR 65
Chan Chi-ming *v.* R [1979] HKLR 491; [1979] HKCU 60
Criminal Practice Directions 2015 [2015] EWCA Crim 1567
DPP *v.* Ping Lin [1976] AC 574
Du Plooy *v.* HM Advocate 2003 SCCR 640
Gall *v.* United States, 552 US 38 (2007)
Gemmell, Robertson, Gibson, and McCourt *v.* HM Advocate [2011] HCJAC 129; 2012 SCCR 176
Gotland Enterprises Ltd *v.* Kwok Chi Yau and Others [2013] 6 HKC 594; [2013] 4 HKLRD 520
Hessell *v.* R [2010] NZSC 135
HKSAR *v.* Abdallah Anwar Abbas [2009] 2 HKLRD 437; [2009] 2 HKC 197
HKSAR *v.* Chan Chun Nam [2018] HKDC 429
HKSAR *v.* Chow Yuen Fai [2010] 1 HKLRD 354; [2010] 1 HKC 181
HKSAR *v.* Fung Chung-keung [2019] HKDC 704
HKSAR *v.* Islam Azharul [2020] HKCA 29
HKSAR *v.* Lam Chor-ping [2010] 1 HKLRD 670
HKSAR *v.* Lam Kai Man [2020] 4 HKLRD 107; [2020] HKCA 624
HKSAR *v.* Lau Wai Wo (2003) HKCFA 624
HKSAR *v.* Lau Wing Fai [2019] HKDC 286
HKSAR *v.* Law Ka-kit [2003] 2 HKC 178
HKSAR *v.* Lo Kam Fai [2016] 2 HKLRD 308; [2016] 4 HKC 204
HKSAR *v.* Ng Kwok Wing [2008] 4 HKLRD 1017
HKSAR *v.* Ngo Van Huy [2005] 2 HKLRD 1; [2004] HKCU 1136
HKSAR *v.* Ngo Van Nam; HKSAR *v.* Abdou Maikido Abdoulkarim [2016] 5 HKLRD 1; [2016] HKCA 397
HKSAR *v.* Shaer Chun-keung [1998] 1 HKLRD 348; [1998] HKCU 137
HKSAR *v.* Wan Wei [2010] 5 HKC 45
HKSAR *v.* Wu Yee-ki [2006] HKCU 1100 CACC 513/2005
Ibrahim *v.* R [1914] AC 599

R *v.* Sang [1980] AC 402
R *v.* Sargeant (1974) 60 Cr App R 74
R *v.* Scales [1987] HKLR 583
R *v.* Thomson and Houlton [2000] NSWCCA 309; (2000) 49 NSWLR 383
R *v.* Turner [1970] 2 QB 321
R *v.* Utton [2019] EWCA Crim 1341
R *v.* Wahab [2003] 1 Cr App R 15; [2002] EWCA Crim 1570
R *v.* Wilson [2012] EWCA Crim 386
R *v.* Wong Man [1993] 1 HKC 80
R *v.* Yu Man-wu [1995] 2 HKLRD 202; [1995] HKCU 450
Scott *v.* R (1989) 89 Cr App R 153
Seabrook *v.* HKSAR [1999] 1 HKLRD 853; [1999] 1 HKC 567
Secretary for Justice *v.* Chau Tsz-tim and Ho Wan-chiu [2015] 2 HKC 88
Secretary for Justice *v.* Hii Siew-cheng [2009] 1 HKLRD 1; [2008] 3 HKC 323
Secretary for Justice *v.* Lam Tat Ming [2000] 2 HKLRD 431
Secretary for Justice *v.* Wong Chi-fung and Others [2018] HKCFA 4; [2018] 2 HKC 50
Secretary for Justice *v.* Yan Shen [2012] 3 HKC 557; [2012] 3 HKLRD 652
Solicitor (24/07) *v.* Law Society of Hong Kong [2008] 11 HKCFAR 117
Spence *v.* HM Advocate [2007] HCJAC 64; 2007 SCCR 592
United States *v.* Booker, 543 US 20 (2005)
Woolmington *v.* DPP [1935] AC 462ss

TABLE OF LEGISLATION

Sentencing Act 2002 (New Zealand)
s. 9
Sentencing Act 2017 (SA)
s. 39
s. 40
Sentencing Act 2020 (UK)
s. 52
s. 59(1)
s. 60(3)
s. 60(4)
s. 65(2)
Sentencing Code 2020 (UK)
s. 52
s. 73
Supreme Court Ordinance (No. 12) of 1873 (Hong Kong)
s. 5

ABBREVIATIONS

BAME	Black, Asian, and minority ethnic
CCSS	Crown Court Sentencing Survey
DAB	Democratic Alliance for the Betterment and Progress of Hong Kong
ICCPR	International Covenant on Civil and Political Rights
PACE	Police and Criminal Evidence Act 1984

1

Introduction

The History of the Problem of 'Cracked Trials'

When the judge, sitting on high in the courtroom, utters the word 'guilty' looking down at the defendant, a sense of dread often emerges. Despite putting the prosecution's case to the test, cross-examining witnesses, and raising legal defences, the state still successfully discharges its burden of proof. The defendant now faces the reality that they have been convicted; the question of guilt or innocence is closed. Thoughts then turn to sentencing: what sentence will the court impose? Are there any prospects for a non-custodial sentence? If it is imprisonment, will it last long?

On the other hand, if the defendant instead utters the word 'guilty' from behind the stand, looking up at the judge, there is likely a sense of relief. The prosecution does not need to prepare their case, witnesses do not need to be called, a trial does not need to be scheduled, and the court can cross another case off its long daily court list. The question of guilt or innocence need not be tested, and the court can proceed immediately from plea arraignment to sentencing. Aside from the question of what sentence the defendant will receive, one now also wonders how much of a sentence discount should be given for the guilty plea.

Guilty pleas supposedly enable the criminal justice system to continue to function by avoiding time-consuming and resource-intensive adversarial trials. In trials, a court is scheduled to hear the case; witnesses are called, examined, and cross-examined; evidence is scrutinised; and legal defences are raised. The court can make a final determination only after this process. On the other hand, when a defendant pleads guilty, all parties understand the charge(s) and agree to the brief facts; unless the court calls for reports, the case jumps to the final stage of sentencing. Indeed, across multiple jurisdictions, guilty pleas are the primary mode of disposing of criminal cases.[1] For instance, in the Crown Court of

[1] A. Ashworth and M. Redmayne, *The Criminal Process*, 4th ed. (Oxford: Oxford University Press, 2010).

England and Wales, the guilty plea rate is around 70 per cent.[2] A similar rate of 70 per cent is found for the higher courts of Australia; the rate for the Magistrates' Courts of Australian states is even higher at over 80 per cent.[3] Likewise, in Hong Kong, the rate is around 75–80 per cent in the District Court and nearly 80 per cent in the High Court.[4] Lastly, the rate in United States District Courts is nearly 97 per cent.[5]

Guilty pleas are so prevalent that some consider them to replace the adversarial trial as the emblematic representation of the criminal justice system. McConville and Mirsky observe that

> [b]oth the English and American systems maintain that they protect the accused from arbitrary accusations of the state ... While both systems celebrate the jury trial as the preferred method of exercising legal rationality, their ideology and structure favours guilty pleas over trials. Thus, while some defendants may assert their right to trial, with a residue of acquittals and favourable rulings, most defendants (regardless of whether there is legally sufficient evidence) are systematically discouraged from testing the state's evidence and relying on traditional notions of adversarialness, as a guarantor of due process. And those who proceed to trial and are convicted are significantly disadvantaged, in the sentences they receive.[6]

Nevertheless, most jurisdictions still regard the right to a fair trial as essential. Article 9 of the International Covenant on Civil and Political Rights (ICCPR) states, 'Anyone arrested or detained on a criminal charge shall be brought promptly before a judge or other officer authorised by law to exercise judicial power and shall be entitled to trial within a reasonable time or to release.' Article 14 further stipulates that '[a]ll persons shall be equal before the courts and tribunals. In the determination of any criminal charge against him, or of his rights and obligations

[2] Ministry of Justice, 'Criminal court statistics quarterly, England and Wales, January to March 2018 (annual 2017)' (2018), available at assets.publishing.service.gov.uk.

[3] A. Freiberg, 'Non-adversarial approaches to criminal justice' (2007) 16 *Journal of Judicial Administration*, 205–22.

[4] S. Lo, K. K. Cheng, and W. H. Chui, *The Hong Kong Legal System*, 2nd ed. (Cambridge: Cambridge University Press, 2020).

[5] Sourcebook of Criminal Justice Statistics, 'Mode of conviction in U.S. District Courts for U.S. Sentencing Commission guideline cases, by primary offense' (2010), available at www.albany.edu/sourcebook/tost_5.html#5_t.

[6] M. McConville and C. Mirsky, 'Looking through the guilty plea glass: the structural framework of English and American state courts' (1993) 2 *Social & Legal Studies*, 173–93, p. 174.

in a suit at law, everyone shall be entitled to a fair and public hearing by a competent, independent and impartial tribunal established by law'.

A long history of scholarly debate exists regarding the merits of guilty pleas. Some claim that guilty pleas are a necessary and pragmatic solution for the system to function efficiently.[7] Others have argued against the caseload pressure rationale, pointing to the fact that high guilty plea rates continue to prevail in jurisdictions with lighter caseloads.[8] Recently, the question is increasingly not just about *whether* a defendant pleads guilty; the question of *when* a defendant pleads is also key. However, the issue of the timeliness of pleas has not received enough attention. Courts welcome guilty pleas if they are timely – that is, *early*. Conversely, *late* guilty pleas are less welcomed. It is asserted that if a defendant pleads guilty on the first day of trial, right before the trial is scheduled to commence, then the time and effort that all parties – the courtroom that has been set aside, the judge who will hear the case, witnesses, all the court staff, and perhaps jurors – have spent in preparing for the case will have been in vain.[9]

7 A. Flynn and A. Freiberg, *Plea Negotiations: Pragmatic Justice in an Imperfect World* (Cham: Palgrave Macmillan, 2018); R. E. Scott and W. J. Stuntz, 'Plea bargaining as contract' (1992) 101 *Yale Law Journal*, 1909–68. Even judges have long argued that guilty pleas and plea bargaining are a 'necessary evil'. For instance, writing specifically about plea bargaining in the United States in his dissenting opinion on the Supreme Court case of *Lafler* v. *Cooper*, 566 US 156 (2012), the late Justice Scalia (joined by Justice Thomas) remarked at 12 that:

> In the United States, we have plea bargaining a-plenty, but until today it has been regarded as a necessary evil. It presents grave risks of prosecutorial overcharging that effectively compels an innocent defendant to avoid massive risk by pleading guilty to a lesser offense; and for guilty defendants it often – perhaps usually – results in a sentence well below what the law prescribes for the actual crime. But even so, we accept plea bargaining because many believe that without it our long and expensive process of criminal trial could not sustain the burden imposed on it, and our system of criminal justice would grind to a halt.

8 M. Heumann, 'A note on plea bargaining and case pressure' (1975) 9 *Law & Society Review*, 515–28; D. Lynch, 'The impropriety of plea agreements: a tale of two counties' (1994) 19 *Law & Social Inquiry*, 115–34; P. F. Nardulli, 'The caseload controversy and the study of criminal courts' (1979) 70 *Journal of Criminal Law and Criminology*, 89–101.

9 An often-cited benefit of guilty pleas is that it spares witnesses, and particularly victims, the distress of having to testify and face cross-examination. With cracked trials, witnesses have a longer period of anxiety while preparing to testify compared to trials with early guilty pleas. See P. Robertshaw, '"Cracked trials" – what is happening?' (1992), 39 *Criminal Law Review*, 867–71.

The United Kingdom's Ministry of Justice has referred to late guilty pleas as '[one] of the worst inefficiencies'.[10] When guilty pleas are entered late, the time and resources they are meant to spare the court are lost. In other words, a late guilty plea wastes the court's time and resources; this cancels out the utilitarian benefits guilty pleas are supposed to achieve. Nevertheless, late guilty pleas lead to 'cracked trials'. A cracked trial is one that does not proceed on the scheduled day of trial, yet does not need rescheduling, as the case has already reached an outcome. Cracked trials are distinguished from 'ineffective trials', which are those rescheduled for other dates.[11] In 2017, the proportion of effective trials in the Crown Court – that is, trials that proceeded as scheduled – was only 51 per cent. That same year, 15 per cent of trials were categorised as 'ineffective', while 34 per cent were considered as having 'cracked'. A similar trend was observed in the Magistrates' Courts, with only 47 per cent of trials being effective, whereas 15 per cent were ineffective and 38 per cent were considered as having cracked.[12] Estimates suggest that in the Magistrates' Courts alone, the combination of ineffective and cracked trials costs the British taxpayer £173 million per year.[13] While trials can 'crack' for several reasons, such as the prosecution withdrawing all charges or the defendant being bound over, the predominant reason is the defendant entering a late guilty plea.[14] In 2017, late guilty pleas accounted for 67 per cent of cracked trials in the Crown Court and half of cracked trials in the Magistrates' Courts.[15]

Playing the System

Why do defendants enter late guilty pleas? According to official discourse, cracked trials are caused by tactical defendants who 'play the system' by delaying their pleas. The clearest indication of this discourse is

[10] Ministry of Justice, *Breaking the Cycle: Effective Punishment, Rehabilitation and Sentencing of Offenders* (London: HMSO, 2010), p. 63.

[11] Ministry of Justice, *Swift and Sure Justice: The Government's Plan for Reform of the Criminal Justice System* (London: HMSO, 2012).

[12] Ministry of Justice, 'Criminal court statistics quarterly'.

[13] J. Bourn, *Crown Prosecution Service: Effective Use of Magistrates' Courts Hearings* (London: National Audit Office, 2006).

[14] Reasons for ineffective trials include the unreadiness of the prosecution or the defence, the absence of prosecution or defence witnesses, the absence of the defendant, and the unavailability of an interpreter.

[15] Ministry of Justice, 'Criminal court statistics quarterly'.

found within the history of the various commissions, committees, and reports that have come out of England and Wales over the past four decades. For instance, referencing an earlier report by the English Bar Association,[16] the Royal Commission on Criminal Justice had this to say:

> As the Seabrook Committee argued, the most common reason for defendants delaying a plea of guilty until the last minute is a reluctance to face the facts until they are at the door of the court. It is often said too that a defendant has a considerable incentive to behave in this way. The longer the delay, the more the likelihood of witnesses becoming intimidated or forgetting to turn up or disappearing. And, if the defendant is remanded in custody, he or she will enjoy the privileges of an unconvicted remand prisoner whereas, once a guilty plea has been entered, the prisoner enters the category of convicted/unsentenced and loses those privileges.[17]

Here, the Royal Commission suggests that factually guilty defendants choose to plead not guilty, hoping that they will nonetheless be legally acquitted. By delaying their pleas and extending the time before the court formally convicts them, they increase the possibility that witnesses may fail to appear and testify, making the state's burden of proving guilt beyond a reasonable doubt more difficult, if not impossible. As a result, by taking advantage of the criminal procedure, guilty defendants may still receive acquittal. Moreover, as long as the court does not convict the defendant, they remain innocent in the eyes of the law. Even if the defendant has been denied bail and remanded in custody, they will not have to serve time in prison.

The image of the tactical defendant was again picked up in Sir Robin Auld's *Review of the Criminal Courts of England and Wales*, commonly known as the Auld Report, which attributed the problem of cracked trials to 'guilty defendants only pleading guilty at the last minute, and of guilty defendants taking their chance with a trial hoping that something may just save them from conviction'.[18] Although the Auld Report acknowledged that other reasons may exist for why defendants do not plead guilty at an earlier stage, such as inadequate preparations by the prosecution or the defence, the delay also has to do with defendants'

[16] R. Seabrook, *The Efficient Disposal of Business in the Crown Court* (London: The General Council of the Bar, 1992).

[17] Royal Commission on Criminal Justice, *Report (Cm 2263)* (London: HMSO, 1993), p. 112.

[18] R. Auld, *Review of the Criminal Courts of England and Wales* (London: Lord Chancellor's Department, 2001), p. 436.

'short-term considerations of retaining as long as possible their right to bail or their privileges as unconvicted remand prisoners'.[19] Instead of presuming innocence, this discourse presumes guilt.[20] In particular, defendants who are granted bail after pleading not guilty can further enjoy their freedom. Yet official discourse also emphasises that remanded defendants also delay their pleas to enjoy the status of a defendant remanded in custody as opposed to that of a convicted offender. Once again, the problem is attributed to guilty defendants tactically taking advantage of the criminal justice system, hoping to escape conviction. In response to the Auld Report, the government of the United Kingdom presented a white paper titled *Justice for All* a year later, which called for 'new procedures which get the case to trial quickly, with reduced chances of the accused "playing the system", and escaping justice'.[21]

Besides England and Wales, other jurisdictions have also attributed late guilty pleas to tactical defendants. In Australia, for example, a report on appropriate early guilty pleas by the New South Wales Law Reform Commission found that defendants who have a prior offence history are more likely to plead guilty late. The report concluded, 'This may suggest that those with a prior offence history, and therefore more knowledge of the system, consider that the benefits of pleading early are not worth the advantages they can get from pleading late.'[22]

Courts have cited the conclusions from these aforementioned reports as evidence to promote change regarding guilty pleas. In the landmark English Court of Appeal case of *Goodyear*, the Royal Commission on Criminal Justice report (1993), the Auld Report (2001), and the *Justice for All* white paper (2002) were all cited to justify the court giving an advanced indication of sentence to defendants who wished to know the maximum sentence that would be imposed if a guilty plea was entered (a topic discussed in greater detail in Chapter 3). The court's rationale,

[19] Ibid.

[20] The presumption of innocence is a longstanding pillar of English common law. This is represented in the often quoted 'golden thread' remark by the House of Lords in *Woolmington* v. *DPP* [1935] AC 462 at 481–2: 'Throughout the web of the English criminal law one golden thread is always to be seen, that is the duty of the prosecution to prove the guilt . . . No matter what the charge or where the trial, the principle that the prosecution must prove the guilt of the [defendant] is part of the common law of England and no attempt to whittle it down can be entertained.'

[21] Home Office, *Justice for All (Cm 5563)* (Norwich: The Stationery Office, 2002), p. 32.

[22] New South Wales Law Reform Commission, *Encouraging Appropriate Early Guilty Pleas (Report 141)* (Sydney: New South Wales Law Reform Commission, 2014), p. 28.

taken verbatim from the Auld Report, was that advanced indication would 'enable the guilty defendant and those advising him to evaluate the judge's indication and assess the advantage or otherwise of proceeding with a plea'.[23]

However, this approach has been criticised. As McConville and Marsh argue, 'The court in *Goodyear* proceeded on the basis that the locus of the problem lay in defendants delaying their plea for *tactical* reasons relating to sentence and [relied on extracts from] the various [Government] Reports cited above without, however, paying *any* attention to the basis of these extracts.'[24] Responding to the Royal Commission on Criminal Justice report (1993), Bridges was even more direct in his critique. He pointedly professed that the report 'is a document that is slip-shod in its use of empirical evidence, slippery in its argumentation, and shameful in its underlying political purposes'.[25] The conclusion that late guilty pleas are caused by defendants whose aim is to play the system thus lacks empirical support. Even though the various reports and the court have referenced each other, the image of the tactical late-pleading defendant was not based on empirical evidence in the first place. Empirical research is therefore still needed to understand why defendants enter late guilty pleas. This book directly addresses that need.

Enhancing Efficiency

The purpose of the guilty plea is clear: to enhance the efficiency of the criminal justice system. Yet guilty pleas have not always dominated the system. Throughout the mercantile era (1800–45), jury trials were the predominant mode of adjudication.[26] At that time, both public and private prosecutions were primarily conducted through jury trials. A shift occurred during the pre-industrialisation period (1850–65), where the guilty plea process replaced jury trials as the predominant mode of adjudication. In a historical quantitative analysis of London's Old Bailey cases, Feeley found that until 1835, virtually all adjudications – between 95 and 98 per cent – were conducted through jury trials. A sharp

[23] *R* v. *Goodyear* [2005] EWCA Crim 888; [2005] 1 WLR 2532 at paragraph 42.

[24] M. McConville and L. Marsh, *Criminal Judges: Legitimacy, Courts and State-Induced Guilty Pleas in Britain* (Cheltenham: Edward Elgar, 2014), p. 100.

[25] L. Bridges, 'Normalizing injustice: The Royal Commission on Criminal Justice' (1994) 21 (1) *Journal of Law and Society*, 20–38, p. 20.

[26] M. McConville and C. Mirsky, *Jury Trials and Plea Bargaining: A True History* (Oxford: Hart, 2005).

increase in guilty pleas then occurred at the turn of the twentieth century, with guilty pleas growing to account for around 40 per cent of case dispositions in the Old Bailey.[27] This trend continued until jury trials became the exception rather than the norm.[28]

Langbein suggests that the increased complexity of trials, with the implementation of complicated procedures and the constant challenging of evidence, made guilty pleas and plea bargaining necessary to deal with heavy caseloads in the criminal courts. In the early nineteenth century, trials were dominated by judges who needed not to resort to the laws of evidence and point to rules regarding inadmissibility, as they had unfettered authority in commenting on the merits of cases and rejecting jury verdicts. Trials were also free of professional lawyers (defendants were typically self-represented), which made early proceedings efficient. The subsequent introduction of the privilege against self-incrimination ensured that defendants came to rely on counsel as their intermediary without saying much in their own defence. Lastly, jury trials at the time resembled present-day sentencing hearings as the trials discussed both guilt and punishment simultaneously.[29] The role of the self-represented defendant was not to challenge evidence or rigorously cross-examine witnesses, but to provide mitigating factors, offer testimony of good character, and plead for mercy in the hope of receiving a lighter

27 M. Feeley, 'Legal complexity and the transformation of the criminal process: the origins of plea bargaining' (1997) 31 *Israel Law Review*, 183–222 at 196. A similar upward trend can be found in the United States. For example, in the New York State Supreme Court in New York City, 75 per cent of cases were disposed through trials in 1846; by 1860, trials only represented around half of all cases. Similarly, in New Haven, Connecticut, trials represented nearly 80 per cent of cases in 1837, but had fallen to half of all cases in 1888 and much further to a dismal 3 per cent by 1934.

28 Trial by jury holds great symbolic value. Lord Devlin famously encapsulated its importance for democracy: 'Each jury is a little parliament. The jury sense is the parliamentary sense. I cannot see the one dying and the other surviving. The first object of any tyrant in Whitehall would be to make Parliament utterly subservient to his will; and the next to overthrow or diminish trial by jury, for no tyrant could afford to leave a subject's freedom in the hands of twelve of his countrymen. So that trial by jury is more than an instrument of justice and more than one wheel of the constitution: it is the lamp that shows that freedom lives.' See P. Devlin, *Trial by Jury* (London: Stevens & Sons Limited, 1956), p. 164. Nowadays, however, the symbolic value of the jury may outweigh its practical significance. See P. Darbyshire, 'The lamp that shows freedom lives – is it worth the candle?' (1991) *Criminal Law Review*, October, 740–52.

29 J. H. Langbein, 'Understanding the short history of plea bargaining' (1979), 13 *Law & Society Review*, 261–72.

punishment.[30] Thus, guilty pleas should not simply be viewed as replacing adversarial trials; instead, it was because trials became more adversarial that courts became more reliant on guilty pleas. As Langbein explains, 'Jury trial was a summary proceeding. Over the intervening two centuries the rise of the adversary system and the related development of the law of evidence has caused common law jury trial to undergo a profound transformation, robbing it of the wondrous efficiency that had characterized it for so many centuries.'[31]

Fisher argues that the rise of guilty pleas occurred because it served the interests of all three major courtroom actors: prosecution, defendants, and judges. For prosecutors, guilty pleas offered a quicker way to handle caseloads and make money, given that many at the time worked part time. For defendants, the newly minted testimony rights led to an unintended increase in pleas. While being allowed to testify in their own trials, veteran offenders instead chose to plea bargain, as they did not want to stand trial for their previous records and face lesser chances of acquittal. Lastly, judges at the time were faced with unbearable caseloads, given their dual responsibility of hearing both criminal and civil matters. As industrialisation caused an enormous number of personal injury cases to arise, plea bargaining offered a quick way for judges to dispose of their criminal obligations.[32]

Efficiency has always been an underlying theme of criminal justice; this certainly remains true in modern times. For instance, the mission of the Royal Commission on Criminal Justice was to scrutinise the effectiveness of the English criminal justice system in the early 1990s with respect to securing the convictions of guilty defendants and acquitting the innocent, paying particular attention to the efficient use of court resources. The commission identified tactical defendants as those who delay the process by not making early pleas, thereby causing inefficiencies in the criminal justice system. Likewise, the Auld Report unwaveringly asserts, 'Guilty defendants seeking to avoid conviction have not the same urgency as the public about the need for an efficient criminal justice

30 Feeley, 'Legal complexity'. Trials at that time combined the determination of guilt and sentencing together, unlike today, where sentencing is considered only after guilt is determined. Moreover, until the nineteenth century, all felonies in England were punishable by death. Therefore, to make a convincing plea for mercy, the defendant had to admit some guilt at trial.

31 Langbein, 'Understanding the short history of plea bargaining', 262.

32 G. Fisher, *Plea Bargaining's Triumph: A History of Plea Bargaining in America* (Stanford: Stanford University Press, 2004).

system.'[33] The courts have also underscored the utilitarian benefits of defendants pleading guilty early. For instance, Hughes LJ had stated:

> The expenditure in public time and money on trials and on preparation for trials is considerable. The case must be thoroughly prepared so that the exacting standard of proof rightly required in a criminal case can be met. Further investigation is likely to be necessary, as may the assembly of a good deal more evidence, lay and expert. Such steps are necessary, but expensive. They are avoided or much reduced by an admission of guilt. The public's limited resources can then be concentrated on those cases where a trial will really be necessary, and such cases will not be delayed, often with accused persons in custody. At present something of the order of 75 per cent of all Crown Court cases result in pleas of guilty; if in all those cases the defendants were out of defiance or otherwise to insist on each detail of the case being proved to the hilt the administration of criminal justice would be in danger of collapse.[34]

Lastly, the theme of efficiency goes hand in hand with the decade of austerity that the English criminal justice system experienced throughout the 2010s.[35]

The pursuit of efficiency in the criminal justice system has also extended beyond England and Wales to other jurisdictions. For instance, the Sentencing Advisory Council of Victoria remarked that 'a plea of guilty can be regarded as the optimum outcome of criminal proceedings'.[36] In Hong Kong, former director of Public Prosecutions Grenville Cross wrote in a major local daily newspaper that 'plea bargaining has traditionally had few friends in Hong Kong'; however, citing the English example as inspiration, he remarked, 'In England and elsewhere, those concerned with criminal justice have asked themselves important questions, of late, concerning the conduct of cases – and Hong Kong cannot afford to be left behind. This, after all, is the era of the proactive judge and effective case management'.[37] Given the close legal heritage that other common law jurisdictions, such as Australia and

[33] Auld, *Review of the Criminal Courts*, p. 395.

[34] *R* v. *Caley and Others* [2012] EWCA Crim 2821 at paragraph 6.

[35] The past decade in Britain has witnessed funding cuts to the police, prisons, and the courts. For example, the Ministry of Justice budget has been reduced by over a quarter. Moreover, funding for legal aid fell by 31 per cent from 2010 to 2018. See FT Editorial Board, 'British criminal justice needs an urgent repair: years of cuts to funding have stretched police, prisons and the courts', *Financial Times*, 27 November 2019.

[36] Sentencing Advisory Council, *Sentence Indication and Specified Sentence Discounts: Final Report* (Melbourne: Sentencing Advisory Council, 2007), p. 15.

[37] G. Cross, 'The case for plea bargaining', *South China Morning Post*, 8 September 2006.

Hong Kong[38], have with England and Wales, reforms that take place in England may proliferate throughout the common law world.

Sentence Discounts

To reduce 'the chances of the accused "playing the system"', the *Justice for All* white paper called for reforms to 'make it clear that early guilty pleas will be matched with appropriate sentence discounts'.[39] Sentence discounts have long been tied to the utilitarian value of saving time and resources. Defendants who plead guilty can expect to receive a lighter sentence compared to the sentence they would have received had they been convicted after trial following a plea of not guilty. This principle is well established in the common law world.[40] This chapter provides an introduction to sentence discounts, while Chapter 2 goes into extensive detail about the sliding scale of sentence discounts in different legal jurisdictions.

Although the final amount for the discount is left to judicial discretion, a one-third sentence discount is usual practice.[41] For example, if a defendant would receive six years of imprisonment if the court convicted them after trial, pleading guilty would lead to them only having to face four years of imprisonment because of a one-third sentence reduction of two years. In England and Wales, sentence discounts were often applied so long as the defendant pleaded guilty before trial.[42] This was the

[38] Hong Kong was under British colonial rule from 1841 until the People's Republic of China (PRC) resumed the exercise of sovereignty in 1997.

[39] Home Office, *Justice for All*, p. 32.

[40] In the case of *Caley* at paragraph 1, Hughes LJ notes that there is a 'long established practice in sentencing which recognises that a distinction should ordinarily be drawn between a defendant who admits his guilt and one who does not'.

[41] The practice of giving a one-third sentence discount for a guilty plea is found in both England and Wales as well as in Hong Kong. See, for example, G. Cross and P. S. W. Cheung, *Sentencing in Hong Kong*, 8th ed. (Hong Kong: LexisNexis, 2018), p. 354. In other jurisdictions, such as New Zealand, the upper limit is a one-quarter discount.

[42] The sentence discount may be reduced from one-third if the defendant pleads guilty during trial. For example, in the Hong Kong case of *HKSAR* v. *Lam Chor-ping* [2010] 1 HKLRD 670, the defendant pleaded guilty after a six-day hearing, changing his plea from an initial plea of not guilty. The trial judge gave the defendant a discount for the plea of less than one-quarter of the sentence. When the defendant later appealed against his sentence, the Court of Appeal rejected it. The court reasoned in paragraphs 16–18 that:

> In the present case, it is true the applicant pleaded guilty in the end, thereby saving expenses in respect of jurors' fees and avoiding inconvenience which

pattern prior to the creation of advisory bodies such as the Sentencing Advisory Panel and the Sentencing Guidelines Council. However, the discount did not account for the stage of the proceedings at which the plea was made. Hence, the practice could not address the problem of late guilty pleas.

Since the 1970s, the Court of Appeal in England and Wales has issued guideline judgments, but they have been rare and only cover a limited number of offences. Eventually, the Crime and Disorder Act 1998 created the Sentencing Advisory Panel to advise the Court of Appeal on sentencing guidelines. The panel consulted on proposals for various guidelines and drafted them for the court's consideration. While the court was not obliged to accept the panel's recommendations, it did so more often than not. This changed under the Criminal Justice Act of 2003. The Sentencing Advisory Panel no longer advised the court, while the newly created Sentencing Guidelines Council became the sole authority to issue definitive sentencing guidelines. This marked a departure from the court being the sole authority to issue sentencing guidelines.

In 2010, the Sentencing Council of England and Wales succeeded both the Sentencing Guidelines Council and the Sentencing Advisory Panel. An independent public body, the council is responsible for developing sentencing guidelines. When sentencing, the courts must now follow the relevant sentencing guidelines for the case in question. This arguably makes the guidelines more binding on the courts.[43] So far, the council has issued definitive sentencing guidelines for most common offences, including assault, burglary, and drug offences, as well as generic guidelines applying to all offences. The goal of these sentencing guidelines is to promote greater consistency in sentencing outcomes and provide a more accurate forecast of prison populations.[44]

To tackle the problem of cracked trials in particular, the Sentencing Guidelines Council introduced a 'sliding scale of sentence discounts' in

> might otherwise be caused to the jurors. However, the applicant had initially objected to his admissions being adduced as evidence, as a result of which the Court had to hold a six-day hearing in order to determine the issue. The applicant's conduct not only wasted the Court's time and prevented the Court from dealing with other cases more expeditiously, but also wasted public money, including expenses arising from prosecutorial work and the provision of legal aid ... [the] decision of not giving the applicant a one-third discount is correct.

[43] Section 125 of the Coroners and Justice Act 2009.

[44] A. Ashworth and J. V. Roberts, 'The origins and nature of the sentencing guidelines in England and Wales', in A. Ashworth and J. V. Roberts (eds.), *Sentencing Guidelines: Exploring the English Model* (Oxford: Oxford University Press, 2013), pp. 1–11.

its definitive guideline on sentence reductions for guilty pleas in 2004, which was revised and made effective in 2007.[45] After succeeding to the Sentencing Guidelines Council, the Sentencing Council for England and Wales revised the guideline on sentence reductions for guilty pleas once again,[46] issuing a new definitive guideline that took effect in June 2017.[47] The 'sliding scale of sentence discounts' can be summarised as follows:

- The maximum sentence reduction for guilty pleas is one-third.
- When a guilty plea is indicated during the first stage of proceedings, a reduction of a one-third sentence discount should normally be made.
- When a guilty plea is indicated after the first stage of proceedings, the maximum reduction for guilty pleas is reduced to one-quarter.
- When a guilty plea is indicated on the first day of trial, the maximum reduction for guilty pleas should be reduced to one-tenth.
- The sentence discount should be reduced further if the guilty plea is entered during trial,[48] and may even be reduced to zero.

A similar sliding scale of sentence discounts has been implemented in Hong Kong. However, unlike England and Wales, Hong Kong never created a sentencing council to establish definitive guidelines for sentence discounts. Instead, legislation has provided some maximum penalties, while the appellate courts have developed sentencing guidelines to provide guidance to the lower courts.[49] These guidelines may be set by guideline judgments through the appeals of convicted defendants, by sentence reviews initiated by the prosecution, or by the appellate court itself taking initiative. Nevertheless, sentencing guidelines are less common

[45] Sentencing Guidelines Council, *Reduction in Sentence for Guilty Plea: Definitive Guideline* (London: Sentencing Guidelines Secretariat, 2007). Sentencing courts in England and Wales are now mandated by the Sentencing Act 2020 – and previously by the Criminal Justice Act 2003 – to take into account the stage in the proceedings at which the defendant indicated their intention to plead guilty.

[46] The Sentencing Council replaced the Sentencing Advisory Panel and the Sentencing Guidelines Council in 2010.

[47] Sentencing Council, *Reduction in Sentence for Guilty Plea: Definitive Guideline* (London: Sentencing Council, 2017).

[48] According to the guideline, a trial is considered to have commenced when pre-recorded cross-examination has begun.

[49] The supervisory role of providing sentencing guidance is often left to the Court of Appeal of the High Court, Hong Kong's second highest court. As the Court of Final Appeal explained in *Secretary for Justice* v. *Wong Chi-fung and Others* [2018] HKCFA 4; [2018] 2 HKC 50 at 115–17:

in Hong Kong. Many offences do not have sentencing guidelines, as they are thought to vary greatly in their nature and circumstances.[50] Even when sentencing guidelines exist for certain offences, they are less systematic than the definitive guidelines for England and Wales, which lay out a step-by-step approach to sentencing. This approach first determines an offender's culpability and the harm they have done, then makes upward and downward adjustments based on a non-exhaustive list of aggravating and mitigating factors, and then makes consideration for a timely guilty plea and (if applicable) the totality principle,[51] as well as time served in custody.

An exception in Hong Kong is the sliding scale of sentence discounts for guilty pleas, for which a specific guideline applies, as discussed earlier.[52] In September 2016, the Hong Kong Court of Appeal issued sentencing guidelines for a quantified sliding scale of sentence discounts in its judgment of two criminal cases, heavily referencing the sentencing guidelines on sentence reductions for guilty pleas.[53] The Hong Kong guidelines can be summarised as follows:

- If a defendant pleads guilty during the plea arraignment or committal proceedings in the Magistrates' Courts, or on the first or subsequent

> The function of sentencing is primarily that of the convicting court of trial, subject to review by the Court of Appeal, whether on an appeal by the convicted person or on review on the application of the Secretary for Justice. The Court of Appeal is therefore the appropriate court to determine if there is a need for appellate guidance as to the levels of sentence for a particular offence and, if so, to set those levels of sentence.

50 Cross and Cheung, *Sentencing in Hong Kong*.

51 The totality principle is relevant when a defendant is convicted of multiple offences. It requires that judges pass an overall sentence that reflects all the offending behaviours while being proportionate. This could result in sentences being structured as concurrent, consecutive, or a mix of both. See Sentencing Council, 'Totality' (2012), available at www.sentencingcouncil.org.uk/overarching-guides/magistrates-court/item/totality/.

52 Another notable exception in Hong Kong is drug trafficking offence, for which the sentence in terms of length of imprisonment corresponds to the type and quantity of drugs. For example, the sentence lengths for ketamine trafficking are: within the sentencer's discretion for up to 1 gm; 2–4 years' imprisonment for 1–10 gm; 4–6 years for 10–50 gm; 6–9 years for 50–300 gm; 9–12 years for 300–600 gm; 12–14 years for 600–1,000 gm; and 14 years or more for over 1,000 gm (*Secretary for Justice* v. *Hii Siew-cheng* [2009] 1 HKLRD 1; [2008] 3 HKC 323). Yet unlike the definitive guidelines in England and Wales, there is no 'step one' for Hong Kong drug trafficking sentencing guidelines that determines the offender's culpability.

53 *HKSAR* v. *Ngo Van Nam*; *HKSAR* v. *Abdou Maikido Abdoulkarim* [2016] 5 HKLRD 1; [2016] HKCA 397. See also *HKSAR* v. *Lam Kai Man* [2020] 4 HKLRD 107; [2020] HKCA 624.

plea day in the District Court, the one-third sentence discount should be maintained.

- If a defendant indicates a guilty plea after a trial date has been fixed but before the first day of trial, the sentence discount is reduced to between one-quarter and one-fifth.
- If a defendant pleads guilty on the first day of trial, the sentence discount is reduced to one-fifth.
- If a defendant pleads guilty during trial, the sentence discount is reduced to less than one-fifth.

The Court of Appeal also noted that, as in England and Wales, judges retain overriding discretion in sentencing and may deviate from the guidelines in cases where they deem it suitable.

Besides being a good case study for comparison with England and Wales, Hong Kong itself is also an interesting case study with respect to guilty pleas. The Hong Kong legal system has especially received significant interest regarding how it is distinct from the PRC's legal system, with Hong Kong citizens enjoying rights and freedoms that mainland Chinese citizens do not possess.[54] As Ip notes:

> The predominance of the common law in Hong Kong entails that its legal system shares few of the Continental European civilian law principles and practices of all nearby jurisdictions. This means, unsurprisingly, that its legal system has been . . . incomprehensible in many ways to jurists and officials from China, who are inured to very different legal traditions, ways of legal interpretation and configurations of law and politics.[55]

Public discourse often cites the rule of law, an independent judiciary, and a robust legal infrastructure as enabling Hong Kong to become the international financial centre that it is. The city has a low crime rate, as measured by both official statistics and crime victim surveys, and is considered one of the safest cities in the twenty-first century[56] – although the 2019 protests may have tarnished this image. Hong Kong has even been described as a 'legal oasis

[54] Article 2 of the Basic Law states, 'The National People's Congress authorizes the Hong Kong Special Administrative Region to exercise a high degree of autonomy and enjoy executive, legislative and independent judicial power, including that of final adjudication, in accordance with the provisions of this Law.'

[55] E. C. Ip, *Law and Justice in Hong Kong*, 2nd ed. (Hong Kong: Sweet & Maxwell, 2016), p. 4.

[56] R. Broadhurst, K. W. Lee, and C. Y. Chan, 'Crime trends', in W. H. Chui and T. W. Lo (eds), *Understanding Criminal Justice in Hong Kong*, 2nd ed. (Abingdon, Oxon: Routledge, 2017), pp. 57–80.

in the region'.[57] However, in 2009, the city's legal system received a rather unflattering comparison to that of another East Asian neighbour. In the preface to the 2010 edition of *Archbold Hong Kong*, general editor and senior counsel Clive Grossman noted that conviction rates in the District Court and the Court of First Instance were 90 per cent or higher, meaning that 'any person who is arrested on a serious or relatively serious charge is almost certain to be convicted'. Such high conviction rates, he warned, were 'probably approaching that of North Korea'.[58] In response, then Chief Justice Andrew Li referred to Grossman's remarks as an 'ill-considered and intemperate outburst by the author', while former director of Public Prosecutions Grenville Cross argued that the referenced statistics were of overall conviction rates, which included guilty pleas alongside trial convictions.[59] However, the question of why so many defendants pleaded guilty remained unanswered.

In Australia, certain state jurisdictions have also adopted a sliding scale of sentence discounts. For instance, South Australia implemented legislation in 2013 to codify sentence reductions for early guilty pleas.[60] In New South Wales, as part of the Early Appropriate Guilty Plea Scheme, new legislation[61] came into force in 2018 that caps the maximum amount of sentence discount a sentencing court may give for a guilty plea on a utilitarian basis.[62] Subject to certain exceptions,[63] these sentence discounts are: one-quarter for a guilty plea in the Local Court before committal, one-tenth for a guilty plea made up to 14 days before the first day of trial, and 5 per cent for a guilty plea made within 14 days before the first day of trial or during trial.

57 SCMP, 'Courts' 90pc conviction rate stirs up row', *South China Morning Post*, 15 September 2009.

58 C. Grossman, 'Preface to the 2010 edition by the general editor', in P. J. Bokhary and C. Grossman (eds.), *Archbold Hong Kong: Criminal Law, Pleading Evidence and Practice 2010* (Hong Kong: Sweet & Maxwell Asia, 2009), p. xi.

59 SCMP, 'Courts' 90pc conviction rate stirs up row'.

60 Sentencing discounts were previously provided for in the Criminal Law (Sentencing) Act 1988. This legislation has since been replaced by the Sentencing Act 2017 (SA), which came into force in April 2018.

61 The Justice Legislation Amendment (Committals and Guilty Pleas) Act 2017 (NSW), which amends existing legislation such as the Criminal Procedure Act 1986 and the Crimes (Sentencing Procedure) Act 1999.

62 Unlike England and Wales and Hong Kong, where the sentence discount has customarily been one-third, under Australian common law, a sentence discount of up to one-quarter was provided for a guilty plea even if the defendant pleaded guilty on the first day of trial. Legislative reform has since changed this custom.

63 For example, judges retain discretion to provide a lesser sentence discount, or even no discount, in cases where the offender's culpability is deemed to be extreme.

Among other common law jurisdictions, Singapore, which has looked to England and Hong Kong for inspiration, has mused openly about adopting a quantified sliding scale of sentence discounts depending on the stage at which a guilty plea is indicated.[64] Other jurisdictions have codified the requirement that the courts consider the timing of the guilty plea when sentencing while refraining from quantified sentence discounts for the stage at which the guilty plea is indicated.[65] Most notably, New Zealand and Scotland have overturned the establishment of a quantified sliding scale for sentence discounts (I discuss this in greater detail in Chapter 2).[66] In summary, although there is variation across different legal jurisdictions in the sentence discounts they provided for, as well as disagreement about whether a quantum should be set, it is evident that any discussion of guilty pleas must address the question of timing.

This Book

As shown earlier, the predominant assumption in official discourse is that cracked trials are caused by defendants who 'play the system' by delaying their pleas in the hope of gaining some tactical advantage, and that a sliding scale of sentence discounts for guilty pleas is necessary to deter such behaviour, as well as encourage early guilty pleas, which offer utilitarian benefits. However, as Ashworth acutely observes: 'Surely it is unwise to make unqualified assertions about the need for the sentence discount without efforts to provide a sound empirical foundation for them.'[67] It is therefore imperative to examine the timing of guilty pleas using an empirical lens. Thus, the central research question of this

64 In his opening address to the Criminal Law Conference 2019, Singapore's Deputy Attorney General Hri Kumar Nair remarked, '[We] can consider the use of structured sentencing discounts to encourage timely pleas of guilt. By this, I mean a structured framework which (i) pegs the quantum of the discount to the stage of the proceedings that the accused elects to plead guilty at; and (ii) specifies the quantum of the discount that will be given at each stage. This framework is by no means novel, having been implemented in both the UK and Hong Kong.' See H. K. Nair, 'Opening address by Deputy Attorney-General, Hri Kumar Nair S.C.: towards a more efficient and just criminal process', *4th Criminal Law Conference 2019* (Singapore: Law Society of Singapore, 2019), available at www.agc.gov.sg.

65 See Section 196(1) of the Criminal Procedure (Scotland) Act 1995.

66 *Gemmell* v. *HMA* 2012 JC 223; *Hessell* v. *R* [2010] NZSC 135.

67 A. Ashworth, *Sentencing and Criminal Justice*, 6th ed. (Cambridge: Cambridge University Press, 2015), p. 186.

monograph is: how do the timing of guilty pleas and the accompanying sliding scale of sentence discounts impact the criminal process?

The aim of this book is a comprehensive investigation of how the timing of guilty pleas affects various facets of the criminal process, from the factors that affect this timing to the effects that the sliding scale of sentence discounts have on sentences and public opinions about them. In particular, this book scrutinises data derived from two jurisdictions, namely England and Wales and Hong Kong, that have adopted a quantified sliding scale of sentence discounts. It presents new statistical analyses of data from the Crown Court Sentencing Survey (CCSS) in England and Wales. This book also presents an original database created specifically for this study through meticulously coding court cases in Hong Kong's District Court. These two datasets underpin the empirical findings of this book.

This book will show that the criminal justice system's reliance on guilty pleas, particularly early guilty pleas, has created an *accelerated guilty plea process* in a system already geared towards the guilty plea as its end goal. Half a century ago, Packer's classic Due Process Model referred to the guilty plea as the 'fulcrum of the entire criminal process'.[68] His other model, the Crime Control Model, holds that when the criminal justice process is stripped down to its bare essentials and is operating at maximum efficiency, it only offers two outcomes: (1) the release of the suspect or (2) the entry of a guilty plea.[69] Moreover, the latest innovation of the quantified sliding scale of sentence discounts for guilty pleas is prescriptive and systematic, as it prescribes an amount of sentence reduction depending on the stage of the criminal justice process, serving to expedite the guilty plea process by encouraging early guilty pleas. Combined with existing pressures from earlier stages in the criminal process, such as confessions to the police, advice from legal representation (especially publicly funded defence lawyers), and pretrial detention, the criminal process is geared towards having defendants pleading guilty and pleading guilty early. The respective sentence differentials between

[68] H. Packer, *The Limits of the Criminal Sanction* (Stanford: Stanford University Press, 1968), p. 224. According to the Due Process Model, the guilty plea acts as a sort of 'iron curtain' that protects any inspection of possible wrongs in the pretrial process, as 'either the possible errors and abuses at the earlier, largely unscrutinised stages of the process are exposed to judicial scrutiny or they are forever submerged in a plea of guilty'. Unlike during trial, once the defendant enters a guilty plea before trial, the evidence against them is not tested.

[69] Ibid., pp. 162–3.

pleas and trials, as well as between early and late pleas, create a 'trial penalty' and 'late-plea penalty' in sentencing that also serve to further this goal.

The sentencing guidelines underpinning the sliding scale for sentence discounts ensure that sentencing judges reflect the timing of guilty pleas in sentence outcomes. The primary justification for all this is the utilitarian benefits that an early guilty plea brings. However, this benefit must be balanced with the necessity for fairness, voluntariness, and public confidence in the criminal justice system. The quantified sliding scale of sentence discounts for guilty pleas has a real risk of exacerbating the pressures on defendants to plead guilty, and to plead guilty early. It puts certain defendants at greater risk of entering a guilty plea that is not fully informed and voluntary, in addition to creating sentence disparities that serve to intensify such pressure; it is thus difficult to argue that the sliding scale is just and proportionate. Moreover, the justification that underpins the sliding scale of sentence discounts, namely that it enhances the efficiency of the criminal justice process, is somewhat dubious. Ultimately, the only way for the criminal justice system to function is for our criminal process to be recalibrated such that it does not emphasise early guilty pleas.

Outline of the Chapters

Chapters 2 and 3 examine the theoretical perspectives regarding sentence discounts and guilty pleas. Chapter 2 goes into extensive detail about the sliding scale of sentence discounts and the forms that it takes in various legal jurisdictions. It examines the justifications that England and Wales and Hong Kong used to adopt a quantified sliding scale of sentence discounts, along with arguments for rejecting such a quantified sliding scale in other comparable legal jurisdictions. The chapter concludes that, despite differences in form across jurisdictions, a strong justification for a sliding scale of sentence discounts exists because of the utilitarian benefits that sentence discounts based on the timeliness of guilty pleas bring.

Chapter 3 scrutinises sentence discounts from another perspective, namely that of implicit plea bargaining, one of the most controversial aspects of criminal case processing. The idea that the defendant receives some concession in return for entering a guilty plea renders opaque a justice system that should be transparent. Advanced sentence indication – in which a judge openly informs a defendant that a sentence will not take a particular form if the defendant pleads guilty – has developed alongside the emergence of the sliding scale of sentence discounts in England and Wales. This chapter argues that requirements for the courts and defence lawyers to communicate the sentence discount to defendants serve as a form of implicit plea bargaining that is actually not so implicit and adds to the pressures on defendants to plead guilty.

Chapter 4 revisits the touted assumptions that cracked trials are caused by tactical defendants playing the system and that the quantified sliding scale of sentence discounts for guilty pleas promotes efficiency in the criminal process. It raises serious doubts about these assumptions based on existing studies of defendants, as well as official data on guilty plea rates, cracked trial rates, and average waiting times for trial. This chapter also outlines the methodology of this book.

Chapter 5 investigates the factors that affect guilty plea decisions under the quantified sliding scale of sentence discounts. It looks at which groups of defendants are more likely to plead guilty, and do so early, through analyses of data from the CCSS and Hong Kong District Court datasets. This chapter also investigates the effects of earlier decisions on guilty plea decisions. A defendant's entry of a plea of guilty or not guilty should not be viewed in isolation. After all, the criminal process is a *process*, and earlier decisions influence subsequent ones. Existing literature finds that defence lawyers, especially legal-aid lawyers, influence their clients into pleading guilty. While this study finds evidence for this claim, it also finds that confession to the police and representation by legal-aid lawyers are significant predictors for a defendant pleading earlier. I also draw on my own previous studies to show that pretrial detention significantly influences defendants into pleading late. Overall, this chapter gives credence to the notion that defendants are pressured to plead guilty and to plead guilty early.

Chapters 6 and 7 examine the impacts of the sliding scale of sentence discounts. Chapter 6 looks at its impact on sentences and demonstrates that there is a 'trial penalty' in Hong Kong and a 'late plea penalty' in England and Wales. This chapter goes beyond the traditional plea-trial distinction in the existing literature to look at the impacts of the timing of guilty pleas on sentences. Chapter 7 examines whether judges (and sentencers) consistently apply the guidelines for the sliding scale of sentence discounts or instead exercise their discretion and depart from the guidelines for their respective jurisdictions. Findings from the analysis of the two datasets reveal that, while judges do apply the guidelines for the sliding scale of sentence discounts, there are also some interesting points of deviation.

Chapter 8 looks at the relationship between public opinion and sentence discounts. Government reports in various countries have emphasised that the public wants efficient justice and that greater sentence discounts should therefore be promoted to encourage early guilty pleas. Yet while many studies and surveys have analysed public opinion towards the courts and sentencing, little is known about public attitudes towards sentence discounts for guilty pleas. This chapter argues that while the public may want swift justice, they are also wary of the courts providing excessive discounts for guilty pleas. Finally, Chapter 9 concludes and summarises the book's primary findings. It suggests certain steps that legal practitioners can take to navigate cracked trials and reduce their adverse impact on the justice system. The chapter also recommends ways to improve the criminal justice process to better ensure that a defendant's decision to plead guilty is indeed voluntary and free from pressure.

2

The Sliding Scale of Sentence Discounts

The sliding scale of sentence discounts for guilty pleas is an innovation in response to the issue of 'cracked trials'. This chapter goes into detail about the quantified sliding scale of sentence discounts for guilty pleas in comparable legal jurisdictions. As discussed in Chapter 1, the sliding scale of sentence discounts sets an amount (or a range) of sentence reduction that corresponds to the stage in the proceedings at which a guilty plea is entered or indicated, making the timing of the guilty plea the crucial factor. This chapter begins with England and Wales, where the sliding scale of sentence discounts was first standardised through the then Sentencing Guidelines Council's definitive guidelines on sentence reductions for guilty pleas. It then looks at Hong Kong, where its sliding scale of sentence discounts was a judicial creation of the appellate court that took inspiration from the developments in England and Wales. Afterwards, this chapter examines the situation in Australia, where certain states have moved towards a quantified sliding scale of sentence discounts. It then discusses the two jurisdictions of Scotland and New Zealand, which have rejected the quantified sliding scale of sentence discounts in favour of greater judicial discretion. Despite varying responses to whether quantified guidelines for sentence discounts for guilty pleas should be implemented, all the jurisdictions surveyed agree that earlier guilty pleas should generally attract higher sentence discounts, primarily justified based on the perceived utilitarian benefits of early guilty pleas.

England and Wales

It had already been established in English common law that defendants who plead guilty would be given a sentence discount, and that an early guilty plea would normally attract a larger sentence discount, but even a late plea would lead to some sentence reduction.[1] For instance, in the case of *Buffrey*,[2] Taylor CJ stated,

> But some reduction, clearly, must be made and because frauds of this kind are complex and do take a long time to unravel, it is well known that they have become a burden on the criminal justice system. They are very costly, both in time and in money . . . All those matters, in our judgment, justify the Court in applying a considerable discount where somebody does, albeit late in the day, face up to what he has done and plead guilty. It would be quite wrong for us to suggest that there was any absolute rule as to what the discount should be. Each case must be assessed by the trial judge on its own facts and there will be considerable variance as between one case and another.[3]

This means that a defendant who pleads guilty would receive a reduction in the sentence that he or she would have otherwise received had he or she been convicted at trial.[4] Back then, however, the amount of sentence discount was left to the trial judge to determine. Following the 1993 Royal Commission on Criminal Justice Report,[5] the timing of guilty pleas and sentence reductions was codified. The report recommended that 'a clearer system of graduated discounts would help to alleviate the problem of "cracked trials"'.[6]

The first iteration of codification came one year later in the form of section 48 of the Criminal Justice and Public Order Act 1994. This section was replaced and replicated in section 144 of the Criminal Justice Act 2003.[7] Its current iteration is found in section 73 of the

1 A. Ashworth, *Sentencing and Criminal Justice*, 6th ed. (Cambridge: Cambridge University Press, 2015).

2 *R* v. *Buffrey* (1993) 14 Cr App R (S) 511.

3 Ibid. at 515. In this case, a sentence discount of one-third was given even for a late guilty plea. As Taylor CJ further stated, 'But as general guidance – and I emphasise only as general guidance – this Court believes that something of the order of one-third would very often be an appropriate discount from the sentence which would otherwise be imposed on a contested trial' at 515.

4 For the perspective of how this should be seen as a 'trial penalty' instead, see Chapter 6.

5 Royal Commission on Criminal Justice, *Report (Cm 2263)* (London: HMSO, 1993).

6 Ibid., paragraph 45.

7 In *Attorney General's References (Nos 14 and 15 of 2006)*, *R* v. *French and Another* [2006] EWCA Crim 1335, it was stated that '[t]he practice of making a reduction in sentence where a Defendant has entered a plea of guilty is judge made. It has received, however, statutory recognition' at 39. In *R* v. *Martin* [2006] EWCA Crim 1035, it was stated that 'no-one can doubt (nor indeed has anyone for many years doubted) that a plea of guilty should produce a reduction in sentence, and that the circumstances in which and the time when indication of an intention to plead guilty should both be taken into account by

Sentencing Code created under the Sentencing Act 2020, which states the following:

(1) This section applies where a court is determining what sentence to pass on an offender who has pleaded guilty to an offence in proceedings before that or another court.
(2) The court must take into account the following matters—
  (a) the stage in the proceedings for the offence at which the offender indicated the intention to plead guilty, and
  (b) the circumstances in which the indication was given.

Furthermore, under section 52 of the Sentencing Code, the courts have a duty to give reasons for and explain the effects of the sentence. In relation to sentence discounts for guilty pleas, subsection 7 states, 'Where as a result of taking into account any matter mentioned in section 73 (2) (guilty pleas), the court imposes a punishment on the offender which is less severe than the punishment it would otherwise have imposed, the court must state that fact.'[8] The legislation, however, never specified the amount of sentence discount that should be given with respect to the timing of guilty pleas.[9] For that, attention needs to be turned to the sentencing guidelines regarding sentence reductions for guilty pleas.

In one of its first sentencing guidelines, the Sentencing Guidelines Council issued a definitive guideline on sentence reductions for guilty pleas in 2004. This guideline was revised in 2007[10] and applies to the Magistrates' Courts, the Crown Court, and, as far as possible, the Youth Courts. Under this guideline, the approach is that the court consider aggravating and mitigating factors when determining a sentence, the court apply the sentence discount for guilty pleas based on the 'sliding

sentencing judges. So, [section] 144 of the 2003 Act does not tell us anything new about sentencing principle' at 14.

8 This wording is replicated from section 174(7) of the Criminal Justice Act 2003, which states, 'Where, as a result of taking into account any matter referred to in section 144(1) (guilty pleas), the court imposes a punishment on the offender which is less severe than the punishment it would otherwise have imposed, the court must state that fact.'

9 Indeed, prior to the establishment of the sliding scale of sentence discounts as set out in the sentencing guidelines, this ambiguity had led to the English Court of Appeal having to handle criminal appeals about the amount of sentence discounts with respect to the stage in the proceedings at which a guilty plea is entered. See, for example *R* v. *Barber* [2001] EWCA Crim 2267; *R* v. *Byrne* [2002] EWCA Crim 479; *R* v. *Rafferty* [1998] 2 Cr App Rep (S) 449; [1998] Crim LR 433.

10 Sentencing Guidelines Council, *Reduction in Sentence for Guilty Plea: Definitive Guideline* (London: Sentencing Guidelines Secretariat, 2007).

scale' provided, and, as required under legislation, the court pronounce the sentence that the defendant would have received had there been no reduction resulting from the guilty plea.[11] The quantified sliding scale of sentence discounts under the 2007 guidelines can be summarised as follows:

- The maximum sentence reduction recommended for guilty pleas is one-third.
- When a guilty plea is indicated at the first reasonable opportunity, a one-third reduction should normally be made; when the first reasonable opportunity occurs will vary from case to case.
- When the guilty plea is admitted later than the first reasonable opportunity but before a trial date has been set, the recommended reduction is reduced to one-quarter.
- When a guilty plea is indicated at the 'door of the court' or after the trial has begun, the recommended reduction is reduced to one-tenth.[12]

It should be highlighted that the sentence discounts do not just pertain to sentence lengths in terms of imprisonment, although such scenarios are where discounts are most likely applicable. The guidelines stipulate that when the sentencer decides on imposing a custodial sentence or a non-custodial one, the amount of sentence discount for the guilty plea ought to be a relevant consideration. Yet where the sentence discount for a guilty plea is among the factors that have led to a non-custodial sentence, there is no need to apply a further sentence discount on account of the guilty plea. A similar approach is to be adopted in cases that led to a financial penalty or discharge instead of a community order.[13]

As noted in Chapter 1, the sentencing guideline regarding sentence reductions for guilty pleas was revised again and came into force a decade later, in 2017. The reasons for a new sentencing guideline are twofold. First, the Sentencing Council for England and Wales, which replaced the former Sentencing Guidelines Council and the Sentencing Advisory Panel, is required by legislation to develop and produce a sentencing guideline on sentence reductions for guilty pleas.[14] Second, the

[11] Ibid., paragraph 3.1.

[12] Ibid., paragraph 4.2.

[13] Ibid., paragraph 2.3.

[14] Section 120(3)(a) of the Coroners and Justice Act 2009, which states: 'The Council must prepare – (a) sentencing guidelines about the discharge of a court's duty under section 144 of the Criminal Justice Act 2003 (reduction in sentences for guilty pleas).'

Sentencing Council found that the former Sentencing Guidelines Council's 2007 guidelines were 'not always applied consistently and that levels of reductions in some cases appear to be higher than those recommended by the guidelines'.[15] Whether the courts have consistently applied the sliding scale of sentence discounts for guilty pleas as per the sentencing guidelines will be examined in detail in Chapter 7. In the 2017 guidelines, the maximum one-third sentence discount is retained;[16] however, the wording has changed from pleading guilty at 'the first reasonable opportunity' to 'the first stage of the proceedings'. So, if a guilty plea is indicated at the first stage of the proceedings, then the court should give a one-third sentence discount.[17] Again, sentence reductions do not just apply to imprisonment length; the stage at when the guilty plea is entered can be considered in reducing a custodial sentence to a community sentence, and in reducing a community sentence to a fine.[18]

The case of *Caley* provides additional guidance on the Sentencing Guidelines Council's 2007 guidelines.[19] For this case, the English Court of Appeal distinguished between the first reasonable opportunity for the defendant to indicate guilt and any subsequent opportunities for the defendant's legal representatives to assess the case and advise the defendant accordingly. The court stated that

> whilst it is perfectly proper for a Defendant to require advice from his lawyers on the strength of the evidence (just as he is perfectly entitled to insist on putting the Crown to proof at trial), he does not require it in order to know whether he is guilty or not; he requires it in order to assess the prospects of conviction or acquittal, which is different.[20]

[15] Sentencing Council, *Reduction in Sentence for Guilty Plea Guideline: Consultation* (London: Sentencing Council, 2016), p. 5.

[16] There were discussions to bring the sentence discount up from one-third to one-half. See discussion in Chapter 8.

[17] Sentencing Council, *Reduction in Sentence for Guilty Plea: Definitive Guideline* (London: Sentencing Council, 2017), paragraph D1. See also *Attorney General's Reference*; *R* v. *Plaku and Others* [2021] EWCA Crim 568.

[18] Sentencing Council, *Reduction in Sentence for Guilty Plea: Definitive Guideline*, paragraph E1.

[19] *R* v. *Caley and Others* [2012] EWCA Crim 2821. Indeed, Hughes LJ notes at the outset of this case: 'The several cases before us raise a number of different questions associated with the long established practice in sentencing which recognises that a distinction should ordinarily be drawn between a Defendant who admits his guilt and one who does not. It has been convenient to hear them together and we believe that it is possible to give some general guidance on some of those questions' at 1.

[20] Ibid. at 14.

Although the court acknowledged that situations exist where a defendant would require proper legal advice to know whether he or she is in fact guilty, such as whether the facts of the case constitute the offence that the defendant is charged with, in most situations, the court believed that such advice is unnecessary.[21] Effectively, the court is stating here that most defendants seek legal advice to assess their odds of convictions only, implicitly suggesting that defendants who are waiting to plead after legal consultation are playing the system. In many cases, defendants need not seek legal advice before knowing whether they are guilty and that should not stop them from indicating their willingness to plead guilty early. The Sentencing Council's 2017 guidelines echo this by stipulating that

> sentencers should distinguish between cases in which it is necessary to receive advice and/or have sight of evidence in order to understand whether the defendant is in fact and law guilty of the offence(s) charged, and cases in which a defendant *merely delays* guilty plea(s) in order to assess the strength of the prosecution evidence and the prospects of conviction or acquittal.[22] (Emphasis added)

Another area of discussion is when the courts can depart from the structure of the quantified sliding scale of sentence discounts laid out in the guidelines. The 2007 guidelines state that where the prosecution's case is overwhelming, the full sentence discount may not be given where it otherwise would have been, especially where the prosecution's case is overwhelming without relying on admissions from the defendant. Although there is a presumption that as long as the guilty plea has been indicated at the first reasonable opportunity, the maximum one-third reduction should be given, the aforementioned situation may be one where departure from the sliding scale of sentence discounts is justified.[23] In such a situation, the guidelines recommend applying a sentence discount of one-fifth.[24] However, in *Caley*, the court cautions a sentencing judge about concluding that a case is overwhelming when the evidence is uncontested. Furthermore, even if the prosecution's case is very strong, some defendants will still elect trial. The court stated, 'It

[21] Ibid.

[22] Sentencing Council, *Reduction in Sentence for Guilty Plea: Definitive Guideline*, paragraph F1. For an illustration where no credit was given for a not guilty plea because the judge had concluded that the defendant maintained the plea for tactical reasons, see *R* v. *Ali (Subhaan)* [2018] EWCA Crim 111.

[23] Sentencing Guidelines Council, *Reduction in Sentence for Guilty Plea: Definitive Guideline*, paragraph 5.3.

[24] Ibid., paragraph 5.4.

cannot be assumed that Defendants will make rational decisions or ones which are born of any inclination to co-operate with the system, but those who do merit recognition.'[25] This is because '[t]he various public benefits which underlie the practice of reducing sentence for plea of guilty apply just as much to overwhelming cases as to less strong ones'.[26] In other words, regardless of whether a guilty plea is made in an overwhelming case or not, there are still utilitarian benefits to defendants pleading guilty.

Even in particularly serious and heinous cases where overwhelming evidence exists, the sliding scale of sentence discounts should still be adhered to. In *Caley*, the court referred to the horrific case of *Wilson*, which involved the rape of a three-year-old child, as well as the making and distribution of indecent photographs of numerous children.[27] The defendant in *Wilson* had pleaded guilty early to the charges. Yet in relation to the most serious charges of oral rape of the child (counts 1 and 2), the trial judge refused to give any credit for the defendant's guilty pleas, stating that the defendant 'had no option but to plead guilty'.[28] The Court of Appeal disagreed, stating that '[e]ven in an overwhelming case the guilty plea has a distinct public benefit. The earlier that it is indicated, the better for everyone'.[29] The court stated several advantages of the guilty plea, including that the repellent video of the victim would not need to be shown, and that a jury would not need to watch it. Moreover, the Court of Appeal held that

> [a]lthough we understand the judge's view, it would be productive of uncertainty, and would ultimately cause chaos if this court were to suggest that an existing definitive guideline could be disregarded or ignored in this case ... If we were to ignore the guilty plea altogether, we would undermine the crucial contribution to the sentencing process of consistency of approach throughout the country, and in this particular context, the value to the victims of crime and the administration of justice of an early indication that the Defendant does not require the issues to be tried ... In our judgment, it follows from these conclusions that it was inappropriate for the judge totally to disregard the guilty pleas on counts 1 and 2. Some allowance should have been made.[30]

[25] *R* v. *Caley and Others* [2012] EWCA Crim 2821 at 24.
[26] Ibid.
[27] *R* v. *Wilson* [2012] EWCA Crim 386.
[28] Ibid. at 25.
[29] Ibid. at 29.
[30] Ibid. at 31–3.

The 2017 Sentencing Council guidelines make this point even more explicitly by stating, 'The strength of evidence should not be taken into account when determining the level of reduction.'[31] Therefore, even in overwhelming cases, the sliding scale of sentence discounts should be observed because of the benefits that early guilty pleas bring to the criminal justice system.

The recent case of *Plaku*[32] further entrenches the rigidness of the 2017 guidelines. Here, the Court of Appeal reiterated that the guidelines deliberately distinguish between the amounts of sentence discount given at the first stage of proceedings and at subsequent stages.[33] Where a defendant does not indicate a guilty plea at the first stage of proceedings, there will be few occasions where the sentence discount should be more than one-quarter, even if an intention to plead guilty is communicated at the next court appearance. The Court of Appeal emphasised, 'It would be wholly inconsistent with the structure of the guideline to introduce an additional sliding scale of reduction between one-third and one-quarter, and we reject the suggestion that such an approach should be routinely, or frequently, adopted.'[34]

Justifications of the Sliding Scale

As seen previously, the courts have referred to the public interest as a justification for adhering to the sliding scale of sentence discounts for guilty pleas. Both the 2007 and 2017 guidelines explicitly outline the benefits of the sliding scale of sentence discounts. The Sentencing Guidelines Council provides four justifications: avoiding the need for trial, shortening the time between charge and sentence, saving cost, and saving victims and witnesses from needing to take the stand and give evidence at trial. Of the four justifications, three relate to the utilitarian benefits of promoting the expediency of cases by way of guilty pleas. The Sentencing Guidelines Council summarises thus: 'The reduction principle derives from the need for the effective administration of justice.'[35] The 2017 guidelines list three benefits: reducing the impact of the

[31] Sentencing Council, *Reduction in Sentence for Guilty Plea: Definitive Guideline*, paragraph B.
[32] *R* v. *Plaku and Others* [2021] EWCA 568.
[33] Ibid. at 6.
[34] Ibid. at 27.
[35] Sentencing Guidelines Council, *Reduction in Sentence for Guilty Plea: Definitive Guideline*, paragraph 2.2.

crime on victims, saving victims and witnesses from the need to testify in court, and serving the public interest in saving the public time and money for both investigations and trials.[36] Here, more emphasis is placed on protecting victims; nonetheless, the practical benefits to the administration of the criminal process remain an important justification.

In *Caley*, Hughes LJ states that the first benefit is for victims and witnesses, assuring them that the defendant will normally still be punished after pleading guilty, as well as avoiding the need for giving evidence in court, which is said to be stressful and uncomfortable.[37] The second major benefit is pragmatic, but 'it is nevertheless vital in the public interest'.[38] Trials are costly and lengthy, since a case has to be prepared carefully to meet the standard of proof required in criminal cases; guilty pleas thereby save time and the public purse. Vitally, the court concedes that 'if in all those cases the Defendants were out of defiance or otherwise to insist on each detail of the case being proved to the hilt the administration of criminal justice would be in danger of collapse'.[39] As it stands, without its reliance on guilty pleas, the criminal process as we know it would not be able to function. Such pragmatism is also emphasised in the case of *R* v. *K*, in which the defendant absconded for 30 years and the Attorney General submitted that full credit should not be given even for the early guilty plea because the defendant had absconded.[40] Treacy LJ stated:

> In our judgment credit for an early guilty plea represents a pragmatic deduction, granted to a Defendant, for steps he has taken to avoid the need for a trial, thus resulting in costs savings and saving victims and witnesses from having to give evidence … therefore, the submission that credit for a guilty plea should be reduced in the light of the absconding fails.[41]

Rather, the issue of absconding should be dealt with separately as an aggravating factor.

Interestingly, remorse is missing as a justification for a sentence discount. Traditionally, a guilty plea is taken as an indication of the

[36] Sentencing Council, *Reduction in Sentence for Guilty Plea: Definitive Guideline*, paragraph B.
[37] *R* v. *Caley and Others* [2012] EWCA Crim 2821 at 5.
[38] Ibid. at 6.
[39] Ibid.
[40] *R* v. *K* [2013] EWCA Crim 130.
[41] Ibid. at 19.

defendant's remorse, therefore warranting a sentence discount. For instance, in *Harper*, Parker CJ remarked, 'It is, however, proper to give an accused a lesser sentence if he has shown genuine remorse, amongst other things by pleading guilty.'[42] Remorse has been regarded as a way to predict future dangerousness and to reflect on the defendant's moral culpability, despite obvious difficulties in determining genuine remorse.[43] It also serves as a way for legal practitioners, including judges, prosecutors, and defence lawyers, to legitimise the pursuit of speedy case dispositions through guilty pleas.[44] If remorse is indicated by way of a guilty plea, then a sentence discount becomes more justifiable. Sentence discounts for guilty pleas nowadays, however, are separated from the issue of remorse. The 2007 guidelines make clear that the issue of remorse is to be dealt with separately by the sentencing court when deciding a sentence before resorting to the sliding scale of sentence discounts for guilty pleas.[45] This is likewise stated in the 2017 guidelines, which make explicit that remorse should not be considered when deciding on the amount of sentence reduction for guilty pleas. Rather, remorse is something that should be addressed separately as a mitigating factor.[46] Therefore, the issue of remorse should be separated from guilty pleas, with the justifications for sentence reductions for guilty pleas based primarily on protecting victims and witnesses, as well as its utilitarian benefits to the process of criminal justice.

42 *R* v. *Harper* [1968] 2Q.B. 108 at 110.

43 S. A. Bandes, 'Remorse and criminal justice' (2015) 8 *Emotion Review*, 14–19. On judicial construction of remorse, see, for example, R. Weisman, 'Being and doing: the judicial use of remorse to construct character and community' (2009) 18 *Social & Legal Studies*, 47–69.

44 J. Gormley and C. Tata, 'Remorse and sentencing in a world of plea bargaining' (2021), in S. Tudor, R. Weisman, M. Proeve, and K. Rossmanith (eds.), *Remorse and Criminal Justice: Multi-disciplinary Perspectives* (London/New York: Routledge/Taylor & Francis Group, 2020).

45 Sentencing Guidelines Council, *Reduction in Sentence for Guilty Plea: Definitive Guideline*, paragraph 2.3.

46 Sentencing Council, *Reduction in Sentence for Guilty Plea: Definitive Guideline*, paragraph B. Such a view has received mixed endorsements by the courts. See, for example, *R* v. *Oosthuizen* [2005] EWCA Crim 1978 at 20 where the court states that remorse should be separated from guilty pleas. However, in *R* v. *Barney and Barney* [2007] EWCA Crim 3181 at 19–20, the court held that questions of remorse should not be entirely divorced from questions of plea. The court was hesitant to say that a remorseful guilty plea would lead to a sentence discount above one-third, only to concede that, in some cases, remorse may be considered as an additional factor.

Hong Kong

Formally under British colonial rule, Hong Kong is now a special administrative region of the People's Republic of China (PRC), with a population of about 7.5 million, which operates under the framework of 'one country, two systems'. English law was imposed in Hong Kong early in the colonial period,[47] and the English-style legal system survived the 1997 handover. Article 8 of the *Basic Law*, Hong Kong's mini-constitution, provides that '[t]he laws previously in force in Hong Kong, that is, the common law, rules of equity, ordinances, subordinate legislation and customary law shall be maintained, except for any that contravene this Law, and subject to any amendment by the legislature of the Hong Kong Special Administrative Region'. Hong Kong is still a common law jurisdiction[48] and previous laws prior to the handover remain in force.[49] In fact, Hong Kong is the oldest continuously functioning legal system in East Asia, predating others in the region.[50] Hong Kong has its own legislature, which enacts its own laws that are distinct from those

[47] In 1841, Hong Kong's legal system started off using the so-called dual legal system based on the Proclamations of Sir Charles Elliot, Chief Superintendent of British Trade in China, in which Chinese customary law would apply to the indigenous Chinese population, whereas English law would apply to all British subjects and foreigners. In 1844, the dual system was abolished and English law was applied to the entire population. The enacting formula for importing English law was settled in 1873. Section 5 of the Supreme Court Ordinance (No 12 of 1873) provides: '[S]uch of the laws of England as existed when the Colony [of Hong Kong] obtained a local legislature, that is to say, on the 5th day of April, 1843, shall be in force in the Colony, except so far as the said laws are inapplicable to the local circumstances of the Colony or of its inhabitants, and except so far as they have been modified by laws passed by the said legislature.' This arrangement lasted until 1966, when the Application of English Law Ordinance (Cap. 88), which defined the extent of English statues prior to 5 April 1843 that still applied to Hong Kong, came into force.

[48] When developing its own jurisprudence, Hong Kong can, and has, referred to other jurisdictions. Article 84 of the Basic Law states, 'The courts of the Hong Kong Special Administrative Region shall adjudicate cases in accordance with the laws applicable in the Region as prescribed in Article 18 of this Law and may refer to precedents of other common law jurisdictions.' Overseas authorities, including the House of Lords and UK Supreme Court decisions, can be and have been treated as persuasive authorities by the Hong Kong courts. See also *Solicitor (24/07)* v. *Law Society of Hong Kong* [2008] 11 HKCFAR 117.

[49] At the time of the handover, 99 per cent of pre-existing laws remained in force.

[50] E. C. Ip, *Law and Justice in Hong Kong*, 2nd ed. (Hong Kong: Sweet & Maxwell, 2016), pp. 3–4.

governing the rest of the PRC.[51] The judicial system in Hong Kong also remains the same today, aside from the establishment of the Court of Final Appeal, which replaced the Privy Council as Hong Kong's highest court.[52] The legal profession in Hong Kong is divided between solicitors and barristers, just like in England and Wales.[53] Hong Kong has an independent judiciary[54] and a prosecution that independently decides whether to prosecute.[55] In criminal cases, the prosecution bears the burden of proving a defendant's guilt beyond a reasonable doubt. Defendants enjoy the right to a fair trial and the presumption of innocence.[56]

Like England and Wales, Hong Kong courts provide a sentence discount for defendants who plead guilty. The courts have stated that it is the policy of the law in Hong Kong to encourage guilty defendants to plead guilty.[57] In the 1980s, Hong Kong courts typically distinguished between guilty pleas made at the first opportunity and guilty pleas made later in the criminal process, where a lower sentence discount was given for guilty pleas entered on the day of trial. This practice seemed to have changed in the 1990s; since then, the courts have provided a one-third

[51] Article 73(1) of the Basic Law states, 'The Legislative Council of the Hong Kong Special Administrative Region shall exercise the following powers and functions: To enact, amend or repeal laws in accordance with the provisions of this Law and legal procedures.'

[52] Article 81 of the Basic Law states, 'The judicial system previously practised in Hong Kong shall be maintained except for those changes consequent upon the establishment of the Court of Final Appeal of the Hong Kong Special Administrative Region.' The court structure for criminal cases in Hong Kong is as follows: Magistrates' Courts, the District Court, the Court of First Instance, the Court of Appeal, and the Court of Final Appeal.

[53] In this respect, Hong Kong shares more similarities with England and Wales, as some other common law jurisdictions have not adopted the split profession for its lawyers.

[54] Article 85 of the Basic Law states, 'The courts of the Hong Kong Special Administrative Region shall exercise judicial power independently, free from any interference.'

[55] Article 63 of the Basic Law guarantees that '[t]he Department of Justice of the Hong Kong Special Administrative Region shall control criminal prosecutions, free from any interference'.

[56] Article 87 of the Basic Law states, 'In criminal or civil proceedings in the Hong Kong Special Administrative Region, the principles previously applied in Hong Kong and the rights previously enjoyed by parties to proceedings shall be maintained. Anyone who is lawfully arrested shall have the right to a fair trial by the judicial organs without delay and shall be presumed innocent until convicted by the judicial organs.' This is further stated in Article XI(1) of the Hong Kong Bill of Rights Ordinance (Cap. 383), which virtually mirrors the International Covenant on Civil and Political Rights: 'Everyone charged with a criminal offence shall have the right to be presumed innocent until proved guilty according to law.' The Hong Kong Bill of Rights Ordinance (Cap. 383) is constitutionally entrenched.

[57] *R* v. *Yu Man-wu* [1995] 2 HKLRD 202; [1995] HKCU 450.

sentence discount to defendants who plead guilty from the first opportunity all the way until the first day of trial.[58] In Hong Kong, the one-third sentence discount is considered a 'high watermark'; only in exceptional circumstances would a sentence discount of more than one-third be given for a timely guilty plea.[59] However, the courts have expressed frustration with this practice. For example, Yeung VP pronounced:

> In order to avoid uncertainty, delay and unnecessary expense arising out of arguments over niceties and subtleties, the court, as a matter of policy, would normally give a defendant a sentence discount of one-third from the starting point as long as he pleads guilty before the trial starts. Such a policy can be abused. Defendants who plead guilty at a very late stage when they should plead guilty at much earlier stages still get the full one-third discount and very often defendants deliberately wait until the last moment before pleading guilty, resulting in a wastage of huge public resources.[60]

Once again, the frustration of 'cracked trials' is attributed to tactical defendants 'playing the system'.[61]

The quantified sliding scale of sentence discounts in Hong Kong is a judicial creation by the Hong Kong Court of Appeal, created in 2016 in the seminal cases of *Ngo Van Nam* and *Abdou Maikido Abdoulkarim*, which were heard jointly.[62] Interestingly, the facts of the case of *Ngo Van Nam* were not about the timing of guilty pleas, but rather about sentence discounts for admissions to the police; the issue in the appeal was whether confessions should lead to another sentence discount in addition to the one-third sentence discount for a guilty plea. In the second case of *Abdou Maikido Abdoulkarim*, the issue in the appeal was about how the trial judge reduced the sentence discount to one-quarter because of an 'untimely' guilty plea. The defendant had first pleaded guilty to a drug trafficking offence at the committal proceedings in the Magistrates' Courts. Yet upon sentencing in the High Court, the defendant claimed he did not know the drugs were inside of the bag he carried. The judge could not accept his guilty plea; the plea was vacated, and the conviction

58 G. Cross and P. S. W. Cheung, *Sentencing in Hong Kong*, 8th ed. (Hong Kong: LexisNexis, 2018), p. 354; *HKSAR* v. *Ngo Van Nam*; *HKSAR* v. *Abdou Maikido Abdoulkarim* [2016] 5 HKLRD 1; [2016] HKCA 397 at 59.

59 *HKSAR* v. *Chow Yuen Fai* [2010] 1 HKLRD 354; [2010] 1 HKC 181 at 31.

60 *HKSAR* v. *Lo Kam Fai* [2016] 2 HKLRD 308; [2016] 4 HKC 204 at 6–7.

61 See discussion in Chapter 1.

62 *HKSAR* v. *Ngo Van Nam*; *HKSAR* v. *Abdou Maikido Abdoulkarim* [2016] 5 HKLRD 1; [2016] HKCA 397.

set aside. During a mention hearing, the defendant indicated he would plead not guilty: however, three days prior to the commencement of the trial, the defence wrote to the court that the defendant would plead guilty. For this, the trial judge reduced the sentence discount. Regarding these two cases, the Hong Kong Court of Appeal adjourned proceedings so that the court could receive *amicus curiae* submissions about the general practice of sentence discounts for defendants who plead guilty.

In its judgment, the Hong Kong Court of Appeal referred to the jurisdictions of England and Wales, Australia, Scotland, and New Zealand. The court heard submissions about the sliding scale of sentence discounts in England and Wales, including the English statutory regime on sentencing, the Sentencing Guidelines Council's sentencing guidelines and its consultation, and the case of *Caley*. Among the submissions from the *amici curiae*, senior counsel[63] Mr Robert Pang, who was appointed by the Court, submitted that the quantified sliding scale of sentence discounts adopted by England and Wales offers the benefit of certainty, given how specified sentence discounts are defined at specific stages of the criminal justice process. Yet Mr Pang warned that 'such certainty carries with it a rigidity, which may create unfairness. A defendant's plea may result in the same utilitarian benefit, but he might receive a lesser discount simply because he missed a particular "waypoint"'.[64] He also pointed out that the time between a defendant's first appearance and trial may be relatively short for proceedings in the Magistrates' Courts, and that the defendant may not have enough time to make a proper decision on entering a guilty plea.[65] It was recommended that rather than the court adopting the English-style sliding scale of sentence discounts, defendants who make a 'timely' plea should be given the full sentence discount, whereas defendants who make an 'untimely' plea should be given a lesser discount. Timeliness ought to be determined based on giving defendants sufficient time to receive legal advice and not in reference to a specific stage of the proceedings.[66]

[63] Senior Counsel, previously Queen's Counsel prior to the handover on 1 July 1997, is appointed by the Chief Justice of Hong Kong for their ability and standing as a barrister and sufficient knowledge of the law. See section 31A of the Legal Practitioners Ordinance (Cap. 159).

[64] *HKSAR* v. *Ngo Van Nam*; *HKSAR* v. *Abdou Maikido Abdoulkarim* [2016] 5 HKLRD 1; [2016] HKCA 397 at 174.

[65] Ibid. at 175.

[66] Ibid. at 176.

The defence counsel for one of the defendants, Mr Michael Blanchflower SC, submitted that the practice in Hong Kong had been considering a guilty plea on the first day of trial a timely plea. He too urged against the adoption of an English-style sliding scale, stating that '[t]o do so, would be to punish a defendant by reducing the discount afforded to him because he might have delayed exercising his right to waive his constitutional rights to a fair trial and presumption of innocence'.[67] His argument essentially was that the sliding scale of sentence discounts would effectively be a trial penalty and late guilty plea penalty, an issue that will be revisited in Chapter 6.

In the submissions by the Department of Justice, the then director of Public Prosecutions Mr Keith Yeung SC noted that a full one-third sentence discount at the door of the court, that is, on the first day of trial, is at odds with the policy reasons for providing a sentence discount for a guilty plea.[68] Even with that said, the Director of Public Prosecutions was against implementing a quantified sliding scale of sentence discounts. He stated, '[T]he approach in England and Wales of having pre-set percentage discounts to be applied mechanically depending principally upon the stage at which the plea was entered was not to be supported.'[69]

Despite opposition against introducing a quantified sliding scale of sentence discounts for guilty pleas in Hong Kong by both the defence and the prosecution, the Hong Kong Court of Appeal did just that. As Lunn VP remarked, the justification was utilitarian:

> There is no doubt that the utilitarian value of a plea of guilty is greater the earlier the plea of guilty is intimated or tendered. The authorities to which we have referred speak with one voice in that respect. We are satisfied that it is not only logical, but also fair to reflect that factor in sentencing, so that a defendant who pleads guilty at an earlier stage is to be afforded a greater discount in sentence than a defendant who pleads guilty at a later stage.[70]

What was missing was mention of how an early guilty plea would protect victims and witnesses, something that was stressed in England and Wales. However, unlike the approach in England and Wales, where a distinction exists between sentence reductions for guilty pleas and

[67] Ibid. at 183.
[68] Ibid. at 189.
[69] Ibid. at 192.
[70] Ibid. at 198.

additional consideration of the defendant's remorse, such a distinction is less clear in Hong Kong. As the Court of Appeal held:

> [I]n Hong Kong to a considerable extent this Court has elided the difference between the utilitarian value of a plea of guilty and the subjective factor of remorse. So, other than in exceptional circumstances, the remorse of a defendant who pleads guilty is taken to be subsumed in the discount of one-third afforded for a plea of guilty. As noted earlier, this Court has used the phrase the 'high watermark' in a number of judgments in reference to the one-third sentence discount to describe the fact that remorse is subsumed in that discount. Notwithstanding that the practice does not reflect a pure, principled approach to sentencing, we are satisfied that it is not only well established but working in practice. Accordingly, we are satisfied that it is appropriate to continue sentencing on that basis.[71]

Although this opinion was not in accordance with any principled reasoning, because of practical applications, the issue of remorse would simply be 'subsumed' within the sentence discount for guilty pleas. Again, utilitarian reasons were enough of a justification for implementing a quantified sliding scale of sentence discounts.

Australia

In all Australian jurisdictions except Tasmania, statutory provisions exist that permit a sentence discount in response to a defendant pleading guilty.[72] However, only the states of South Australia, Western Australia, and New South Wales have a quantified sliding scale of sentence discounts.[73] The most generous sentence discount for a timely guilty plea is provided for in South Australia, where for summary offences or minor indictable offences that have been tried in the same way as a summary, the sentence discount can go up to 40 per cent if the defendant pleads guilty no more than four weeks after the first court

[71] Ibid. at 200. In *HKSAR* v. *Wan Wei* [2010] 5 HKC 45 at 12 for example, it was said that 'the significance of remorse said to be implicit in a plea of guilty has been the subject of debate. There is force in the suggestion that in many cases it is not a sign of remorse at all but that the plea is advanced for different reasons, which will vary from case to case; very often because of the strength of the case or for similarly pragmatic reasons.'

[72] See, for example, Part 2 Section 6AAA of the Sentencing Act 1991 (Vic); section 13 of the Penalties and Sentences Act 1992 (Qld).

[73] See sections 39 and 40 of the Sentencing Act 2017 (SA) and section 9AA of the Sentencing Act 1995 (WA).

appearance.[74] In New South Wales, a mandatory quantified sliding scale of sentence discounts was implemented for indictable offences since 30 April 2018.[75] Tellingly, the statutory provisions explicitly point out the utilitarian benefits of sentence discounts for guilty pleas; as section 25D(1) of the Crimes (Sentencing Procedure) Act 1999 (NSW) stipulates: 'In determining the sentence for an offence, the court is to apply a sentencing discount for the *utilitarian value* of a guilty plea in accordance with this section if the offender pleaded guilty to the offence at any time before being sentenced' (emphasis added). The courts have also noted that the earlier the plea is entered, the greater the utilitarian benefit to the administration of the criminal process.[76]

Under the sliding scale in New South Wales, there is to be a sentence discount of one-quarter if the magistrate accepted the defendant's guilty plea during committal proceedings for the offence. The sentence discount is reduced to one-tenth if the defendant was committed for trial and he or she either pleaded guilty at least 14 days prior to the first day of the trial or complied with pretrial notice requirements and pleaded guilty at the first available opportunity. Where these situations do not apply, the sentence discount is reduced to 5 per cent for the defendant's guilty plea.[77] However, the sentencing court has the discretion to reduce the sentence discount, despite the stage at which the defendant enters the guilty plea, if it is determined that the defendant's level of culpability is so extreme that community interests in the sentencing principles of retribution, punishment, community protection, and deterrence cannot be met.[78] Ultimately, when providing the sentence discount for a guilty plea, the sentencing court should explicitly state that a guilty plea was considered, demonstrating that it has been given weight. Judges are also encouraged to quantify the sentence discount, which can encompass all relevant matters including remorse, witness vulnerability, and utilitarian

[74] Section 39(2) of the Sentencing Act 2017 (SA). In Western Australia, the maximum sentence discount is set at one-quarter under legislation.

[75] For summary offences, the court may impose a lesser penalty after considering the fact of the guilty plea, the timing of the guilty plea or the indication of intention to plead guilty, and the circumstances of the intention, as per section 22(1) of the Crimes (Sentencing Procedure) Act 1999 (NSW).

[76] *R* v. *Thomson and Houlton* [2000] NSWCCA 309; (2000) 49 NSWLR 383. See also *R* v. *Borkowski* [2009] NSWCCA 102.

[77] Section 25D(2) of the Crimes (Sentencing Procedure) Act 1999 (NSW).

[78] Section 25F of the Crimes (Sentencing Procedure) Act 1999 (NSW).

value, although encouragement is given particularly to quantifying the utilitarian aspect.[79]

The utilitarian justification is expressed vividly in the High Court of Australia case of *Cameron*, in which it was emphasised that remorse is not necessarily a prerequisite for a sentence discount for a guilty plea. Instead, other features exist that are in the public interest.[80] Kirby J plainly states that

> [t]he main features of the public interest, relevant to the discount for a plea of guilty, are 'purely utilitarian'. They include the fact that a plea of guilty saves the community the cost and inconvenience of the trial of the prisoner which must otherwise be undertaken ... Given that under our criminal justice system it is the right of the accused to put the state to the proof of the crime charged; given that by pleading guilty the accused surrenders any chance of being acquitted, even undeservedly ... it is in the public interest to facilitate pleas of guilty by those who are guilty and to conserve the trial process substantially to cases where there is a real contest about guilt. Doing this helps ease the congestion in the courts that delay the hearing of such trials as must be held.[81]

Here is a clear acknowledgement that the criminal justice system relies on guilty pleas to operate, even though the justice system is supposedly built upon the premise that a defendant has the right to put the prosecution to the test and the right to a fair trial. Nonetheless, it is asserted that the utilitarian benefits of guilty pleas, especially early ones, are so strong that it is in the public interest for there to be sentence discounts for guilty pleas.

Scotland

Like other comparable jurisdictions, Scottish legislation requires the courts to consider the stage in the proceedings at which the defendant indicates a willingness to plead guilty and the circumstances of that indication when sentencing.[82] A justification primarily focused on the

[79] *R* v. *Thomson and Houlton* [2000] NSWCCA 309 at 160; (2000) 49 NSWLR 383.

[80] *Cameron* v. *R* (2002) 187 ALR 65 at 65. The court noted that a sentence discount for remorse may serve the public interest as a reinforcement for the defendant to avoid reoffending and serve as an example to others. The Hong Kong Court of Appeal has also cited this case.

[81] Ibid. at 66–7.

[82] Section 196 of the Criminal Procedure (Scotland) *Act* 1995.

utilitarian benefits of early guilty pleas is also endorsed.[83] Moreover, the courts have outlined a sliding scale of sentence discounts for guilty pleas modelled after the English definitive guidelines. The major difference, however, is that in Scotland emphasis is placed on the sliding scale not being mandatory, and that sentencing ought to be left to judicial discretion.

Like its English counterpart, the Scottish statutory provision requiring the courts to consider the timing of guilty pleas does not specify the exact amount of sentence discounts for guilty pleas. In the case of *Du Plooy*, the court was reluctant to state what a 'normal' or fixed sentence discount would be, arguing that it is a matter for the sentencer to decide for each individual case; however, the court did note that a sentence discount for a guilty plea should not normally exceed one-third.[84] In *Spence*, the High Court of Justiciary went further to give general guidance on the amount of sentence discounts corresponding to the stage in the criminal proceedings at which the defendant indicated a guilty plea.[85] The court held that '[t]he extent of the discount will be on a sliding scale ranging at its greatest from one-third, or in exceptional circumstances possibly more, to nil'.[86] This correspondence between the amount of sentence discounts and the different stages of criminal proceedings mirrors the sentencing guidelines found in England and Wales. Nevertheless, the court in *Spence* indicated that the levels of sentence discounts it provided are intended for guidance only and are not prescriptive. The exact amount of sentence discount for guilty pleas is dependent on the circumstances of individual cases.[87]

[83] See, for example, *Du Plooy* v. *HM Advocate* 2003 SCCR 640.

[84] Ibid. at 26.

[85] *Spence* v. *HM Advocate* [2007] HCJAC 64; 2007 SCCR 592.

[86] Ibid. at 14. More specifically: 'After an accused has appeared on petition, investigation and preparation will to an increasing extent be undertaken by the Crown prior to the service of an indictment. Among other courses open to an accused person during that period is the giving of written intimation to the Crown under section 76 of the 1995 Act of his intention to plead guilty and his desire to have his case disposed of at once. If a clear indication of an intention to plead guilty is given during that period (and is adhered to), we would expect that a discount in the order of one-third might be afforded. Such an indication at the first calling of a case at a preliminary hearing (or in the sheriff court at a first diet) might attract a discount in the order of one-quarter. Thereafter, any discount can be expected to reduce further. A plea at the trial diet should not ordinarily exceed one-tenth and in some circumstances may be less than that or nil.'

[87] Ibid. at 15.

In *Gemmell*, the court stressed the discretion of sentencers in providing for a sentence discount for guilty pleas and the amount of the discount.[88] The court noted that in appeals for cases before them and from courts of first instance, an expectation had developed since *Du Plooy* and *Spence* that defendants who pleaded guilty were 'entitled to' a sentence discount. The court stated that this was 'a careless use of language'.[89] It stressed that the level of sentence discount, if any, is always a matter at the sentencer's discretion; this had always been stressed in previous case law, but was neglected by legal practitioners and the courts.[90] The then Lord Justice Clerk Gill went further to criticise the quantified sliding scale of sentence discounts:

> In my opinion the sliding scale approach exemplified in the Definitive Guideline [In England and Wales] carries a risk of rigidity. That approach was favoured by this court in *Spence v HM Advocate*, but with the clear reservation that the amount of the discount, if any, would depend in every case on the circumstances. As it happens, the sliding scale mentioned in *Spence v HM Advocate* coincides with the Definitive Guideline. I think that the approach in *Spence v HM Advocate* is sound, but only so long as sentencers do not overlook that reservation. In my view, the broad principle that, in general, the discount will be the greater the earlier the plea is probably a sufficient statement of guidance for most purposes.[91]

Clearly, in Scotland the approach to leave sentence reductions for guilty pleas to the discretion of sentencers is favoured.[92]

What remains the same in Scotland as in other comparable jurisdictions is the plain acknowledgement, perhaps more plainly than others, that sentence discounts for guilty pleas are given for practical reasons. In *Gemmell*, the court declared:

> The euphemism 'utilitarian value' may be thought to give the principle of discounting some ethical content; but sentence discounting is not an exercise in Benthamite philosophy. It is not based on any high moral principle relating to the offence, the offender or the victim. On the contrary, it involves the court's passing a sentence that, in its considered judgment, is less than the offence truly warrants. It is a statutory

[88] *Gemmell, Robertson, Gibson and McCourt* v. *HM Advocate* [2011] HCJAC 129; 2012 SCCR 176.

[89] Ibid. at 30.

[90] Ibid. at 31.

[91] Ibid. at 78.

[92] See also J. Gormley, R. McPherson, and C. Tata, *Sentence Discounting: Sentencing and Plea Decision-Making* (Edinburgh: Scottish Sentencing Council, 2020).

> encouragement of early pleas. In some cases, there is a saving of inconvenience to complainers and witnesses. In a small minority of cases there is a saving in jury costs. There is also a benefit to the criminal justice system in the avoidance of undue delay between arrest and sentencing. But the primary benefit that is realised in every case is the saving of administrative costs and the reduction of the court's workload.[93]

Therefore, the amount of sentence discount in any given case is directly related to the extent of the utilitarian benefits from a guilty plea, given that some benefit from an early guilty plea is always likely.[94] It is not surprising, then, that the court stated that other factors, including the strength of the prosecution's case and the defendant's remorse, are not relevant to the sentence discount.[95]

The Lord Justice General Gill reiterated these principles in *Murray*, where it was again emphasised that a defendant who pleads guilty in Scotland is not entitled to a one-third sentence discount. However, he also stated that the sentence discount should be greater the earlier the plea is entered, and that at least a token discount should be given for an early plea. The overall utilitarian benefit from an early guilty plea would depend on the individual circumstances of each case.[96] The Lord Justice General emphasised that the earlier case of *Spence* did not set down a mandatory sliding scale of sentence discounts, as it reserved the decision on the amount of sentence discount for a guilty plea, if any, to the discretion of the sentencer in every case.[97] In contrast to the quantified sliding scale of sentence discounts adopted by England and Wales, Hong Kong, and some Australian states, the approach in Scotland is case-oriented and gives pre-eminence to the discretion of the sentencer.[98]

New Zealand

In New Zealand, the Sentencing Act 2002 lists 'whether and when the offender pleaded guilty' as one of the mitigating factors that the sentencing judge is to consider, among other mitigating factors including the offender's age, the victim's conduct, whether there was limited

93 *Gemmell, Robertson, Gibson and McCourt* v. *HM Advocate* [2011] HCJAC 129; 2012 SCCR 176 at 34.

94 Ibid. at 43.

95 Ibid. at 48–52.

96 *Murray* v. *HM Advocate* [2013] HCJAC 3; 2013 SCCR 88 at 17.

97 Ibid. at 24.

98 G. Brown, *Criminal Sentencing as Practical Wisdom* (Oxford: Hart, 2017), p. 203.

involvement in the offence on the offender's part, and any remorse shown by the offender.[99] The court is also to consider aggravating factors including whether the offence involved actual or threatened violence or the use of a weapon, whether it involved unlawful entry into or unlawful presence in a dwelling place, and whether it was committed while the defendant was on bail or still subject to a sentence.[100] Listing a guilty plea and when the guilty plea was entered as mitigating factors reflects the traditional approach adopted by New Zealand courts to leave the amount of sentence discount for a guilty plea to the discretion of the sentencing judge. There had been a refusal to set out a quantum for the sentence discount for guilty pleas because of the view that there would be widely varying circumstances for which a defendant might enter a guilty plea in individual cases. Nevertheless, the general principle remains that the earlier the guilty plea, the more generous the sentence discount may be.[101]

This changed with the case of *R* v. *Hessell* in the New Zealand Court of Appeal in 2009, where it was recognised that since about 2005, the New Zealand courts had shifted towards more definitive guidelines in response to defendants pleading guilty. A major influence behind this change in attitudes was the publication of the definitive guidelines by the Sentencing Guidelines Council in England and Wales on sentence reductions for guilty pleas.[102] Nevertheless, the adoption of a sliding scale for sentence discounts is not in line with the principles that a guilty plea is a mitigating factor, and that any sentence discount is left to the discretion of the sentencing judge. In *Hessell*, the New Zealand Court of Appeal took the opportunity to set out a guideline judgment on this issue by appointing a Full Court to hear the case.[103]

The Court of Appeal set out a sliding scale of sentence discounts for guilty pleas, where a one-third sentence reduction would be given to defendants who enter a guilty plea, or communicate a willingness to enter one, at the first reasonable opportunity. The sentence discount would reduce to one-fifth if the defendant enters a guilty plea, or communicates a willingness to enter one, at a status hearing or equivalent stage of proceedings in summary cases, or at the first committal callover in

[99] Section 9(2) of the Sentencing Act 2002.
[100] Section 9(1) of the Sentencing Act 2002.
[101] *R* v. *Mako* [2000] 2 NZLR 170.
[102] *R* v. *Hessell* [2009] 4 NZCA 450 at 3.
[103] Ibid. at 5.

indictable cases. The sentence discount would reduce further to one-tenth if the defendant enters a guilty plea, or communicates a willingness to enter one, three weeks prior to the commencement of the trial or hearing.[104] A sentence discount of less than one-tenth may be given after the commencement of trial, whereas no reduction would be given after the conclusion of the prosecution's case.[105] Since a sliding scale is to be adopted, between the first reasonable opportunity and the status hearing or first callover, the sentence discount would range from one-fifth to one-third. Between the status hearing or first callover and the commencement of the trial or hearing, the sentence reduction would range from one-tenth to one-fifth. The extent of the sentence discount depends on the stage in the proceedings at which the guilty plea is entered and 'the degree to which the plea prevented further trauma, stress, and inconvenience for victims and witnesses and save resources'.[106] Essentially, the New Zealand Court of Appeal adopted a quantified sliding scale of sentence discounts that mirrors the English model.

However, *Hessell* was appealed at the Supreme Court of New Zealand, which overturned the quantified sliding scale of sentence discounts.[107] The Supreme Court acknowledged that the motivation behind the Court of Appeal's adoption of a sliding scale and its justification had to do with utilitarian benefits. Writing the judgment for the Supreme Court, McGrath J pointed out: 'In the administration of criminal justice, courts give credit in sentencing for a guilty plea principally for policy reasons ... Avoiding the need for a trial saves the government costs associated with the judiciary and providing prosecution and defence services.'[108] However, the Supreme Court noted that encouragement for defendants to plead guilty, namely by way of a sentence discount, is premised on the assumption that defendants who plead guilty are in fact guilty. Otherwise, 'if that assumption is wrong, the incentives distort the criminal justice system and are contrary to the public interest. More fundamentally, they risk infringement of human rights',[109] since all defendants are presumed innocent until proven guilty. The Court further explained: 'The concern is that the pressure this puts on the accused can, potentially,

[104] Ibid. at 15.
[105] Ibid. at 18.
[106] Ibid. at 17.
[107] *Hessell* v. *R* [2010] NZSC 135.
[108] Ibid. at 45.
[109] Ibid. at 46.

lead to persons charged pleading guilty to offences they may not have committed.'[110] By focusing just on the timing of the plea, the Court underscored that 'pressure of this kind could lead to a guilty plea being entered in haste, by someone who may not be guilty of the offence charged and pleaded to'.[111]

Instead, the approach that the Supreme Court of New Zealand prefers is for '*[a]ll* circumstances in which the plea was entered must be addressed, not merely the timing'.[112] These include the strength of the prosecution's case and the defendant's remorse.[113] Moreover, the extent of the sentence discount should be left to the sentencing judge's discretion after considering the degree to which the guilty plea facilitates the administration of the criminal justice process and the objective circumstances in which the guilty plea is made.[114] Thus, it is not that the Supreme Court does not accept the justification of utilitarian benefits, but that they reject rigidly adhering to a quantified sliding scale of sentence discounts based solely on the stage at which the guilty plea is entered to the neglect of other factors.[115]

Conclusion

England and Wales, Hong Kong, and some Australian states have adopted a quantified sliding scale of sentence discounts, whether by way of definitive guidelines issued by an agency such as the Sentencing Council, sentencing guidelines handed down by the appellate court, or statutory provisions. The amount of sentence discount is determined primarily based on the timing of the guilty plea, whereas other factors, such as the strength of the prosecution's case or the defendant's remorse, are dealt with separately or subsumed in the sentence discount for the guilty plea. This unmistakably makes when the defendant pleads guilty

110 Ibid. at 48.
111 Ibid. at 60.
112 Ibid. at 51.
113 Ibid. at 52.
114 Ibid. at 57.
115 Ibid. at 70. In the recent case of *Moses* v. *R* [2020] NZCA 296 at 46, the New Zealand Court of Appeal stated that a two-step methodology should be used in sentencing. The first step is to calculate the adjusted starting point of the sentence, incorporating the aggravating and mitigating factors of the offence. The second step is to incorporate the aggravating and mitigating factors personally relevant to the defendant, together with any sentence discount for guilty pleas, which should be calculated as a percentage of the adjusted starting point.

the crucial factor. Other jurisdictions, namely Scotland and New Zealand, reject the quantified sliding scale of sentence discounts for guilty pleas, even though they acknowledge that an early plea should attract a greater sentence discount. The various jurisdictions, however, agree that the prevailing justification of sentence differentials for guilty pleas is the utilitarian benefits of saving time and costs. The Supreme of New Zealand pointed out that the assumption is that guilty defendants plead guilty, otherwise such incentives to plead guilty risk pressuring innocent defendants to plead guilty. For a long time, scholars and commentators have pointed to how sentence discounts for guilty pleas and related initiatives should be examined from the viewpoint of pressures on defendants to plead guilty, which will be discussed in Chapter 3.

3

Implicit (and Explicit) Plea Bargaining

Chapter 2 examined sentence discounts for guilty pleas in several comparable common law jurisdictions. Whereas the various jurisdictions differ regarding implementation, with some adopting a quantified sliding scale of sentence discounts for guilty pleas and others opting to leave the issue to judicial discretion, where they all agree on is the rationale for needing to include the timing of guilty pleas into sentencing considerations. Such a rationale is based on calculating defendants 'playing the system' by delaying their pleas, and the justification is utilitarian benefits to the criminal justice system. This chapter offers an alternative perspective on this rationale. First, it discusses how the sentence discount for guilty pleas can be viewed as a form of implicit plea bargaining. After all, as illustrated in Chapter 2, the courts aim to inform defendants of the sentence discount. Moreover, operating in tandem with advanced sentence indications and other stages of the criminal process, sentence discounts for guilty pleas arguably serve as pressure for defendants to plead guilty. This chapter begins by stepping back to consider the voluntariness of guilty pleas. It then examines the creation of advanced sentence indications, along with explicit communications of sentence discounts for guilty pleas to defendants by both the courts and defence lawyers. The chapter then explores plea bargaining and how communicating the sentence discount serves as implicit plea bargaining. Finally, this chapter concludes by arguing that the sliding scale of sentence discounts for guilty pleas operates in such a way that it leads to pressure defendants to plead guilty.

Voluntariness of Guilty Pleas

A defendant's entry of a guilty plea is equated as a formal admission of guilt. The legal principle governing such an admission appears straightforward: the defendant must be given the freedom of choice regarding whether to plead guilty. This principle is illustrated in the classic

1970 case of *Turner*,[1] in which the appellant (Turner) was convicted of car theft. The facts of this case are peculiar because the car actually belonged to Turner. The appellant had left his car at a garage for repairs; however, the garage staff who had parked the repaired car on the street subsequently found the car missing. It was later found on the street where the appellant lived. The garage owner thus took the car back, removed the repaired engine, and placed the car back on the street where it was found. After police were called, the appellant lied, saying he had never taken the car to the garage. He had initially pleaded not guilty and instructed his counsel to attack the prosecution's case;[2] however, on advice from his counsel, he entered a guilty plea and was subsequently convicted.

The issue in the appeal was whether the defendant had free choice in pleading guilty. During an adjournment in the trial, the defence counsel for Turner expressed to his client, in the solicitor's presence, that if he entered a guilty plea, the sentence may be non-custodial; conversely, if he contested in trial, where his previous convictions would be exposed, and was convicted, he risked a prison term. The defence counsel did this in strong terms and on more than one occasion. However, the English Court of Appeal did not find the counsel's view to amount to improper pressure on the appellant to plead guilty, as the counsel had stressed that the appellant maintained final say regarding the plea. Instead, the issue was that the counsel had given the appellant advice after having visited the judge together with the prosecutor. Consequently, the advice the counsel had given presented the impression that the counsel was reiterating the judge's views. The Court of Appeal, albeit with some reluctance, accepted that the appellant did not have free choice in retracting his plea of not guilty and thus quashed the conviction.

In this case, the English Court of Appeal laid down guidance that has been subsequently referred to as the *Turner* guidelines:

- The defence counsel must be completely free to give the best advice to the defendant and, if need be, give such advice 'in strong terms'.[3]

1 *R* v. *Turner* [1970] 2 QB 321.

2 The prosecution's case was based on the notion that the garage owners had a proprietary interest, specifically a lien, on the car and that because of the lies told to police, the taking of the car was done dishonestly.

3 *Turner* at 327.

- The defendant, after considering such legal advice, must be free to choose whether to plead guilty.
- Access must be maintained between the defence counsel and the judge, and discussions must take place with the prosecution present and, if so desired, with the defence's solicitor present.
- With one exception, the trial judge should never indicate the sentence that they are thinking about imposing. This includes supposing a certain sentence upon a conviction following a guilty plea, while also supposing a more severe sentence upon a conviction following a not guilty plea. Such a statement 'could be taken to be *undue pressure* on the accused, thus depriving him of that complete freedom of choice which is essential' (emphasis added).[4]
- The only exception to the previous is that the judge may say whether the sentence will not be of a certain form if the defendant pleads guilty or not guilty.
- Where any discussions between defence counsel and the judge occur, these should be disclosed to the defendant and the defendant should be informed of what took place.

Overall, the defendant's voluntariness in pleading guilty is considered essential, and emphasis is placed on preventing judges from indicating sentences in advance. This is partly to respond to the perception of 'plea bargaining', which this book will revisit in greater detail later, but more importantly, a prematurely indicated sentence is considered undue pressure on the defendant to plead guilty.

Advanced Sentence Indications

In the seminal case of *Goodyear*,[5] the English Court of Appeal held that judges no longer needed to adhere to the practice of never indicating the sentence they are thinking about imposing if the defendant seeks an advanced sentence indication. In this case, the appellant (Goodyear) appealed against his sentence following his guilty plea for corruption. During the trial judge's chambers meeting with the appellant's counsel and the prosecution, the judge indicated that the case would not result in a custodial sentence. The appellant and his co-defendants were re-arraigned, and they pleaded guilty. Subsequently, the appellant was

[4] Ibid. at 328.

[5] *R* v. *Goodyear* [2005] 3 All ER 117; [2005] EWCA Crim 888.

sentenced to six months' imprisonment suspended for two years and ordered to pay a fine.

The grounds of the appeal rested on the notion that a custodial sentence, even a suspended one, should not have been imposed, especially given the judge's indication.[6] Citing the then Sentencing Guidelines Council's definitive guidelines on sentence reductions for guilty pleas and past government reports,[7] Wolff CJ noted that 'a very different culture'[8] had emerged since *Turner* and that it was time to reconsider advanced sentence indications. The court in *Goodyear* subsequently drew a distinction between a sentence indication sought by the defendant and an unsolicited sentence indication given by the judge. The former was deemed appropriate, the reason being that '[t]he judge is simply acceding to the defendant's wish to be fully informed ... by having the judge's views about sentence available to him rather than the advice counsel may give him about what counsel believes the judge's views would be likely to be'.[9]

The current guidelines for an advanced sentence indication prior to the defendant pleading guilty, also known as a *Goodyear* indication, can be summarised as follows:

- Defendants in the Crown Court[10] may seek from the judge the maximum sentence that would be imposed if a guilty plea was entered at that stage in the proceedings.
- The judge, however, must refrain from indicating a maximum possible sentence following conviction post-trial.
- The judge can remind the defence of its entitlement to seek such an indication.
- When asked, the judge may refuse to give an indication of a sentence or reserve their position to give it at a later time.[11]

6 Ibid. at 18.

7 Home Office, *Justice for All (Cm 5563)* (Norwich: The Stationery Office, 2002); R. Auld, *Review of the Criminal Courts of England and Wales* (London: Lord Chancellor's Department, 2001); Royal Commission on Criminal Justice, *Report (Cm 2263)* (London: HMSO, 1993).

8 *R* v. *Goodyear* [2005] 3 All ER 117 at 47; [2005] EWCA Crim 888.

9 Ibid. at 49.

10 *Goodyear* indications are not applicable in the Magistrates' Courts.

11 This can be because the judge wants to wait until they obtain a pre-sentence report or that they would like more time to become familiar with the case. If the judge refuses to give an advanced sentence indication at that time, the defendant can seek another indication later on.

- Save for exceptional circumstances,[12] an indication is binding on the presiding judge and subsequent judges once given.
- The indication will only be valid for a reasonable period.[13]
- An indication should be given in open court.[14]

The objective of these changes is clear, as the court in *Goodyear* acknowledges: 'Experience tends to suggest that this would result in an increased number of early guilty pleas, which a consequent reduction in the number of trials, and the number of cases which are listed for trial, and then, to use current language, "crack" at the last minute.'[15] Once again, the assumption is that defendants are 'playing the system' and delaying their guilty pleas. The application procedure for an advanced sentence indication in the Crown Court is specified in the Criminal Procedure Rules.[16]

Besides England and Wales, other jurisdictions have also adopted advanced sentence indications. In New Zealand, for instance, a defendant may request a sentence indication in writing from the relevant court any time before trial. If granted, the court will then issue a statement about the likely sentence should the defendant plead guilty at that stage of the proceedings. The statement may include indications about the type and quantum of the sentence, such as duration or monetary amounts.[17] However, before the court issues a sentence indication about quantum, the judge must have information about the summary of facts that the prosecution and the defendant have agreed on, any previous convictions of the defendant, and copies of any victim impact statements.[18] The

[12] See, for example, *R* v. *Newman* [2010] EWCA Crim 1566; [2011] 1 Cr App R (S) 68.

[13] *R* v. *Utton* [2019] EWCA Crim 1341 states, 'If the court gives a Goodyear indication, the defendant has a reasonable opportunity to consider his position in light of the indication. If he does not do so, within that period, the indication ceases to have effect' at 14. What a 'reasonable period' is depends on the circumstances.

[14] See also Division VII: Sentencing of the *Criminal Practice Directions 2015* [2015] EWCA Crim 1567.

[15] *Goodyear* at 53.

[16] Rule 3.31 of the Criminal Procedure Rules 2020 states that where a defendant wishes to seek an indication for the maximum sentence that would be passed should a guilty plea be entered when the indication is sought, the application should be made in writing and submitted to the court officer and the prosecutor. The application must specify the offence(s) to which the defendant pleads guilty and the factual basis on which the guilty plea would be entered, as well as include the prosecution's agreement to, or other representations of, the proposed basis of the guilty plea.

[17] Section 60 of the Criminal Procedure Act 2011 (New Zealand).

[18] Ibid., section 61.

sentence indication is in effect until the close of the date specified by the judge or, if no date is specified, five working days after the date when it was issued.[19]

Similarly, in both the County Court and Supreme Court of Victoria, Australia, upon the defendant's application with the prosecutor's consent, the judge may indicate whether the court would likely impose an immediate imprisonment sentence should a guilty plea be given at the time of application.[20] However, a sentence indication can only be given once, unless the prosecution agrees otherwise.[21] In the Magistrates' Courts, advanced sentence indications may be broader, as the court can indicate whether it would likely impose immediate imprisonment or another sentence of a specified type should the defendant plead guilty to charges at that time.[22]

In jurisdictions such as Hong Kong, no advanced sentence indication schemes exist. Yet this does not mean that sentence discounts for guilty pleas cannot still be communicated.

Communicating the Sentence Discount

As discussed in Chapter 2, when sentencing a defendant in England and Wales, there is a statutory requirement for the courts to state in open court, in ordinary language and in general terms, its reasons for the imposed sentence and to explain to the defendant the effects of the sentence and the effects of non-compliance, if any orders have been imposed.[23] Furthermore, where the court has passed a less-severe sentence on a defendant who has pleaded guilty because of the guilty plea, the court must explicitly state that fact.[24] In effect, the court must clearly state that the defendant has received a sentence discount because of their guilty plea.[25]

19 Ibid., section 64.

20 Sections 207 and 208 of the Criminal Procedure Act 2009 (Victoria).

21 Ibid., section 208(1).

22 Ibid., section 60.

23 Sections 52(2) and 52(3) of the Sentencing Act 2020.

24 Ibid., section 52(7). See also R. Henham, 'Bargain justice or justice denied? Sentence discounts and the criminal process' (1999) 62 *Modern Law Review*, 515–38. For this study, the author observed 310 cases across different Crown Court Centres throughout 1997 and found that only about half of the judges would state in open court that they had given a sentence discount as a result of the defendant pleading guilty.

25 See also *R* v. *Fearon* [1996] 2 Cr App R (S) 25, where the English Court of Appeal, 'We would like to stress that it is highly desirable in every case where a defendant pleads guilty

In the case of *Saffa*,[26] the English Court of Appeal criticised the trial judge for making excessively brief sentencing remarks, including not explaining what sentence discount was applied in response to the defendant's guilty plea. The Crown Court Compendium, which aims to provide Crown Court judges with guidance for sentencing, reiterates this need to explain to convicted defendants, including defendants who pleaded guilty, the reasons for passing sentence and its effects in ordinary language.[27] Furthermore, sentencing remarks should give adequate explanations for the guideline category of the offence with respect to the sentencing guideline in question, reasons for any upward or downward adjustment from the relevant guideline's starting point for sentencing, reasons for considering a factor as an aggravating one, and reasons for applying a sentence discount for any guilty plea.[28] Consequently, Lord Burnett of Maldon CJ noted that sentencing remarks have gotten longer and longer, with sentencing judges 'craft[ing] sentencing remarks with the eye to the Court of Appeal',[29] something that should be avoided. Save for exceptional circumstances, sentencing remarks need not refer to authorities. However, the Lord Chief Justice stated the following:

> The sentence must be located in the guidelines. In general, the court need only identify the category in which a count sits by reference to harm and culpability, the consequent starting point and range, the fact that adjustments have been made to reflect aggravating and mitigating factors, where appropriate *credit for plea (and amount of credit)* and the conclusion.[30] (emphasis added)

In Hong Kong, the courts also have a duty to communicate sentence discounts to defendants. The sentencing court should explicitly state the starting point for the sentence adopted for the offence in question and the sentence discount given as a result of the guilty plea. Upon appeal,

in the Crown Court for the sentencing judge invariably to say so in his sentencing remarks. Then not only does the defendant know that it has been taken into consideration, but should the matter come to be considered by this Court, we also know that it has been taken into consideration' at 27.

26 *R* v. *Saffa* [2021] EWCA Crim 661.

27 D. Maddison *et al.*, *The Crown Court Compendium – Part II: Sentencing*, M. Picton, J. Cooper, and L. Harris (eds.), rev December 2020 (London: Judicial College, 2021), section 1.8(1).

28 Ibid., section 1.8(4).

29 *R* v. *Chin-Charles and Cullen* [2019] EWCA Crim 1140; [2020] 1 Cr App R (S) 6 at paragraph 7.

30 Ibid. at paragraph 10.

having information on the precise starting point for sentencing and the specific amount of sentence discount given would allow the appellate court to decide whether the discount was appropriate.[31] Where a sentencing judge does not provide the maximum sentence discount, that is, a one-third discount, it is important for the judge to indicate why. For example, in the case of *Shaer Chun-keung*,[32] where the defendant pleaded guilty to drug trafficking, the trial judge had initially stated that he would reduce the sentence by one-third or nearly one-third without further elaboration. The Hong Kong Court of Appeal stated, 'Here the full discount would have resulted in a sentence of nine years four months, and we are unable, in the absence of any reason given by the judge, to see why that sentence should not have been imposed.'[33] The Court of Appeal reiterated that it is important for the courts to give reasons for why they did not provide a full sentence discount in response to defendants' guilty pleas. This reasoning is not only useful in appeals but also useful to let defendants know that credit is given for guilty pleas, especially for timely guilty pleas. After all, the Hong Kong courts have clarified that 'it is the policy of the law to encourage guilty pleas by guilty persons'.[34]

Communications of the sentence discount may not just be directed at the defendant in a particular case. By imposing a duty on the courts to state in open court their reasons for sentences, including sentence discounts for guilty pleas,[35] the courts are essentially communicating the sentence discount for 'the courts; repeat clientele',[36] the audience in the courtroom, including other defendants present, and to the general public. The message is clear that all defendants who plead guilty will receive sentence discounts, and those who plead earlier will receive greater sentence discounts.

Besides explicit communications of sentence discounts for guilty pleas to individual defendants, past ethnographic research on criminal courts has also found that courts communicate the consequences of not pleading guilty implicitly to all defendants. For instance, a study by McConville and Mirsky observed over 250 felony cases in the 'guilty plea

[31] G. Cross and P. S. W. Cheung, *Sentencing in Hong Kong*, 8th ed. (Hong Kong: LexisNexis, 2018), p. 355.
[32] *HKSAR* v. *Shaer Chun-keung* [1998] 1 HKLRD 348; [1998] HKCU 137.
[33] Ibid. at 349.
[34] *R* v. *Yu Man-wu* [1995] 2 HKCLR 202; [1995] HKCU 450 at 203.
[35] Section 52(2) of the Sentencing Act 2020.
[36] L. Welsh, L. Skinns, and A. Sanders, *Sanders and Young's Criminal Justice*, 5th ed. (Oxford: Oxford University Press, 2021), p. 361.

court' of New York City between 1984 and 1987.[37] The authors found that defendants appearing before their plea arraignment are first shown, through watching other defendants preceding them, the consequences of a more severe punishment if a defendant chooses to plead not guilty. Subsequent defendants are then given '15 seconds to accept or reject the pleas and sentences offered to them by calendar judges'.[38] As a result, defendants witness for themselves the consequences of not pleading guilty.

In another ethnographic study of the Australian Magistrates' Courts, Roach Anleu and Mack found that while magistrates are prohibited from directly participating in plea bargaining and constrained by the expectation of judicial impartiality, they can still indirectly influence guilty pleas through their actions and communications.[39] The authors identified four strategies that magistrates adopt to encourage a guilty plea from the defendant: granting routine adjournments, granting reluctant adjournments attached with explicit expectations, setting a pretrial conference date or a trial date, and letting the defendant know that a guilty plea would lead to a lesser sentence or resolving the matter immediately that day.[40] In routine adjournments, for example, magistrates would comment that these were opportunities for the defendant to seek legal advice and learn about different aspects of the case, knowing that such advice would likely lead to a guilty plea.[41] Magistrates have also been found to express frustration when previous adjournments did not lead to a resolution in terms of a guilty plea or a decision to go to trial. This may be accompanied by a statement that expresses the expectation for a decision in the next hearing and hints that no further adjournments will be granted, usually meaning the expectation for a guilty plea.[42] In situations where adjournments do not reach a resolution, the magistrate may set a pretrial conference date. Moving the case to the next procedural stage in the criminal process indicates a stronger expectation for resolving the

37 M. McConville and C. Mirsky, 'Guilty plea courts: a social disciplinary model of criminal justice' (1995) 42 *Social Problems*, 216–34.

38 Ibid., 217.

39 S. Roach Anleu and K. Mack, 'Intersections between in-court procedures and the production of guilty pleas' (2009) 42 *Australian and New Zealand Journal of Criminology*, 1–23.

40 Ibid., 8.

41 See Chapter 5.

42 Roach Anleu and Mack, 'Intersections between in-court procedures and the production of guilty pleas,' 12.

case.[43] Lastly, in conjunction with the previous strategies, the magistrate can communicate that a sentence discount will accompany a guilty plea and, most importantly, that an earlier guilty plea would lead to a more generous discount.[44]

Communications by Defence Lawyers

Under the Code of Conduct for English barristers in the Bar Standards Board Handbook, a barrister has the core duty of 'act[ing] in the best interests of each client'.[45] The case of *Turner* discussed earlier laid down the principle that '[c]ounsel must be completely free to do what is his duty, namely to give the accused the best advice he can and if need be, advice in strong terms. This will often include advice that a plea of guilty . . . may well enable the court to give a lesser sentence than would otherwise be the case'.[46] While it may appear to always be in the client's best interest for the defence lawyer to test the state's case at trial and aim for acquittal, sometimes this best interest may very well be advising the defendant to plead guilty and receive a sentence reduction. This is because it is also the defence lawyer's ethical duty to draw the defendant's attention to the sentence discount for guilty pleas.[47] Therefore, like judges, defence lawyers are also obligated to ensure that defendants are well informed about the sentence discount.[48] The effects that defence lawyers and their advice may have on defendants pleading guilty will be further investigated in Chapter 5.

The *Turner* guidelines do stipulate that it is ultimately up to the defendant to make their choice of plea. However, Blake and Ashworth acutely observe that '[i]n reality the English system, with its large discount for pleading guilty, militates against the "free choice" of the defendant. The committed defence lawyer should recognise this, and strive to maximise client choice within the structure of the legal system

[43] Ibid., 15.
[44] Ibid., 17–18.
[45] Section CD2 of the Bar Standards Board Handbook.
[46] *Turner* at 327.
[47] M. Blake and A. Ashworth, 'Ethics and the criminal defence lawyer' (2004) 7 *Legal Ethics*, 167–89.
[48] Section rC15 of the Bar Standards Board Handbook states that a barrister's duty to act in the best interests of each client is to provide a competent standard of work and service to each client. The guidance to Rule C15 at section gC38 explains that a competent standard of work includes 'seeking to advise your client, in terms they can understand'.

as it exists'.[49] Tata also points out that the lawyer–client relationship is not one of equals; while this does not mean that defendants have no choice in their plea decisions, it does mean they rarely question their legal advisor's legal knowledge and advice.[50] Given explicit sentence discounts and the unequal relationship between lawyers and clients, one ought to wonder how much confidence can be placed in the notion that after considering legal advice, the defendant is completely free to make their plea decisions.

While defence lawyers are often given the image of zealous defenders standing up on behalf of individual defendants against the might of the state, in many ways, they have the same goals as other legal professionals in the criminal process. The most vivid example is again found in Code of Conduct in the Bar Standards Board Handbook, which states that the first core duty of barristers is to 'observe [their] duty to the court in the administration of justice'.[51] Although the Code of Conduct does not list the Core Duties in any order of precedence, it specifically states that the barrister's duty to the court overrides any other core duty.[52] Furthermore, Rule C4 clearly states that a barrister's duty to act in the best interests of each client is 'subject' to the barrister's duty to the court, which includes taking all reasonable steps to avoid wasting the court's time.[53] This rule is a clear indication that the defence counsel should have the same goal of efficiency as the courts. The same requirement is also set out for solicitors in England, where the Code of Conduct for English Solicitors simply and unequivocally states, 'You do not waste the court's time'.[54]

Similar provisions for barristers and solicitors in Hong Kong are also set out in ethical codes of conduct. For barristers, the Code of Conduct of the Hong Kong Bar Association echoes what has been set out in the *Turner* guidelines, stating that the duty of the defence counsel is to advise the client generally about pleading guilty to the charge, although prefaced

[49] Blake and Ashworth, 'Ethics and the criminal defence lawyer', 182.

[50] C. Tata, 'In the interests of clients or commerce? Legal aid, supply, demand, and "ethical indeterminacy" in criminal defence work' (2007) 34 *Journal of Law and Society*, 489–519.

[51] Section CD1 of the Bar Standards Board Handbook.

[52] Ibid., section gC1.

[53] Ibid., section rC3. Rule C3 reiterates that a barrister 'owe[s] a duty to the *court* to act with independence in the interests of justice. This duty overrides any inconsistent obligations which [they] may have (other than obligations under the criminal law)'.

[54] Section 2.6 of the Solicitors Regulation Authority's Code of Conduct for Solicitors, RELs and RFLs.

by the statement that the client has 'the responsibility for and complete freedom of choice in his plea'. However, the Code of Conduct subsequently says that in giving legal advice regarding pleas, the barrister may refer to all aspects of the case when giving advice. The barrister may also advise the client that acquittal may be unlikely and that the courts generally treat a guilty plea as a mitigating factor, meaning that a guilty plea will probably lead to a more lenient sentence. Most importantly, the Code of Conduct permits the defence counsel to express such legal advice, if need be, 'in strong terms'.[55] Similarly, for solicitors in Hong Kong, the Solicitors' Guide to Professional Conduct emphasises that the defendant has the right to choose whether to plead guilty and must clearly understand that the plea decision is ultimately theirs to make. Yet solicitors may offer legal advice regarding pleas 'in a strong and persuasive manner'[56] so long as the defendant understands that 'he has a right to choose how to plead'.[57] Ultimately, the ethical codes for both barristers and solicitors in Hong Kong demonstrate that their duties do not include drawing the defendant's attention to the possibility of a sentence discount for a guilty plea; however, they can advise on the guilty plea in a 'strong' manner. Moreover, like their English counterparts, Hong Kong barristers have a duty to the court where they 'must in every case use [their] best endeavours to avoid unnecessary expense and waste of the Court's time'.[58]

Implicit Plea Bargaining

Both prosecutors and defence counsel routinely engage in plea bargaining across various common law jurisdictions. However, the term 'plea bargaining' carries negative connotations. Lynch, for instance, notes: 'For all but the most doctrinaire free market micro-economists, the very term "plea bargaining" is distasteful .... "To bargain" is different than "to present reasoned arguments," and to reach a "bargain" or even an "agreement" is different than to obtain a "judgment" .... Something called "plea bargaining" can hardly be other than an expedient stepchild

[55] Paragraph 10.56(a) of the Code of Conduct of the Hong Kong Bar Association.

[56] Commentary 2 on Rule 10.16 of the Hong Kong Solicitors' Guide to Professional Conduct, vol. 1.

[57] Ibid.

[58] Paragraph 10.36 of the Code of Conduct of the Hong Kong Bar Association.

in a judicial system.'[59] Therefore, in jurisdictions such as England and Wales and Hong Kong, plea bargaining is not officially recognised as a practice despite the frequent informal use of the term.[60] Instead, such jurisdictions recognise what is referred to as 'charge bargaining'. For instance, in cases with multiple charges, the prosecution can reach an agreement with the defence to drop certain charges in exchange for the defendant pleading guilty to the remaining charges. Another example is the prosecution proceeding with a less serious charge in exchange for a guilty plea, such as reducing a drug-trafficking charge to a possession charge.[61]

To avoid the impression that justice is dispensed through some back-door 'bargaining' between the prosecution and defence counsel, such arrangements are referred to as 'plea negotiations' in England and Wales and in Australia,[62] or 'resolution discussions' in Canada.[63] In Hong Kong, the Prosecution Code refers to 'plea negotiation and agreement', while defence lawyers use the phrase 'make representations to the Department of Justice to see if this matter can be dealt with in another way' in court proceedings.[64] Nevertheless, judges have tried to distance themselves from the practice. In *Goodyear*, the court held that when providing for an advanced sentence indication,

> [a] judge should never be invited to give an indication on the basis of what would appear to be a 'plea bargain'. He should not be asked or become involved in discussions linking the acceptability to the prosecution of a particular plea or bases of plea and the sentence which might be imposed

[59] G. E. Lynch, 'Our administrative system of criminal justice' (1998) 66 *Fordham Law Review*, 2117–51, pp. 2129–30.

[60] An exception to this convention in England and Wales concerns formal powers that have been granted to the Serious Fraud Office to negotiate plea agreements in serious fraud cases. See D. Alge, 'Negotiated plea agreements in cases of serious and complex fraud in England and Wales: a new conceptualization of plea bargaining?' (2013) 19 *European Journal of Current Legal Issues*, 1–18.

[61] See, for example, Paragraphs 9.1–9.7 of the Code for Crown Prosecutors in England and Wales, as well as paragraphs 13.1–13.5 of the Prosecutions Code for Hong Kong. For instance, Paragraph 13.1 of the latter states, 'The prosecution may be invited by the defence to resolve a matter by agreeing to the accused pleading guilty to fewer or lesser charges than those already laid. In rare circumstances, the prosecution may itself put this suggestion to the defence.'

[62] C. A. Brook *et al.*, 'A comparative look at plea bargaining in Australia, Canada, England, New Zealand, and the United States' (2016) 57 *William & Mary Law Review*, 1147–224.

[63] Ibid., 1157.

[64] K. K. Cheng, 'The practice and justifications of plea bargaining by Hong Kong criminal defence lawyers' (2014) 1(2) *Asian Journal of Law and Society*, 395–412, p. 400; paragraph 13 of the Prosecutions Code (2020).

> and he should not be asked to indicate levels of sentence which he might have in mind depending on possible different pleas.[65]

In other words, any plea discussions are left to the prosecution and the defence with no judicial involvement. In *McKinnon*, Lord Brown unambiguously stated that '*Goodyear* forbids are *judicial*, not prosecutorial, indications of sentence' (emphasis in original).[66]

In the Hong Kong case of *Scales*, the trial judge heard a discussion in his chambers, where he was informed that the defendant was considering pleading guilty to certain charges in exchange for the prosecution dropping the remaining charges. The judge was also asked if a suspended sentence as opposed to an immediate imprisonment sentence was possible. Yet after the defendant pleaded guilty, the judge eventually imposed an immediate prison term. The defendant appealed, arguing that it was necessary to give effect to the judge's promise of a suspended sentence. However, the Hong Kong Court of Appeal dismissed the appeal, emphasising that '[i]t is of major importance that there be no appearance of a defendant striking a bargain with the court'.[67] The court went on to state that 'plea bargaining is not part of our jurisprudence',[68] explaining that '[w]hat transpired here was not, in our view, *true plea bargaining* for this we take to mean an indication from a trial judge that if a man pleads guilty he will get one sentence and if he does not, and is convicted after trial, he will get another and more severe one' (emphasis added).[69] Interestingly, whereas Hong Kong has no mechanism for advanced sentence indications by judges unlike England and Wales, as previously mentioned, the Court of Appeal was attempting to narrow the definition of plea bargaining, even denying its existence altogether.

However, if we adopt a wider definition of plea bargaining to mean where a defendant pleads guilty in exchange for some concessions, then charge bargaining, along with any sentence indications by judges and sentence discounts for guilty pleas, would all fit this definition. After all, if a defendant pleads guilty in exchange for a reduction in charges – which will probably lead to a reduced sentence given that the defendant will be convicted of fewer or less-severe offences – or does so knowing that a guilty plea will amount to a lighter sentence because of the sentence discount, these events very much amount to plea bargaining because a

65 *Goodyear* at 67.
66 *McKinnon* v. *US* (2008) UKHL 59 at 34.
67 *R* v. *Scales* [1987] HKLR 583 at 587.
68 Ibid.
69 Ibid. at 587–8.

clear concession, via a more lenient sentence, is given in exchange for pleading guilty. As Welsh, Skinns, and Sanders remark, 'plea bargaining by any other name smells just as sour to us'.[70]

Consequently, the sentence discount for guilty pleas can be regarded as 'implicit plea bargaining', where although no direct negotiations take place between the judge and the defendant, the defendant knows they will receive a more lenient sentence because the sentence discount for guilty pleas is made *explicit* to them.[71] Heumann observed the following half a century ago:

> Whether or not actual discussions took place between prosecutors and defence attorneys as the old timers asserted, the plea of guilty itself probably earned the defendant – or was perceived as likely to earn the defendant – a more favourable disposition than if he insisted on trial. Pleading guilty was (and is) tantamount to engaging in 'implicit plea bargaining'. Today perhaps defence attorneys are more forceful in insuring that the reward is forthcoming, and perhaps their efforts in the 'explicit plea bargaining' encounter yield even greater rewards, but the difference is one of degree and not of kind.[72]

Mack and Roach Anleu go further to state that '[w]hen a judge advises an accused person of the availability of the sentence discount, this judicial offer of a lesser sentence in return for a plea of guilty is, in effect, a plea bargain in its crudest form'.[73] With the development of the advanced sentence indications, sentencing guidelines on sentence discounts for guilty pleas, and an increasing emphasis on saving court time and resources, the implicit nature of receiving a concession for pleading guilty is becoming increasingly not that implicit. The effects of all these developments increase pressure on defendants to plead guilty.

Pressures to Plead Guilty

Feeley's seminal work on the lower criminal courts in the American state of Connecticut points to how 'the process is the punishment'.[74] Although

[70] Welsh, Skinns, and Sanders, *Sanders and Young's Criminal Justice*, p. 370.

[71] L. M. Friedman, 'Plea bargaining in historical perspective' (1979) 13 *Law & Society Review*, 247–60.

[72] M. Heumann, 'A note on plea bargaining and case pressure' (1975) 9 *Law & Society Review*, 515–28, p. 526.

[73] K. Mack and S. Roach Anleu, 'Sentence discount for guilty plea: time for new look' (1997) 1 *Flinders Journal of Law Reform*, 123–44, p. 124.

[74] The title of Feeley's book effectively presents his thesis. See M. Feeley, *The Process Is the Punishment: Handling Cases in a Lower Criminal Court* (New York: Russell Sage Foundation, 1979).

the work was published decades ago, its message still resonates today, especially regarding the timing of guilty pleas and the pressure on defendants to get the matter over with quickly. The dominant theme of Feeley's Pretrial Process Model is that the costs of a defendant having to go through criminal proceedings outweigh the eventual sentences that the court will impose following conviction. As he explains:

> In the lower courts, it is the cost of being caught up in the criminal justice system itself that is often most bothersome to defendants accused of petty offences, and it is this cost which shape their subsequent course of action once they are entrapped by the system . . . And for every defendant who would like a trial, there are dozens who do not even bother to appear in court. Under such circumstances, even a decision to engage in protracted negotiations could *increase* rather than decrease costs to the defendant intent on getting his case over with the least possible effort.[75]

While Feeley's model is meant to apply to lower courts where the eventual sentence is less severe, thus rendering pretrial costs disproportionate, his observations can also apply to higher courts where a sliding scale of sentence discounts is enforced. This is because defendants in higher courts must bear the same costs – probably even higher costs – because of the longer and more complex court proceedings. Moreover, with a sliding scale of sentence discounts in effect, greater emphasis is placed on the timing of guilty pleas, where an early plea would incur the least costs associated with a sentence, that is, the most discounted sentence. This adds a major incentive for defendants to get their cases over with as quickly as possible, the quickest way to do so being through an early guilty plea.

The costs that defendants must bear while going through the criminal process serve as pressures for them to plead guilty. For instance, the defendant may be held in pretrial detention, meaning that they are locked up even before a formal conviction from the court.[76] Even if the defendant is granted bail, bail conditions must be imposed, including posting sureties,[77] reporting to a police station, or even undergoing electronic monitoring.[78] Such conditions can make life cumbersome for the defendant, even if they are released on bail.

[75] Ibid., p. 30.
[76] This is further discussed in Chapter 5.
[77] Section 8 of the Bail Act 1976.
[78] Ibid., section 3AB.

Another significant cost that defendants face during the pretrial phase is that associated with obtaining a lawyer, which goes beyond legal costs. They may experience a lot of confusion in finding the right defence lawyer, deciding on whether to hire a private lawyer or seek a publicly funded one, and applying for and undergoing merits[79] and means testing to see if they are eligible for legal aid should they choose the latter. In England and Wales, free legal advice without means testing is limited to 'initial advice and initial assistance' for individuals held in custody at a police station or similar premises.[80] Unrepresented defendants who appear in the Magistrates' Courts can also receive assistance from a duty solicitor for their first appearance without means testing if they are charged with an offence for which imprisonment is a possibility.[81] The fact of the least restrictive legal assistance being limited to police station custody or the first hearing only further supports the notion that pretrial costs are minimised the most if the case is concluded as soon as possible.

Repeated interviews with lawyers and the weighing of legal advice can also take their toll on the defendant. Court appearances, especially when more than one is required, as is the case if the defendant pleads not guilty, means that the defendant will have to take time off work and lose potential earnings. This last point is vividly illustrated in Cheng's observations of the Magistrates' Courts in Hong Kong, where defendants were discovered wanting to plead guilty at the earliest opportunity to avoid needing to reappear in court and losing income from taking time off work. Cheng's observations of a typical shoplifting case involving an

79 See Section 17 of the Legal Aid, Sentencing and Punishment of Offenders Act 2012. The merits test is in 'the interests of justice'. Section 17(2) lists the factors for the purposes of such determination. It includes: (a) whether, if any matter arising in the proceedings is decided against the individual, the individual would be likely to lose his or her liberty or livelihood or to suffer serious damage to his or her reputation, (b) whether the determination of any matter arising in the proceedings may involve consideration of a substantial question of law, (c) whether the individual may be unable to understand the proceedings or to state his or her own case, (d) whether the proceedings may involve the tracing, interviewing or expert cross-examination of witnesses on behalf of the individual, and (e) whether it is in the interests of another person that the individual be represented.

80 Ibid., section 13. Moreover, section 13(7) states that '"initial advice" means advice as to how the law in relation to a matter relevant to the individual's arrest applies in particular circumstances and as to the steps that might be taken having regard to how it applies' and that '"initial assistance" means assistance in taking any of those steps which the individual might reasonably take while in custody, including assistance in the form of advocacy'.

81 Similarly, the Duty Lawyers Scheme offers free legal representation without means testing for first appearances in the Hong Kong Magistrates' Courts; however, the Hong Kong legal system does not provide for free legal advice at police stations.

unrepresented middle-aged woman illustrate this desire. The following extract is taken from the exchange regarding plea mitigation after the unrepresented defendant entered a guilty plea at the first opportunity:

DEFENDANT: I bought many things that day. I forgot to put back the toothpaste.
MAGISTRATE: When you were leaving, did you know you had the toothpaste?
DEFENDANT: Sorry. Sorry. It was my fault. I only knew when the alarm went on.
MAGISTRATE: I cannot accept your plea then.
DEFENDANT: Oh no. I plead guilty. I need to go to work. Because I work in the hospital, it's hard to get a day off. I plead guilty.
MAGISTRATE: Case stood down. Go see the duty lawyer.

After the defendant returned to court with a duty lawyer later that day, she continued to plead guilty until the magistrate ultimately accepted her plea.[82]

Whereas proceedings in the criminal process already pressure defendants into pleading guilty, the quantified sliding scale of sentence discounts is the definitive pressure for defendants to plead guilty sooner rather than later. Notably, the Sentencing Council for England and Wales prefers using the term 'incentive' when referring to sentence discounts and not 'reward', and certainly does not want the sliding scale to be perceived as pressure for defendants to plead guilty.[83] The Sentencing Council emphasises in their definitive sentencing guidelines on sentence reductions for guilty pleas that '[t]he purpose of this guideline is to encourage those who are going to plead guilty to do so as early in the court process as possible. Nothing in the guideline should be used to put pressure on a defendant to plead guilty'.[84] Moreover, in the House of Lords decision on *McKinnon*, Lord Brown remarked, 'In one sense all discounts for pleas of guilty could be said to subject the defendant to pressure, and the greater the discount the greater the pressure.' However,

[82] K. K. Cheng, 'Pressures to plead guilty: factors affecting plea decisions in Hong Kong's magistrates' courts' (2013) 53 *British Journal of Criminology*, 257–75.

[83] The Sentencing Council for England and Wales noted: 'There is an understandable reluctance to provide those who are guilty with a "reward" for pleading guilty, especially when they have little or no prospect of being acquitted. However, it is important to recognise that the guilty plea reduction is in place to provide an incentive (with all the benefits outlined above) and not a reward.' See Sentencing Council, *Reduction in Sentence for a Guilty Plea Guideline: Consultation* (London: Sentencing Council, 2016).

[84] Ibid., p. 4.

he further emphasised, '[T]he discount would have to be very substantially more generous than anything promised here (as to the way the case would be put and the likely outcome) before it constituted *unlawful pressure* such as to vitiate the process' (emphasis added).[85] While a one-third sentence discount on a 15, 20, or 30-year sentence as a starting point indeed sounds 'generous', the House of Lords rejected the notion that the actual amount of the sentence discount itself would constitute undue pressure, as how the discount was put forth is also important. Lastly, certain defendants may be more vulnerable to such 'incentives', including ethnic minorities, women, younger defendants, and defendants with mental illness, who are more susceptible to pleading guilty because of these incentives. Even so, defendants caught up in the criminal process are disproportionately represented by the disadvantaged and vulnerable in society.[86]

Innocent Defendants Pleading Guilty

The courts typically accept a guilty plea without questioning the rationale behind it. Unlike a trial, where evidence is heard and contested to reduce the probability of convicting innocent defendants, such protection is not afforded to those who plead guilty.[87] Since so many instances of wrongful convictions resulting from trials have occurred, it can be surmised that a strong probability of defendants being wrongfully convicted through guilty pleas exists. Moreover, given the pressures to plead guilty described earlier, especially that brought by the sliding scale of sentence discounts, a significant risk of innocent defendants plead guilty exists. After all, Feeley observes: '[P]retrial costs do not distinguish between innocent and guilty; they are borne by all'[88] For the

[85] *McKinnon* at 38.

[86] R. K. Helm, 'Conviction by consent? Vulnerability, autonomy and conviction by guilty plea' (2019) 83(2) *The Journal of Criminal Law*, 161–72; K. Mack and S. Roach Anleu, 'Choice, consent and autonomy in a guilty plea system' (2000) 17 *Law in Context*, 75–95; J. Peay and E. Player, 'Pleading guilty: why vulnerability matters' (2018) 81 *Modern Law Review*, 929–57.

[87] Bridges acutely points out, 'The not guilty plea serves to reaffirm the burden of proof on the prosecution and the proper role of the court in determining guilt or innocence. By contrast, the guilty plea is almost always immediately determinate of the legal outcome of the case, effectively supplanting the role of the court both in adjudicating guilt or innocence.' See L. Bridges, 'The ethics of legal representation on guilty pleas' (2006) 9 *Legal Ethics*, 80–100.

[88] Feeley, *The Process Is the Punishment*, p. 31.

certain prospect of a reduced sentence, innocent defendants are often highly tempted to plead guilty.[89]

Evidence of the likelihood of innocent defendants pleading guilty is found in the 1993 Crown Court Study conducted by the Royal Commission on Criminal Justice. For the study, Zander and Henderson took a snapshot of nearly all English Crown Courts to capture the practices involved in over 3,000 criminal cases. Questionnaires were handed out to various parties, including defence lawyers, judges, police, jurors, and defendants. A question that was posed to lawyers asked: 'An innocent defendant sometimes decides to plead guilty to achieve a sentence discount or reduction in the indictment. Were you concerned that this was the case?'[90] The authors found that lawyers responded 'yes' to 53 cases where such a concern existed. Extrapolating this finding to a full year suggests that 1,400 innocent defendants plead guilty annually, allegedly because of the sentence discount for guilty pleas or some other concession.[91] However, Zander subsequently tried to downplay this finding by arguing that closer inspection of the 53 cases revealed most of the defendants to have previous criminal convictions. He interpreted this discovery as indicating that more experienced defendants were perhaps not so innocent and would tactically plead guilty.[92] In short, Zander's interpretation reveals another belief based on the assumption that defendants with a criminal history 'play the system' through guilty pleas.

In a more recent survey of criminal law practitioners across England and Wales conducted by Helm from 2017 to 2018, of the 90 legal professionals surveyed, 90 per cent replied that they thought defendants pleaded guilty because it would be easier and quicker than going to trial. Thirty-four per cent of respondents thought that this occurred

89 See L. E. Dervan and V. A. Edkins, 'The innocent defendant's dilemma: an innovative empirical study of plea bargaining's innocence problem' (2013) 103 *Journal of Criminal Law and Criminology*, 1–48. The authors conducted an experimental study where student participants were accused of cheating. They found that both guilty and innocent students accepted plea offers, with over half of the innocent students being willing to falsely admit guilt for a reduced punishment.

90 The wording of this question was criticised for presuming that innocent defendants who plead guilty exists, exactly what the question sought to validate. See M. McConville and L. Bridges, 'Pleading guilty while maintaining innocence' (1993) 143 *New Law Journal*, 160–4.

91 M. Zander and P. Henderson, *The Royal Commission on Criminal Justice: Crown Court Study (Research Study No. 19)* (London: HMSO, 1993), p. 139.

92 M. Zander, 'The "innocent"(?) who plead guilty' (1993) 143 *New Law Journal*, 85–6.

frequently, while 56 per cent thought that this occurred not too often. Yet when asked whether they believed that both guilty and innocent defendants plead guilty because it would be easier and quicker than going to trial, 61 per cent of respondents replied yes. An additional 13 per cent replied that it was impossible to know, since they did not know whether their clients were factually guilty.[93]

Further evidence of false guilty pleas by innocent defendants is found in a recent content analysis of 139 Australian appellant court cases in which a guilty plea conviction was overturned. In this analysis, Nash, Dioso-Villa, and Porter examined the types of errors resulting in these wrongful convictions. They discovered that in 58 per cent of cases, the appellate court overturned the guilty plea conviction because the defendant may not have been legally culpable for the convicted offence, including cases where the appellate court found that the defendant's actions did not constitute the offence specified in the charge or that there was an arguable defence to the charge.[94] Thirty per cent of wrongful convictions occurred because of procedural errors, which included undue pressure by the courts, such as inappropriate comments on the likelihood of conviction. Lastly, 12 per cent of cases were overturned because the appellate court deemed the defendant factually innocent.[95]

Conclusion

This chapter offers an alternative perspective on the sliding scale of sentence discounts for guilty pleas. Instead of looking at sentence discounts through the lens of the utilitarian benefits it purports to bring, it considers sentences discounts as a form of implicit plea bargaining. Despite the courts' hesitation toward being seen as a party to the plea bargaining process, the notion of a sentence discount for guilty pleas is essentially a form of plea bargaining, as are the requirements on the

[93] R. K. Helm, 'Constrained waiver of trial rights? Incentives to plead guilty and the right to a fair trial' (2019) 46 *Journal of Law and Society*, 423–47, pp. 443–4.

[94] The latter refers to cases where defendants had their guilty plea convictions overturned because they were considered legally innocent in addition to factually innocent.

[95] C. Nash, R. Dioso-Villa, and L. Porter, 'Factors contributing to guilty plea wrongful convictions: a quantitative analysis of Australian appellate court judgments' (2021) *Crime & Delinquency*, advanced online publication. On the reluctance of the English Court of Appeal to overturn guilty plea convictions, see R. Nobles and S. Schiff, 'The supervision of guilty pleas by the Court of Appeal of England and Wales – workable relationships and tragic choices' (2020) 31 *Criminal Law Forum*, 513–52.

courts and defence lawyers to communicate the sentence discount directly, in some cases alongside advanced sentence indications in certain jurisdictions. Moreover, as with any form of plea bargaining, sentences discounts bring with them the associated risks of plea bargaining. Compounding existing costs on defendants regarding being caught up in the criminal process, the sliding scale of sentence discounts for guilty pleas adds to the pressures on defendants to plead guilty, aiming to extract a guilty plea as soon as possible.

4

Revisiting the Assumptions and Methodology

As outlined in Chapter 1, the sliding scale of sentence discounts for guilty pleas is based on the two prevailing assumptions that criminal defendants 'play the system' by delaying their guilty pleas and that 'cracked trials' leads to a waste of resources. The aim of a quantified sliding scale of sentence discounts for guilty pleas is to encourage defendants to plead guilty, and to plead guilty sooner rather than later. A sliding scale is ultimately enacted to resolve the criminal justice system's problem of cracked trials. One major criticism against this notion is that various government reports and court cases have cited no empirical evidence that late guilty pleas are indeed the product of cunning experienced defendants 'playing the system'. This chapter aims to take a step back and scrutinise these two assumptions. First, it investigates whether defendants did 'play the system' before the implementation of the quantified sliding scale of sentence discounts. From the limited studies available, the answer to this question is mixed at best. Second, this chapter investigates whether the sliding scale of sentence discounts has helped the courts resolve their problem of cracked trials. Data before and after the introduction of the sliding scale of sentence discounts suggest that not much has changed in terms of guilty plea rates, cracked trial rates, and average waiting time until trial, bringing into question the usefulness of the sliding scale in promoting efficiency. The rest of the chapter details the methodology and datasets for this book, paving the way for the analyses in proceeding chapters.

Playing the System?

What does it mean for defendants to 'play the system'? What potential advantages might defendants gain from waiting until closer to the trial date or the day of trial (or even during trial) to plead guilty, instead of doing so at the earliest opportunity? Perhaps the defendant is waiting in hopes of a more favourable sentencer at a subsequent hearing, or that additional evidence may turn up in their favour. Whatever the reason, the assumption exists that experienced defendants who have been through the criminal process before are best placed to 'play the system'.

Studies on the causes of cracked trials and late guilty pleas are scarce. The limited studies that were conducted prior to the implementation of the quantified sliding scale for sentence discounts for guilty pleas provide important insights. Despite being decades old, one of the most seminal studies on 'cracked trials' is the study of defendants in the Birmingham Crown Court during the 1970s by Baldwin and McConville, titled *Negotiated Justice*. They interviewed 121 plea-changers for their reasons in going from an initial not guilty plea to entering a late guilty plea.[1] The study discovered that it was not defendants using the criminal procedure to their tactical advantage, but the defendants' own legal counsel pressuring them to change their pleas. This pressure was at times manifested in plea bargaining with the prosecution. 18.2 per cent of the interviewed sample cited a plea bargain being made and accepted as their reason for their late guilty pleas, while 13.2 per cent stated that there was no explicit plea bargain, but they thought a plea deal had been struck on their behalf. Most strikingly, nearly 40 per cent of the defendants interviewed disclosed that no specific offer of a plea bargain was made, but they had pleaded guilty because of pressure from their barristers.[2]

Alge's thesis offers another rare picture of the potential causes for late guilty pleas prior to the implementation of the quantified sliding scale of sentence discounts in England and Wales. From the Crown Prosecution Service files, Alge analysed 119 cases heard at Manchester Minshull Street Crown Court between June and December 2006 involving 151 defendants, which served as the unit of analysis. Ten interviews with legal practitioners were also conducted.[3] Among the 151 defendants, all had initially pleaded not guilty, with only 23.2 per cent of cases ending in a conviction or acquittal after trial. This meant that most of the sample could be said to have at least one 'cracked' criminal charge. For nearly half of the defendants, their entire case was disposed of either by way of a

[1] J. Baldwin and M. McConville, *Negotiated Justice: Pressures to Plead Guilty* (London: Martin Robertson, 1977).

[2] Ibid.

[3] D. Alge, 'Pressures to plead guilty or playing the system? An exploration of the causes of cracked trials', unpublished PhD thesis, The University of Manchester (2009).

late guilty plea or by the prosecution offering no evidence, with the former accounting for most of the cases.[4]

A closer examination of the recorded reasons for cracked trials within the sample of case files reveals that 28 per cent was because of the defendant's plea to the original offence, 16 per cent because of the defendant's plea to an alternative offence, 28 per cent because the prosecution offered no evidence, and 28 per cent because of a combination of reasons.[5] The case files for approximately 41 per cent of the defendants recorded a plea bargain of some form, with the defence making an offer in 16.56 per cent of the cases and the prosecution making an offer in 7.28 per cent of the cases. Moreover, counteroffers between the prosecution and defence were recorded for over 10 per cent of the cases.[6] This stresses the role that plea bargaining may play in a defendant's decision to enter a late guilty plea. Alge observes that how officials record what is a 'cracked trial' is problematic. A 'cracked trial' is a trial where all the charges in a particular case have cracked, with the reason attributed to the defendant if one charge 'cracks' because of the defendant's guilty plea. This definition ignores how 28 per cent of the cases that Alge studied cracked because of multiple reasons, and that cracked trials caused by defendants entering a late guilty plea are likely overrepresented. More importantly, this overrepresentation contributes to the (false) assumption that defendants are 'playing the system'.[7] Alge's study also found that the number of previous convictions a defendant had was irrelevant to whether the case cracked. An equal number of defendants with a previous conviction stood in a cracked trial and in an effective trial.[8] This raises doubts about the assumption that more experienced defendants are cracking their trials.

In Hong Kong, the most direct study of cracked trials prior to the introduction of the sliding scale of sentence discounts for guilty pleas is the one by Cheng and colleagues. They conducted courtroom observations to elicit quantitative data in the Magistrates' Courts from January to October 2015, one year before the sliding scale of sentence discounts was

[4] Ibid., pp. 121–3.
[5] Ibid., p. 125.
[6] Ibid., p. 150.
[7] Ibid., p. 158.
[8] Ibid., pp. 139–40.

introduced in Hong Kong; data were collected for 427 defendants.[9] Each defendant was tracked from initial court appearance to trial date to determine whether their cases would crack.[10] Nearly three-quarters of the sample resulted in a cracked trial where the defendant entered a late guilty plea.[11] Additionally, criminal record was used as a proxy variable in a binary logistic regression to test whether experienced defendants were more likely to enter a late guilty plea (the outcome variable). Regression analysis found that the number of criminal convictions was not a significant factor affecting the timing of guilty pleas.[12]

Cheng and colleagues subsequently conducted semi-structured interviews with 58 defendants referred by non-governmental organisations to gain a deeper understanding of their experiences with and views regarding the criminal justice process. Of particular interest was whether defendants entered late guilty pleas to 'play the system'. Most responded that they had not tried to 'game the system' with their plea decisions or that they did not know how to tactically take advantage of the system. Some defendants, however, disclosed that they had tried to delay their guilty plea, hoping that they would come before a more lenient magistrate in sentencing. The idea was that if the magistrate sitting at the initial plea arraignment had a reputation for being a harsh sentencer, then the defendant would initially plead not guilty, leading the magistrate to set a trial date at another court where there would hopefully be a more lenient magistrate sitting. The defendant would then plead guilty on the new trial date and have the supposedly more lenient magistrate sentence them. Yet the defendants stressed that this was difficult to do. One defendant explained he had tried this tactic before but, given how difficult it was to accomplish, had given up:

> Yes, I did use this tactic. It's a matter of luck. Sometimes, it's not possible to avoid a particular judge even if I employed this method. In one of my previous cases, the case ended up being handled by another judge who gave me an even heavier punishment. This is my personal experience. Another defendant who continued to be handled by the original judge was given a more lenient punishment, just half the length of mine . . .

[9] K. K. Cheng, W. H. Chui, S. N. M. Young, and R. Ong, 'Why do criminal trials "crack"? An empirical investigation of late guilty pleas in Hong Kong' (2018) 13 *Asian Journal of Comparative Law*, 1–25.

[10] The study noted the defendants' names, trial dates, and courtrooms set for their trial so that each defendant could be tracked using the Hong Kong Judiciary's daily cause list.

[11] There were no cases in the sample where the prosecution offered no evidence.

[12] Cheng *et al.*, 'Why do criminal trials "crack"?', 17.

> I gave up (on this tactic). I did not care who the judge was in my next hearing. Sometimes, when I was assigned to a lenient judge, he might be on holiday on the date of my trial session. It's really difficult for me to arrange for myself to be heard by a kind judge.[13]

Of particular difficulty is that when a case is set for trial in another courtroom, the defendant would not know beforehand which court is available for his or her eventual trial date, thus making it difficult to predict which judge or magistrate would eventually hear the case. In short, 'playing the system' is more difficult than it sounds.

Resolving 'Cracked Trials'

Prior to the introduction of the sliding scale of sentence discounts for guilty pleas, how did the courts deal with cracked trials? In the 1990s, the Royal Commission commissioned one of the largest studies on the Crown Court; its findings remain relevant today. It is especially insightful to understand how the English Crown Court operated before the era of the sliding scale. The Crown Court Study in 1993 took a snapshot of almost every Crown Court within a two-week period to capture over 3,000 criminal cases. It also surveyed the views of legal practitioners, including judges, prosecutors, and lawyers, as well as defendants.[14] Over 80 per cent of judges in the study responded that they did not think cracked trials wasted court time. Prosecutors also did not seem to hold detrimental views towards cracked trials, as many of them did not find cracked trials to affect the efficiency of the court process.[15] One major reason why judges and prosecutors did not find cracked trials inefficient is that a strategy was already in place to address them.

In different courts, particularly at large court centres, there would be several 'floating' cases. These were cases that were not immediately assigned to a courtroom, but rather kept on a waiting list. The courts knew that some cases would inevitably crack, so they did not immediately list all cases. Once a case did crack, making a courtroom and court staff available, these 'floating' cases would then be assigned to the vacant courtroom, thus minimising losses in judicial resources.[16] This would

[13] Ibid., 21.
[14] M. Zander and P. Henderson, *The Royal Commission on Criminal Justice: Crown Court Study* (Research Study No. 19) (London: HMSO, 1993).
[15] Ibid., pp. 154–6.
[16] Ibid.

avoid situations where a defendant entering a late guilty plea on the day of trial suddenly leaves the assigned judge and court staff, as well as prosecutors, with nothing to do.

The courts in Hong Kong have adopted a similar strategy. In interviews with legal practitioners, Cheng discovered that strategies have been in place to mitigate any disturbances that cracked trials may bring to the court process.[17] The courts in Hong Kong also overbook court dates and courtrooms by overscheduling cases to be heard. When a defendant pleads not guilty, the magistrate or judge at the plea arraignment will have on hand an overview of upcoming cases that require a trial. With ample experience in case processing and knowledge of which cases would likely crack, the presiding magistrate or judge can schedule cases considering the probability that some will eventually crack. Moreover, defence lawyers have a duty to notify the courts[18] if their clients intend to change their pleas, as one solicitor stated:

> If you believe you should plead guilty because you've been given proper legal advice, it's the defence lawyer's duty to write to the court to request a date for an early plea. It is possible to ask for a date for an early plea of guilty in all levels of courts, including the High Court, District Court, and Magistrates' Courts. We can state in the letter that the client is going to plead guilty and hope it can help the save the time of the prosecutor in the preparation and the court's time. We can request for a time which is convenient to the court.[19]

In this way, cracked trials do not always take the courts by surprise and they can adjust accordingly.

Another related court strategy used alongside overscheduling is different magistrates and judges offering assistance to each other. For instance, when a defendant enters a late guilty plea on the day of trial, the magistrate or judge in question will no longer have to hear the originally scheduled case. A particular trial may have been booked for a single day or several days; however, the trial magistrate or judge cannot just take those days off when the trial has cracked. As mentioned previously, since the court list is overbooked, other cases can be transferred to the now

[17] K. K. Cheng, 'Navigating through the effects of "cracked trials": how Hong Kong legal practitioners deal with late guilty pleas' (2018) 47 *Common Law World Review*, 136–49.

[18] For instance, paragraph 10.36 of the Hong Kong Bar Association Code of Conduct states, 'A practising barrister must in every case use his best endeavours to avoid unnecessary expense and waste of the Court's time.'

[19] Cheng, 'Navigating through the effects of "cracked trials"', 143.

vacant courtroom for hearing. When that is not possible, the vacant courtroom may be called upon to assist with other matters, such as bail hearings.[20] Speaking about the Magistrates' Courts, a magistrate disclosed how this works in practice:

> All the magistrates would have a morning break every day. For example, if on one day, both cases scheduled in my court are settled and finished with a plea of guilty, I would have nothing to do the rest of the day. Then, I would [tell] my clerk to ask to see if anyone needs help. And then, the case can be transferred to my court. When the trial is re-fixed in my court, the prosecution has to assign manpower to handle the case.[21]

These morning breaks allow court clerks to communicate with each other behind the scenes to reallocate cases and minimise any adverse effects that cracked trials may bring.

Another problem that cracked trials are said to bring is wasting lawyers' trial preparations. In comparison with preparing for plea mitigation following a guilty plea, it takes more time and effort to prepare a case for trial (e.g. to challenge the state's evidence, to examine witnesses, and to raise potential legal defences). However, interviews with defence lawyers revealed that they may not think this way. One barrister stated, 'I would not say that it's a waste of time [to have prepared for trial] because not as a very senior barrister, as a junior [counsel], I will say you learn while you are preparing each case. So, you benefit from it, from your research and preparation.'[22] Even if the case does not eventually get to trial, a barrister still benefits from having to prepare for the case as a learning experience.[23]

What about remuneration? Barristers, for instance, earn their remuneration through the brief fee and the refresher. The brief fee is for appearing in court on the first day of the hearing or trial; it usually includes fees for preparation work, such as the perusal of documents and legal research, and must be agreed to beforehand.[24] The refresher, usually

[20] Ibid., 144.

[21] Ibid.

[22] Ibid., 141.

[23] Around 27 per cent of the Junior Bar (junior counsels) in Hong Kong has less than five years of post-qualification experience. This percentage was calculated by filtering the Bar List provided by the Hong Kong Bar Association, available at www.hkba.org/Bar-List/junior-counsel.

[24] Paragraph 9.2 of the Hong Kong Bar Association Code of Conduct states, 'Unless otherwise expressly agreed between the barrister and the instructing person before the hearing/trial, the fee marked on a brief covers the barrister's appearance in Court on the

lower than the brief fee, is for each subsequent day of court appearances until the hearing or trial is complete. Thus, a barrister whose client pleads guilty before or on the first day of trial would lose refresher fees. Interviews with legal practitioners in Hong Kong did reveal that while barristers will suffer some financial losses for cracked trials, the brief fee is still guaranteed, and the barrister can negotiate the refresher fee even if there are no subsequent days of court appearance.[25] A barrister remarked:

> I reserved these five days for you, and I don't take any other cases during those five days. So, I should be entitled to my brief and the refresher. That's in principle. But, when you ask your client to pay, the client will say, 'Why do you charge me for the rest of the four days? Now, I changed my plea.' They will argue to negotiate with the instructing solicitor and the instructing solicitor will negotiate with us. It may end up [that] we will charge, maybe, only the brief, or for the rest of the refresher, we will charge like half of it. Half of [the amount].[26]

In Hong Kong, an interesting historical understanding exists between the Law Society of Hong Kong and the Hong Kong Bar Association over unused refreshers that are payable to the barrister, dating back to the 1960s. This arrangement is referred to as the Vine Formula, named after then president of the Law Society of Hong Kong, Mr Peter Vine; no equivalent formula exists in England. The details of the Vine Formula are outlined in an old circular of the Law Society of Hong Kong, which states that '[i]f a solicitor requests counsel to reserve five days or more fixed for the hearing of any proceedings, and counsel undertakes to appear during such days to conduct such proceedings, the solicitor agrees to pay counsel's brief fee and half the unused refreshers in the event'.[27]

first day of the hearing/trial as well as the preparation beforehand including the perusal of papers and the drafting or settlement of skeleton argument/written submissions. Refreshers, if any, must be agreed before the hearing/trial and should be marked on the brief.'

25 In Hong Kong, a barrister cannot sue for his or her fees since there is no contractual relationship between the barrister and the instructing solicitor or between the barrister and the lay client. The remedy is for the barrister to lodge a complaint with the Law Society against the instructing solicitor. The Bar Council and the Council of the Law Society have set up a Joint Tribunal to adjudicate such disputes regarding barristers' fees. Failure by a solicitor to pay barristers' fees may become a case of professional misconduct.

26 Cheng, 'Navigating through the effects of "cracked trials"', 141.

27 Law Society Circular (No 58/66), cited in *Gotland Enterprises Ltd* v. *Kwok Chi Yau & Ors* [2013] 6 HKC 594, paragraph 11; [2013] 4 HKLRD 520.

Although the Vine Formula is not explicitly stated nowadays, according to the Hong Kong Bar Association,

> [a] barrister is only entitled to a refresher fee if he attends court on a subsequent day. Any entitlement of a barrister to 'unused' refreshers would depend on the expressed agreement he has made with the solicitor. In a long case, it is not uncommon for a barrister to agree with the solicitor that a portion of the 'unused' refreshers is payable if the hearing collapses within a specified time of the delivery of the brief. This is to compensate the barrister for the lost opportunity of being available to take up other cases within the period reserved for the hearing.[28]

Through this, the barrister's loss of remuneration resulting from a cracked trial is mitigated.

Writing about barristers in England and Wales, Alge points out it may be more beneficial financially for barristers to have cases crack than having to appear in court for trial. For legal-aid cases in England, the Criminal Legal Aid (Remuneration) Regulations 2013 is structured such that the barrister receives a basic fee per case and an 'uplift' for additional trial days, witnesses, and evidence beyond what was set out in the basic fee.[29] Moreover, the time between when a case is first listed and the actual trial date is divided into three equal periods. Once the 'first third' is passed, the barrister is entitled to the cracked trial fee instead of the guilty plea fee, which is lower. Therefore, it may be in the barrister's interest to have cases 'crack' early before substantial preparations have been made for trial. By doing so across multiple cases, barristers might earn a higher income than if they focused on a single case that goes to trial.[30] In sum, the adverse effects that cracked trials supposedly have on the court system and on defence lawyers may have been overstated.

In fact, strictly reserving the maximum sentence discount only for guilty pleas at the first opportunity may increase inefficiencies in other parts of the criminal justice process. For instance, defence lawyers in Hong Kong revealed they would ask the court to adjourn cases and not take pleas at the defendant's first court appearance to delay the plea arraignment. This practice allows the defence to receive all papers from the prosecution and buy time to advise their clients, while preserving the

[28] Hong Kong Bar Association, 'How barristers charge their fees', available at www.hkba.org/content/how-barristers-charge-their-fees.

[29] The basic fee depends on the complexity of the case and the seniority of the barrister.

[30] D. Alge, 'The effectiveness of incentives to reduce the risk of moral hazard in the defence barrister's role in plea bargaining' (2013) 16 *Legal Ethics*, 162–81, p. 172.

full sentence discount by not having their clients take a plea. This effectively 'front-loads' cases and creates more work for the court of first appearance, since defendants would need to return to court and take a plea at a subsequent time.[31]

Sliding Scale on Guilty Plea Rates

The Sentencing Council for England and Wales recently published a report on the impact and implementation of its 2017 definitive guidelines on reductions in sentences for guilty pleas.[32] As previously discussed, the 2017 definitive guidelines provide a more stringent quantified sliding scale of sentence discounts for guilty pleas compared with the Sentencing Guidelines Council's (SGC) 2007 definitive guidelines. However, this report does not compare pre- and post-implementation data for the sliding scale of sentence discounts or its impact on the timing of guilty pleas in England and Wales. The data from the UK Ministry of Justice that the report draws on goes back only to 2010.[33] Therefore, the report can only analyse the time after the SGC's guidelines were implemented and compare it to the time encompassed by the more recent guidelines. Nonetheless, its results provide valuable insight into the effectiveness of the sliding scale of sentence discounts.

The Sentencing Council report referenced the UK Ministry of Justice's quarterly statistics about criminal courts. These statistics cover guilty plea rates in the Crown Court and the stages at which these guilty pleas were entered. The report used trend data to determine any changes since the revised guidelines had come into force. In terms of the overall plea rate, it found that the proportion of defendants who pleaded guilty in the Crown Court remained stable even with the introduction of the revised guidelines. This suggests that the new sliding scale of sentence discounts has

[31] Cheng, 'Navigating through the effects of "cracked trials"', 146.

[32] P. Jooman and A. Issac, *Assessing the Impact and Implementation of the Sentencing Council's Reduction in Sentence for a Guilty Plea Definitive Guideline* (London: Sentencing Council, 2020). This report represents part of the Sentencing Council's responsibility to monitor the use of sentencing guidelines and assess the impact of guidelines on sentencing practice. See sections 128 and 129 of the Coroners and Justice Act 2009.

[33] The UK Ministry of Justice's quarterly criminal court statistics are available at www.gov.uk/government/collections/criminal-court-statistics. While these statistics cover both adults and minors under the age of 18 without a breakdown by age, almost all defendants who would appear in the Crown Court are adults.

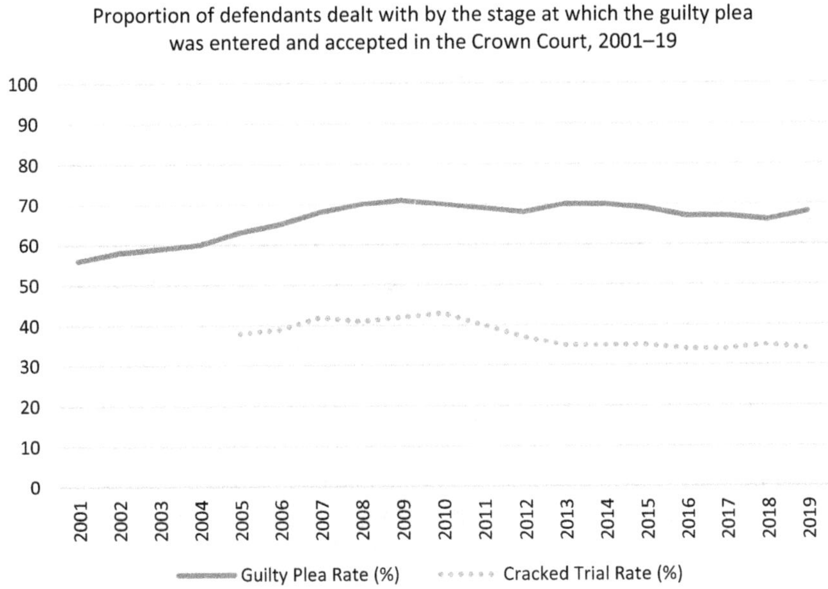

Figure 4.1 Sliding scale of sentence discounts on the guilty plea and cracked trial rate in the Crown Court

no impact on guilty plea rates.[34] Looking more specifically at the stage at which a guilty plea was entered, the Sentencing Council plotted the proportion of Crown Court cases that resulted in a guilty plea prior to trial and the proportion of cracked trials, reporting quarterly data from 2010 until the first quarter of 2019. Figure 4.1 presents a similar graph that includes additional data from before 2010 sourced from the UK Ministry of Justice's published statistics.

Three years are of particular importance: 2004 marks the introduction of the sliding scale of sentence discounts, which was revised in 2007 and again in 2017. As Figure 4.1 illustrates, the proportion of defendants

[34] Jooman and Issac, *Assessing the Impact and Implementation of the Sentencing Council's Reduction*, 9. The Council further broke down the statistics to compare whether implementing the sliding scale resulted in any differences regarding the gender and ethnicity of defendants who pleaded guilty. No significant pre- and post-implementation differences were observed for either male or female defendants. Regarding ethnicity, no such differences were found for White or Black defendants, nor for defendants classified as being of 'Other' ethnicities. The only slight difference was observed for Asian defendants; while 85 per cent pleaded guilty in 2013, the proportion decreased to 81 per cent in 2018, one year after the revised guideline had come into force.

pleading guilty prior to trial in the Crown Court increased between 2001 and 2009 from 56 per cent to 71 per cent. Despite the introduction of the sliding scale, this upward trend continued at relatively the same rate. This suggests that the sliding scale of sentence discounts had little, if any, impact on the guilty plea rate in the Crown Court. A similar trend can be observed from 2010 to 2019, during which the guilty plea rate hovered between 66 per cent and 70 per cent, suggesting that the more stringent 2017 definitive guidelines also did not appear to make any difference. As for the proportion of cracked trials, the proportion increased slightly from 38 per cent in 2005 to a high of 43 per cent in 2010. Looking at the years before and after 2007, it also appears that the cracked trial rate in the Crown Court did not change significantly after the sliding scale of sentence discounts was first revised. The cracked trial rate decreased from the 2010 peak to 34 per cent in 2019; however, from 2013 to 2019, the rate remained steady between 34 per cent and 35 per cent, again suggesting that the 2017 guidelines did not affect the trend.

Ultimately, trend analyses reveal that the sliding scale of sentence discounts did not have the desired impact of encouraging early guilty pleas. Existing trends continued for guilty plea rates prior to trials and for cracked trials.[35] Similar findings were observed for the Magistrates' Courts in England and Wales; although no statistics are provided for the timing of guilty pleas in the Magistrates' Courts, information about the number of cracked trials due to acceptable guilty pleas being entered late is available. It was discovered that the percentage of late guilty pleas decreased from 21 per cent in 2010 to 18 per cent to 2015, and then slightly increased to 19 per cent in 2018, one year after the revised guidelines came into force.[36]

The Sentencing Council report also examined the number of hearings held at the Crown Court. One would expect that to save judicial resources, more stringent sentence discounts for guilty pleas would decrease the number of hearings needed because defendants would plead guilty earlier; this was not the case. From 2014 to the end of 2018, the average number of Crown Court hearings for closed cases stood between

[35] Ibid., 11. The Sentencing Council additionally looked at the UK Ministry of Justice's n3 statistics, finding that the proportion of legal-aid fee claims for early guilty pleas had decreased between 2014 and 2017 and continued to decrease after the implementation of the revised sentencing guidelines. This further confirms that implementing the revised guidelines had no impact on existing guilty plea trends.

[36] Ibid., 13.

three and four hearings. This number peaked at 3.7 hearings in 2015, remaining stable afterwards in 2017 and 2018 at an average of 3.3 hearings. This figure shows that the revised sentencing guideline did not affect the number of Crown Court hearings.[37] Likewise, similar findings were observed for the Magistrates' Courts, where the average number of hearings remained at around 1.5 hearings before and after the revised guideline came into place.[38]

Unlike the UK Ministry of Justice, the Hong Kong Department of Justice does not publish results on the timing of guilty pleas; however, it does publish conviction rates and the number of defendants who pleaded guilty annually.[39] This allows for comparisons of the guilty plea rates before and after the implementation of the sliding scale of sentence discounts for guilty pleas in Hong Kong by looking at the guilty plea rates and conviction rates before and after 2016, the year the sliding scale of sentence discounts for guilty pleas came into effect (see Table 4.1).

As Table 4.1 shows, the guilty plea rate for defendants across three levels of Hong Kong criminal courts, namely the Magistrates' Courts, the District Court, and the Court of First Instance, actually decreased after the implementation of the sliding scale of sentence discounts. This means that more defendants opted for trial instead of pleading guilty after the sliding scale came into effect. In the Magistrates' Courts, the lowest criminal court in Hong Kong,[40] the guilty plea rate went from being steady at around 47–49 per cent before the sliding scale to decreasing each year after 2016 to around 30–34 per cent. Similarly, in the District Court, the guilty plea rate dropped to about 75 per cent for both 2017 and 2018 before rising back to 78.2 per cent in 2019. The Court of First Instance, which deals with the most serious criminal cases in

[37] Ibid., 11–12.

[38] Ibid., 13–14. For similar findings, see J. V. Roberts and J. Pina-Sánchez, 'Sentence reductions for a guilty plea: the impact of the revised guideline on rates of pleas and "cracked trials"' (2021) *Journal of Criminal Law*, advanced online publication.

[39] These statistics can be found in the 'Prosecutions Hong Kong' series of annual reports by the Hong Kong Department of Justice, available at www.doj.gov.hk/en/publications/prosecution_and_criminal_law.html.

[40] The Magistrates' Courts hear both summary and indictable offences. All criminal cases begin in the Magistrates' Courts and most end there. More serious indictable offences are transferred to the District Court or the Court of First Instance upon application by the Secretary for Justice. The normal sentence that a magistrate can impose is two years' imprisonment (up to three years where two or more indictable offences are being dealt with simultaneously) and a fine up to HK$100,000.

Table 4.1 *Guilty plea rates and conviction rates in Hong Kong*

	No. of defendants					
Year	Convicted of own plea	Convicted after trial	Acquitted after trial	Total	Guilty plea rate (%)	Conviction rate including guilty pleas (%)
Magistrates' Courts						
2014	4,490	2,358	2,330	9,178	48.9	74.6
2015	4,038	2,357	2,180	8,575	47.1	74.6
2016	3,944	2,061	2,114	8,119	48.6	74.0
2017	1,766	1,909	1,543	5,218	33.8	70.4
2018	1,644	1,925	1,423	4,992	32.9	71.5
2019	1,471	1,867	1,550	4,888	30.1	54.6
District Court						
2014	930	229	28	1,187	78.3	97.6
2015	952	191	81	1,224	77.8	93.4
2016	1,012	182	68	1,262	80.2	94.6
2017	888	227	62	1,177	75.4	94.7
2018	872	171	118	1,161	75.1	89.8
2019	1,032	194	94	1,320	78.2	92.9
Court of First Instance						
2014	439	77	43	559	78.5	92.3
2015	430	77	35	542	79.3	93.5
2016	419	61	47	527	79.5	91.1
2017	412	75	31	518	79.5	94.0
2018	328	89	42	459	71.4	90.8
2019	357	74	48	479	74.5	90.0

Hong Kong,[41] also saw its guilty plea rate decrease after the implementation of the sliding scale of sentence discounts for guilty pleas.

These official statistics, however, do not tell the entire story. Not only is information about the timing of guilty pleas unavailable, but the overall

[41] The Court of First Instance hears serious indictable offences such as murder, manslaughter, armed robbery, and large amounts of drug trafficking. There is no limit to the length of imprisonment it can impose. Criminal cases in the court are heard before a jury. The court may also hear criminal appeals from the Magistrates' Courts, during which a judge will sit alone. The Court of First Instance also has unlimited civil jurisdiction.

acquittal statistics also include 'bound over' cases. A bind over order is a court order under which a defendant appearing before the court enters into a recognisance, promising to be of good behaviour and to keep the peace for a period not exceeding three years.[42] If the defendant breaches the recognisance, then he or she is liable to pay a sum of money into court. The bind over order specifies what type of conduct the defendant promises not to commit during the specified time. Such an order is neither a conviction nor a punishment, and the courts and the prosecution regard it as a preventive measure. Since a bind over order will not result in a criminal record – and in some cases, the prosecution will agree to offer no evidence proving its case in return for the defendant agreeing to be bound over – it can technically be regarded as an acquittal. However, grouping bound-over cases into overall acquittal statistics may not be entirely appropriate, as it inflates the total number of acquitted individuals, thereby lowering the guilty plea rate. After all, persons who enter into a recognisance before the courts do not leave unscathed in the sense of a normal acquittal, as they have to observe certain behaviours or face the consequences.[43] Ultimately, these official statistics reveal that the trends in Hong Kong's guilty plea rates are unlikely to be affected by the sliding scale of sentence discounts.

The Hong Kong Judiciary also publishes the average waiting times at the different levels of court (see Table 4.2).[44] In the Magistrates' Courts, average waiting time refers to the average number of days from plea to trial date. Supposedly, the sliding scale of sentence discounts would lead to more defendants pleading guilty early, thus reducing the waiting time for defendants heading into trial. This notion is based on the assumption that through encouraging early guilty pleas in exchange for sentence reductions based on the sliding scale, court and prosecution resources can be devoted to cases that need to appear for trial. Such a reduction did

42 Section 109I of the Criminal Procedure Ordinance (Cap. 221). See also *HKSAR* v. *Lau Wai Wo* (2003) HKCFA 624.

43 A magistrate can impose up to six months' imprisonment for failure to comply with the undertaking, as per Section 61 of the Magistrates Ordinance (Cap. 227). A former Director of Public Prosecution even stated that a bind over should not be perceived as a 'let-off'. Instead, it 'is a vital aspect of preventive justice. It operates as a rehabilitative measure in its own right, which serves to keep the defendant on the straight and narrow'. From the Hong Kong Department of Justice, 'To bind over, or not?' (2001), 2, available at www.doj.gov.hk/en/community_engagement/speeches/pdf/art200103e.pdf.

44 These statistics can be found in the Hong Kong Judiciary's annual reports, available at www.judiciary.hk/en/publications/publications.html#annu_report.

Table 4.2 *Average waiting time for cases in Hong Kong*

	Average waiting time (days)			
Year	Magistrates' Courts (on bail)	Magistrates' Courts (remanded)	District Court	Court of First Instance
2014	44	36	63	227
2015	49	39	79	272
2016	41	36	118	291
2017	40	31	152	164
2018	57	47	187	167
2019	51	41	191	167

not occur among the Hong Kong courts after the implementation of the sliding scale for sentence discounts in late 2016. For the Magistrates' Courts, the average waiting time actually increased for both defendants on bail and those remanded in custody. The average for the former group rose from 44 days in 2014 to a high of 57 days in 2018; likewise, the average for the latter group rose from 36 days in 2014 to a high of 47 days in 2018, before dropping slightly to 41 days in 2019. These increases in waiting time still occurred despite the number of defendants appearing in the Magistrates' Courts having decreased significantly during this period. As illustrated in Table 4.1, over 9,000 defendants appeared in the Magistrates' Courts in 2014, with that number dropping to below 5,000 in 2018 and 2019. The increase in average waiting time was even more prominent in the District Court, where an annual increase was observed. In the District Court, average waiting time refers to the average number of days from the defendants' first appearance in court to the hearing date. The increase was rather staggering, with the average waiting time more than tripling from 63 days in 2014 to 191 days in 2019, even as the number of defendants appearing in the District Court remained pretty consistent throughout this period. The only exception to the trend was the Court of Frist Instance, where the average waiting time from the filing of the indictment to the hearing date decreased from 227 days in 2014 to 167 days in both 2018 and 2019.

Despite questionable assumptions and the lack of an empirical basis for it, the sliding scale of sentence discounts was still implemented in England and Wales as well as in Hong Kong. Overall, the trends in these two jurisdictions raise doubts about the intended effects of efficiency promised by the sliding scale of sentence discounts. Attention will now turn to a deeper empirical examination of the effects that the regime of the sliding scale of sentence discounts for guilty pleas has on the criminal processes in England and Wales, as well as in Hong Kong, from defendants' decision to plead guilty to their sentencing. The methodology and the datasets for this book, which allow for more in-depth investigation into the timing of guilty pleas, will now be further elaborated, paving the way for the analyses in subsequent chapters.

Methodology and Data Collection

Between October 2010 and March 2015, the Sentencing Council conducted the Crown Court Sentencing Survey (CCSS), asking sentencing judges and other sentencers at the Crown Court to complete paper-based questionnaires when imposing a sentence. The Crown Court hears serious criminal cases, including cases sent for trial from the Magistrates' Courts, when the offence is 'indictable only' or is an 'either way' offence, but the defendant opts for a jury trial. It also deals with the sentencing of defendants convicted in the Magistrates' Courts but sentenced in higher courts because of the serious nature of their offences. The CCSS collected factual information about defendants that appeared in the Crown Court and the seriousness of their offences. It also collected information about sentencing factors, including the timing of guilty pleas measured by the stage at which the defendant entered the guilty plea, which sentencers considered when sentencing. The CCSS served to fulfil the duties of the Sentencing Council to 'monitor the operation and effect of its sentencing guidelines'.[45] The survey was ended after an external review, but the data collected was made publicly available after being anonymised.[46]

So far, the CCSS data has been used primarily to examine consistency in the application of sentencing guidelines in practice.[47] Yet few analyses have used it to examine the effects of sentencing factors on sentence outcomes, as Irwin-Rogers and Perry observe: 'The CCSS dataset

45 Section 128 of the Coroners and Justice Act 2009.

46 See CCSS underlying data on the Sentencing Council website, www.sentencingcouncil.org.uk/research-and-resources/data-collections/crowncourt-sentencing-survey/.

47 See, for example, J. Pina-Sanchez and R. Linacre, 'Sentencing consistency in England and Wales: evidence from the Crown Court Sentencing Survey' (2013) 53 *British Journal of Criminology*, 1118–38.

provides researchers with the opportunity to conduct in-depth explorations of many other issues . . . despite there being much debate in recent years about the impact that sentencing factors ought to have on sentence severity, little empirical research has explored the impact of these factors on sentence severity in practice.'[48] This book offers new statistical analyses that investigate not only the consistency in the application of the sentencing guidelines regarding sentence reductions for guilty pleas, but also the various factors that influence the timing of pleas and the effects that this timing has on sentences. Data for the most recently surveyed year of 2014 is used here for analyses. The CCSS sample comprises 41,480 cases; Table 4.3 presents the descriptive statistics for this sample.

As Table 4.3 shows, in 2014, the CCSS recorded that most defendants in England and Wales pleaded guilty at the first opportunity (72.42 per cent). Looking further at the timing of guilty pleas, most defendants pleaded guilty at the early stage (78.21 per cent), and only a minority pleaded guilty at the intermediate (5.59 per cent) or late stages (12.22 per cent).[49] The CCSS did not record defendants that pleaded not guilty and went to trial. The survey distinguishes twelve categories of offence types, with most cases in 2014 involving assault (22.95 per cent), drugs (20.09 per cent), and theft (14.26 per cent). Regarding the demographic characteristics of defendants, most were males (89.75 per cent), with females making up only 10.14 per cent of the sample. Most defendants also tended to be younger, with the youngest age group of 18- to 24-year-olds comprising 30.86 per cent of the sample and the next youngest age group of 25- to 34-year-olds comprising 34.47 per cent of the sample. There is an even split between defendants with a previous criminal conviction (47.36 per cent) and those without (46.83 per cent). Finally, slightly more convicted defendants received immediate imprisonment sentences (54.53 per cent) than those who did not (45.47 per cent), with the median sentence length ranging between over 18 months and up to three years.

The Hong Kong data was extracted from the 'Reasons for Sentence' database, which collects written explanations from sentencing judges

48 K. Irwin-Rogers and T. W. Perry, 'Exploring the impact of sentencing factors on sentencing domestic burglary', in J. V. Roberts (ed.), *Exploring Sentencing Practice in England and Wales* (London: Palgrave Macmillan, 2015), pp. 212–13.

49 Early pleas are pleas entered at the Magistrates' Court prior to or at the Plea and Case Management Hearing (PCMH). Intermediate pleas are pleas entered after the PCMH but before trial. Late pleas are pleas entered on or after the day of trial.

Table 4.3 *Descriptive statistics for the CCSS 2014 dataset*

Measure	Count (%) (N = 41,480)
Age group (years)	
18–24	12,804 (30.86%)
25–34	14,300 (34.47%)
35–44	7,839 (18.89%)
45–54	4,495 (10.84%)
≥54	1,996 (4.81%)
Gender	
Male	37,230 (89.75%)
Female	4,204 (10.14%)
Existing illness	
Yes	3,248 (7.83%)
No	38,232 (92.17%)
Offense type	
Arson	645 (1.55%)
Assault	9,520 (22.95%)
Burglary	5,454 (13.15%)
Death	366 (0.88%)
Driving	1,737 (4.19%)
Drugs	8.333 (20.09%)
Fraud	354 (0.85%)
Indecent photography of children	688 (1.66%)
Robbery	2,073 (5.00%)
Sex	2,358 (5.69%)
Theft	5,917 (14.26%)
Other	4,035 (9.73%)
Criminal history	
Yes	19,636 (47.34%)
No	19,427 (46.83%)
Guilty plea entered	
Yes	30,041 (72.42%)
No	11,439 (27.58%)
Timing of guilty plea	
Early	32,441 (78.21%)
Intermediate	2,317 (5.59%)
Late	5,067 (12.22%)
Confession	
Yes	22,698 (54.72%)
No	18,782 (45.28%)

Table 4.3 (*cont.*)

Measure	Count (%) (N = 41,480)
Sentencing outcome	
Immediately imprisoned	22,621 (54.53%)
Not immediately imprisoned	18,860 (45.47%)
Median sentence length (months)	$18 \leq 36$

about case particulars and their sentencing processes. The Hong Kong Judiciary started this database in 2009 for archival purposes and to give the public insight into the rationale behind judges' sentencing decisions. These 'Reasons', which are uploaded shortly after a sentence has been imposed, are sourced directly from the Hong Kong Judiciary's Legal Reference System and are publicly available.[50] Such explanations differ from typical court judgments in that the former focus on the judicial reasoning for handing out sentences, whereas the latter describe the facts of the case, which encompass the judicial reasoning regarding the nature of the applicable laws and the court's decision about guilt or innocence. The data examined in this book were derived from criminal cases heard in Hong Kong's District Court from January 2018 to the end of 2019; the sample comprises 1,533 cases heard by 39 judges. Being a lower court of record, the District Court hears a wide range of criminal cases that are more serious compared to those heard in the Magistrates' Courts; it can thus be considered Hong Kong's intermediate criminal court. Cases are heard before a single judge, and only individuals with at least five years of practice – whether as a solicitor, barrister, or advocate – are eligible for appointment as a District Court judge.[51] The maximum sentence the District Court can impose is seven years of imprisonment.[52] There is only one District Court in Hong Kong, which is located at Wan Chai in the city centre.

Unlike for the CCSS, where Crown Court sentencers filled out questionnaires, in the 'Reasons for Sentence', Hong Kong judges write out their explanations in either English or Chinese.[53] This means that the

[50] The 'Reasons for Sentence' are available on the Legal Reference System website, legalref .judiciary.hk/lrs/common/rs/rs.jsp.

[51] Section 5 of the District Court Ordinance (Cap. 336).

[52] Section 82 of the District Court Ordinance (Cap. 336).

[53] Both English and Chinese are the official languages of Hong Kong and both are used by the courts.

reports are less systematic; the written judgments must therefore be meticulously coded for data analysis. For this book, data regarding offence details, defendant characteristics, the stage at which a guilty plea was entered, and the sentence were coded into an original database. The 'Reasons for Sentence' reports also contain information that the CCSS does not document. They therefore provide greater insight, for instance, into the sentencing process, given that the sentencing judge notes the starting point of sentence, which is adopted after considering sentencing factors such as the sentence discount for guilty pleas and the final sentence. Table 4.4 presents the descriptive statistics for the Hong Kong sample.

Similar to England and Wales, most defendants in Hong Kong's District Court sample pleaded guilty at the earliest stage (80.62 per cent), with much fewer defendants pleading guilty at a later stage (6.78 per cent). A minority of defendants did not plead guilty but were eventually convicted after trial (12.60 per cent). Defendants in the Hong Kong sample faced an average of 2.3 charges. The dataset covered seven categories of offence type, the most common being drug-related offences (32.09 per cent). As in the CCSS, most defendants in the Hong Kong sample were male (88.13 per cent). Looking at the ethnicity of defendants as extracted from the 'Reasons for Sentence' reports, most defendants were local Hong Kong Chinese (82.13 per cent); 11.55 per cent of defendants were foreigners, while 6.32 per cent were Mainland Chinese. In terms of age, defendants were distributed rather evenly across the five defined age groups, with most falling under the 35- to 44-year-old group (26.55 per cent). A majority of defendants had previous convictions (61.12 per cent), and even more were represented by legal-aid lawyers (85.52 per cent). An even distribution was observed for prosecution type, where only slightly more defendants were prosecuted by a public prosecutor (51.01 per cent) as opposed to a prosecutor on fiat[54] (48.99 per cent). Lastly, the vast majority of convicted defendants received immediate imprisonment (94.46 per cent) with a mean sentence length of 28.80 months.

[54] Prosecutors on fiat refers to private practicing barristers or solicitors who are briefed by the Department of Justice to act as prosecutors.

Table 4.4 *Descriptive statistics for the Hong Kong District Court 2018–19 dataset*

Measure	Count (%) (N = 1,533)
Age group (years)	
18–24	246 (16.05%)
25–34	372 (24.27%)
35–44 (R)	407 (26.55%)
45–54	274 (17.87%)
≥54	234 (15.26%)
Gender	
Male (R)	1,351 (88.13%)
Female	182 (11.87%)
Ethnicity	
Local (R)	1,259 (82.13%)
Foreigner	177 (11.55%)
Mainland Chinese	97 (6.32%)
Existing illness	
None (R)	1,329 (86.69%)
Mental illness	80 (5.22%)
Physical illness	124 (8.09%)
Offense type	
Assault/Sex	117 (7.63%)
Burglary/Robbery	291 (18.98%)
Death/Driving	82 (5.35%)
Drugs (R)	492 (32.09%)
Fraud	172 (11.22%)
Theft	203 (13.24%)
Other	176 (11.48%)
Criminal history	
Yes	937 (61.12%)
No (R)	596 (38.88%)
Timing of guilty plea	
Early (R)	1,236 (80.62%)
Late	104 (6.78%)
No plea	193 (12.60%)
Confession	
Yes	879 (57.34%)
No (R)	206 (13.44%)
Represented by legal aid	
Yes	1,311 (85.52%)

Table 4.4 (*cont.*)

Measure	Count (%) (N = 1,533)
No (R)	222 (14.48%)
Prosecution type	
On fiat (R)	751 (48.99%)
Public prosecutor	782 (51.01%)
Sentencing outcome	
Immediately imprisoned	1,448 (94.46%)
Not immediately imprisoned	85 (5.54%)
Mean sentence length (months)	28.80
Mean number of charges	2.3

Conclusion

This chapter first revisited the assumptions underlying the need for creating and implementing a quantified sliding scale of sentence discounts for guilty pleas. The assertion that experienced defendants 'playing the system' is the reason for late guilty pleas, thus contributing to cracked trials, appears to be mixed at best. While certain defendants may try delaying their pleas for some tactical advantage, such as waiting for sentencing from a more lenient judge, such a strategy is difficult to achieve and does not seem widespread. Another assumption that cracked trials harm the efficiency of the criminal process also seems to be overblown. Prior to the sliding scale of sentence discounts, the courts had strategies in place to minimise any inefficiencies that cracked trials may cause. These include overscheduling court lists considering that some trials will crack, alongside diverting vacant judges and courtrooms to assist with other matters when necessary. Defence lawyers also have mechanisms in place to mitigate financial losses from cracked trials, with some even suggesting that legal-aid barristers may benefit financially from cracked trials. Overall, the sliding scale of sentence discounts appears to have no impact on guilty plea rates and cracked trial rates in England and Wales or in Hong Kong.

The second part of this chapter detailed the methodology of collecting data derived from the CCSS and the 'Reasons for Sentence' reports for sentences in the Hong Kong District Court. This data will pave the way for subsequent chapters to make empirical examinations of the impacts that the sliding scale of sentence discounts for guilty pleas has on the criminal process.

5

Factors Affecting the Timing of Guilty Pleas

In Chapter 4, doubts were cast about the prevailing assumption that late guilty pleas are due to tactical defendants 'playing the system'. This chapter now turns to the question of what factors affect the timing of guilty pleas for defendants under the current regime of a quantified sliding scale of sentence discounts. Extant empirical studies have pointed to both legal and extra-legal factors affecting plea decisions. However, attention should be paid not just to these variables but also to key decisions made prior to the guilty plea during the criminal process, such as a defendant's confession and the type of legal representation afforded. These prior decisions pressure defendants into ultimately pleading guilty, even into doing so earlier. Since the criminal process is, after all, a process, previous decisions will significantly affect subsequent decisions.[1] Most existing studies have understandably focused on sentences as an outcome, since sentencing is considered as the final stage of the criminal process.[2] Regrettably, much less attention has been given to guilty pleas as the dependent variable. Using the datasets from the Crown Court Sentencing Survey (CCSS) and the Hong Kong District Court, this chapter focuses on the factors that affect not just the dichotomous distinction between guilty pleas and not guilty pleas but also the timing of guilty pleas. The chapter concludes by discussing reasons for why certain factors are significant.

[1] 'Cumulative disadvantage' in the criminal process can be defined as 'a process that encompasses the cumulative impact of a specific form of disadvantage over time and/or the accumulation of multiple, interactive forms of disadvantage, both within and across time points': M. C. Kurlychek and B. D. Johnson, 'Cumulative disadvantage in the American criminal justice system' (2019) 2 *Annual Review of Criminology*, 291–319, p. 292. For further discussions, see also B. L. Kutateladze *et al.*, 'Cumulative disadvantage: examining racial and ethnic disparity in prosecution and sentencing' (2014) 52 *Criminology*, 514–51; J. Wooldredge *et al.*, 'Is the impact of cumulative disadvantage on sentencing greater for black defendants?' (2015) 14 *Criminology & Public Policy*, 187–223.

[2] This assumption will be revisited in Chapters 6 and 7.

Demographic Characteristics

When considering age in the criminal justice system, a distinction usually falls between juvenile and adult defendants. Most jurisdictions have a distinct juvenile (or youth) justice system for juvenile defendants. In England and Wales and in Hong Kong, the age of criminal responsibility is 10,[3] as in all Australian states[4] and in New Zealand.[5] In Scotland, this age was recently raised to 12,[6] as it is in Canada.[7] Under most circumstances, defendants in England and Wales between ages 10 and 17 appear in the Youth Court.[8] Likewise, the Juvenile Court in Hong Kong typically deals with defendants between ages 10 and 16.[9] In both jurisdictions, Youth/Juvenile Court proceedings are less formal and cater to the needs of young defendants. However, no jurisdiction distinguishes young adult defendants (typically referring to those aged 18–25) from other adult defendants.

Among the few studies that have focused on age in relation to the intention and timing of pleading guilty, most compared differences between juvenile and young adult defendants. For instance, Grisso and colleagues compared samples of 'youths' (ages 11–17) and 'young adults' (ages 18–24), measuring their legal decision-making using vignettes. They discovered significant differences regarding the plea bargaining vignette, where youths were much more likely than their young adult counterparts to accept a plea bargain.[10] In another hypothetical scenario presented to both youths and young adults, Redlich and Shteynberg found that when participants were asked to assume guilt, they observed no differences regarding plea decisions across both groups. However,

3 Section 50 of the Children and Young Persons Act 1933 (England and Wales) and section 3 of the Juvenile Offenders Ordinance (Cap. 226) (Hong Kong).

4 For instance, section 5 of the Children (Criminal Proceedings) Act 1987 (New South Wales).

5 Section 21 of the Crimes Act 1961.

6 See section 1 of the Age of Criminal Responsibility (Scotland) Act 2019, which amends section 41 of the Criminal Procedure (Scotland) Act 1995.

7 Section 13 of the Criminal Code.

8 Serious crimes such as murder are transferred to the Crown Court.

9 Section 3A of the Juvenile Offenders Ordinance (Cap. 226). In Hong Kong, the Juvenile Court also has jurisdiction over care and protection cases for individuals under the age of 18.

10 T. Grisso *et al.*, 'Juveniles' competence to stand trial: a comparison of adolescents' and adults' capacities as trial defendants' (2003) 27 *Law and Human Behavior*, 333–63.

when participants were asked to assume innocence, juvenile participants were nearly 2.5 times more likely to plead guilty than young adults.[11] Lastly, Viljoen, Klaver, and Roesch compared guilty pleas among juvenile defendants held in a pretrial detention facility, stratifying them into three age groups (ages 11–13, 14–15, and 16–17). They found that across all age groups, the defendant's lawyers and parents influenced their decision to plead guilty; influence from peers was also found for the older adolescent age group.[12]

Gender is another demographic characteristic of interest to researchers. Studies have found that while female defendants plead guilty more often than male defendants, they are less involved in the plea bargaining process. Contrary to the first observation, Figueira-McDonough found that male defendants plead guilty to a lesser charge almost twice as often as female defendants. Nevertheless, she opined that female defendants tended to commit less serious crimes and are therefore processed through the criminal justice system more expediently, reducing their engagement in plea bargaining;[13] this claim aligns with the second observation. Another study by Berdejó showed that for less serious crimes, female defendants are more likely to have their charges dropped or reduced compared to male defendants.[14] Other gender-specific reasons may exist for why female defendants plead guilty. Through interviews with 50 women incarcerated in an English prison, Jones found that women face various pressures to confess and plead guilty, including family responsibilities, coercion by their male partners, and the desire to protect male co-defendants (i.e., 'stand by your man'). Given that women tend to be primary caregivers for their families, they face considerable stress when separated from their children and other close family members. They therefore see pleading guilty as a way to receive a lesser sentence, perhaps avoiding imprisonment and thus separation.[15]

[11] A. D. Redlich and R. V. Shteynberg, 'To plead or not to plead: a comparison of juvenile and adult true and false plea decisions' (2016) 40 *Law and Human Behavior*, 611–25. See also R. K. Helm *et al.*, 'Too young to plead? Risk, rationality, and plea bargaining's innocence problem in adolescents' (2018) 24 *Psychology, Public Policy, and Law*, 180–91.

[12] J. L. Viljoen, J. Klaver, and R. Roesch, 'Legal decisions of preadolescent and adolescent defendants: predictors of confessions, pleas, communication with attorneys, and appeals' (2005) 29 *Law and Human Behavior*, 253–77.

[13] J. Figueira-McDonough, 'Gender differences in informal processing: a look at charge bargaining and sentence reduction in Washington, D.C.' (1985) 22 *Journal of Research in Crime and Delinquency*, 101–33.

[14] C. Berdejó, 'Gender disparities in plea bargaining' (2019) 94 *Indiana Law Journal*, 1247–303.

[15] S. Jones, 'Under pressure: women who plead guilty to crimes they have not committed' (2011) 11 *Criminology & Criminal Justice*, 77–90.

Compared to other demographic characteristics, the defendant's ethnicity or race has garnered more attention with respect to guilty pleas. Studies in the American context have pointed to how, after controlling for legally relevant variables such as the severity of the offence, ethnic minority defendants are less likely to plead guilty compared to white defendants; this is especially pronounced for Black defendants.[16] For example, examining 907 felony cases in Florida, Metacalfe and Chiricos found black defendants, particularly males, were much less likely to plead guilty than white defendants.[17] Similar findings were also observed for Toronto, Canada,[18] as well as in England and Wales, where Black, Asian, and minority ethnic (BAME) defendants disproportionally plead not guilty compared to their White counterparts.[19] Likewise, comparing straight guilty pleas, negotiated pleas, and trials using Pennsylvania Sentencing Commission data collected in 1998, Frenzel and Ball found that black defendants were less likely to receive a negotiated guilty plea or make a non-negotiated guilty plea than go to trial.[20] They posit that under a criminal justice system dominated by plea bargaining, ethnic minority defendants have greater distrust for conviction outcomes made behind-the-scenes and would rather have their cases heard in an open court or before a jury.[21] Lastly, Mileski suggests that black defendants may more likely be wrongly charged, have less-favourable plea bargains offered to them,[22] and have stronger resistance to the 'white man's justice' of plea bargaining;[23] they thus would rather opt for trial. Beyond plea bargaining, the general lack of trust in the criminal process has been cited as the primary reason why BAME defendants in England

[16] C. A. Albonetti, 'Race and the probability of pleading guilty' (1990) 6 *Journal of Quantitative Criminology*, 315–34; G. D. LaFree, 'Adversarial and nonadversarial justice: a comparison of guilty pleas and trials' (1985) 23 *Criminology*, 289–312.

[17] C. Metacalfe and T. Chiricos, 'Race, plea, and charge reduction: an assessment of racial disparities in the plea process' (2018) 35 *Justice Quarterly*, 223–53.

[18] G. Kellough and S. Wortley, 'Remand for plea: bail decisions and plea bargaining as commensurate decisions' (2002) 42 *British Journal of Criminology*, 186–210.

[19] D. Lammy, *The Lammy Review: An Independent Review into the Treatment of, and Outcomes for, Black, Asian and Minority Ethnic Individuals in the Criminal Justice System* (London: Lammy Review, 2017), p. 26.

[20] E. D. Frenzel and J. Ball, 'Effects of individual characteristics on plea negotiations under sentencing guidelines' (2008) 5 *Journal of Ethnicity in Criminal Justice*, 59–82.

[21] Ibid.

[22] See also B. L. Kutateladze, N. R. Andiloro, and B. D. Johnson, 'Opening Pandora's box: how does defendant race influence plea bargaining?' (2016) 33 *Justice Quarterly*, 398–426.

[23] M. Mileski, 'Courtroom encounters: an observation study of a lower court' (1971) 5 Law & Society Review, 473–538, p. 495.

and Wales plead not guilty. Interestingly, while BAME defendants are more likely to request legal advice at police stations compared to White defendants, many of them do not trust the advice they are given, particularly from publicly funded defence lawyers.[24]

Little is known about the role that demographic characteristics may play in guilty plea decisions across Asian contexts. A study by Laidler, Peterson, and Emerton on the experiences of Mainland Chinese sex workers caught up in Hong Kong's criminal justice system offers some interesting insights regarding gender and ethnicity as they relate to guilty pleas. They found that the sex workers were processed bureaucratically and charged with the generic offences of soliciting for an immoral purpose or breaching their conditions of stay.[25] Although the defendants were assigned publicly funded lawyers and charged separately, the lawyers interviewed and advised them as a group and the court even heard their cases together. Given these bureaucratic processes, virtually all the defendants ended up pleading guilty.[26]

Confessions

Strength of evidence is a factor relevant to the decision to plead guilty, as it directly relates to the likelihood of conviction or acquittal. However, not all evidence exerts positive effects on the likelihood of the defendant pleading guilty. Physical evidence and prior confession may significantly increase this likelihood, whereas eyewitness identification and the number of prosecution witnesses have been found to negatively correlate with the probability of the defendant entering a guilty plea.[27] The defence may consider witnesses to be more manageable; when they take the stand in trial to provide their testimonies, they are open to cross-examination by the defence, during which they may be discredited and help the

[24] Lammy, *The Lammy Review*, p. 27.

[25] While prostitution is not a crime in Hong Kong, related activities such as soliciting 'for an immoral purpose' are illegal, as per section 147 of the Crimes Ordinance (Cap. 200). Moreover, mainland Chinese sex workers are often charged with the immigration offence of breaching their conditions of stay for being visitors who are working without valid employment visas. See section 41 of the Immigration Ordinance (Cap. 115).

[26] K. J. Laidler, C. Petersen, and R. Emerton, 'Bureaucratic justice: the incarceration of Mainland Chinese women working in Hong Kong's sex industry' (2007) 51 *International Journal of Offender Therapy and Comparative Criminology*, 68–83.

[27] Albonetti, 'Race and the probability of pleading guilty'.

defence's case. Conversely, physical evidence and confessions provide leverage for the prosecution as they pursue trial or a guilty plea.[28]

A confession is not a guilty plea. Although a guilty plea also involves the defendant's admission of guilt, the two are distinct. Section 82(1) of the Police and Criminal Evidence (PACE) Act 1984 defines a confession as including 'any statement wholly or partly adverse to the person who made it, whether made to a person in authority or not and whether made in words or otherwise'. Notably, no equivalent to the PACE Act applies to Hong Kong, which maintains the common law approach that a confession is made to a 'person in authority'.[29] In any case, a confession is the defendant – or suspect before charges are issued – admitting to the alleged crime. While a confession is an admission to the factual basis of the underlying crime, it does not automatically lead to conviction; nevertheless, it is potentially a powerful piece of evidence that may be used in trial and ultimately lead to a conviction. Despite this, like other evidence, confessions can be challenged in court.

Regarding the nature of a guilty plea, Garrett acutely points out,

> The defendant agrees to receive a conviction and sentence, which can bring with it prison time and a range of collateral consequences. These consequences formally attach to the conviction itself and are not a confession to the underlying facts of the crime because those facts may not have been determined with any specificity. If a plea bargain is a confession or an admission, it is often one stating, 'I did it', with 'it' being the legal definition of the crime, but not what was actually done or how or why.[30]

In essence, a guilty plea is the defendant admitting to the legal elements of the crime. Moreover, the English Court of Appeal ruled in *Price* that an admission of guilt at the police interview is not equivalent to a guilty plea at the first opportunity.[31] In that case, the defendant did not receive the full one-third sentence discount for his guilty plea because it was not indicated at the first opportunity in the Magistrates' Courts. The Court of

[28] Ibid., 324.

[29] *Ibrahim* v. *R* [1914] AC 599. While an exhaustive list of who is considered a 'person in authority' does not exist, the term generally includes law enforcement personnel such as the police.

[30] B. L. Garrett, 'Why plea bargains are not confessions' (2016) 57 *William & Mary Law Review*, 1415–44, p. 1421. Although Garrett was writing with regard to the context of the United States, his distinction between confessions and guilty pleas/plea bargains is applicable in other jurisdictions.

[31] *R* v. *Price* [2018] EWCA Crim 1784 [2019] 1 Cr App R (S) 24.

Appeal also held that admissions to the police may be regarded as potential mitigating factors and should not determine the level of sentence reduction for guilty pleas.[32] This further solidifies the distinction between a confession and a guilty plea.[33]

Despite this distinction, empirical studies have found a connection between confessions and guilty pleas. For instance, Redlich and colleagues examined prosecutors' case files between 2005 and 2006 for two counties in New York, resulting in a sample of 502 cases.[34] They discovered that confessions influenced plea decisions, with virtually all defendants who had made a full or partial confession pleading guilty. In contrast, only about 70 per cent of defendants who initially denied their alleged crimes to the police later pleaded guilty.[35] This proportion represents a significant anomaly, given that in the United States, nearly all criminal cases result in a guilty plea, usually by way of a plea bargain. Scherr, Redlich, and Kassin go further to assert that a process of 'cumulative disadvantage' unfolds; suspects who make false confessions cause police to assume their culpability with certainty, resulting in biased evidence collection and ultimately ending in wrongful convictions or false guilty pleas.[36] This disadvantage underscores how the criminal process is one in which a prior decision affects subsequent stages of the criminal proceedings.

Legal Representation

One of the most astounding significant variables affecting guilty pleas, especially in the English context, is legal representation. Studies have

[32] Ibid., paragraph 9.

[33] See also A. D. Redlich, 'False confessions, false guilty pleas: similarities and differences', in G. D. Lassiter and C. Meissner (eds.), *Police Interrogations and Confessions: Current Research, Practice, and Policy* (Washington, DC: APA Books, 2010), pp. 49–66. In this context, guilty pleas are primarily discussed as plea bargains: 'A false confession is defined here as a statement provided to the police in which the person partially or fully admits guilt, or otherwise takes responsibility, for a crime he or she did not commit. A false guilty plea is defined as the acceptance of a plea offer from the prosecutor for a crime the person did not commit.'

[34] A. D. Redlich *et al.*, 'The influence of confessions on guilty pleas and plea discounts' (2018) 24 *Psychology, Public Policy, and Law*, 147–57.

[35] Ibid., 152.

[36] K. C. Scherr, A. D. Redlich, and S. Kassin, 'Cumulative disadvantage: a psychological framework for understanding how innocence can lead to confession, wrongful conviction, and beyond' (2020) 15 *Perspectives on Psychological Sciences*, 353–83. See also K. Wynbrandt, 'From false evidence ploy to false guilty plea: an unjustified path to securing convictions' (2016) 126 *The Yale Law Journal*, 545–63.

pointed to the defendant's own legal representative as a source of pressure regarding pleading guilty. Baldwin and McConville conducted a seminal and controversial study[37] on this factor in the 1970s, interviewing 121 defendants in the Birmingham Crown Court. All these defendants had changed their plea decisions from initially pleading not guilty to entering a late guilty plea.[38] Baldwin and McConville discovered that nearly 40 per cent of defendants responded that the single most important factor for why they changed their pleas was pressure from their barristers; many did not actually want to plead guilty, but were swayed by their counsels. One defendant said, 'The barrister turned around and says, "If I were you, I'd forget my pride. I know you think you're innocent but if you're proved guilty, I think you'll go down – I can't guarantee it, but I think you will."'[39]

Nearly two decades later, McConville and colleagues supplemented his earlier study through directly observing solicitor–client interactions, shadowing almost 50 law firms across Britain and conducting further interviews. They found a distinction between representation for privately funded clients and legally aided defendants. Compared to paying clients, legal-aid defendants were treated hastily and with indifference, as many solicitors and paralegals would adopt a presumption of guilt towards those they were tasked to represent. Legally aided defendants were told that they occupied the bottom rung of the criminal justice hierarchy in terms of credibility and were persuaded to plead guilty by their legal representatives without careful examination of the evidence at hand.[40] Another study also found the same guilt-presumptive attitudes in barristers, prosecutors, law clerks, and even magistrates.[41]

Following McConville *et al.*, a more recent study by Newman continued ethnographic research on English law firms focusing on legal-aid criminal lawyers and their interactions with defendants. Newman found that even after another two decades, nothing much had changed from the

[37] This early study created such controversy that attempts were made to block its publication. See J. Baldwin, 'Research on the criminal courts', in R. D. King and E. Wincup (eds.), *Doing Research on Crime and Justice*, 2nd ed. (Oxford: Oxford University Press, 2007), pp. 375–98.

[38] J. Baldwin and M. McConville, *Negotiated Justice: Pressures to Plead Guilty* (London: Martin Robertson, 1977).

[39] Ibid., p. 66.

[40] M. McConville *et al.*, *Standing Accused: The Organisation and Practices of Criminal Defence Lawyers in Britain* (Oxford: Clarendon Press, 1994).

[41] A. Mulcahy, 'The justifications of "justice": legal practitioners' accounts of negotiated case settlements in magistrates' courts' (1994) 34 *British Journal of Criminology*, 411–30.

findings of McConville *et al.* Legal-aid lawyers displayed negative attitudes towards their clients, considering them as lacking intelligence, being of questionable moral character, and being presumptively factually guilty.[42] Given these attitudes that defence lawyers possess, it is not surprising that they are inclined to persuade their clients to plead guilty. Although the lawyers would not openly call on their clients to plead guilty, Newman observed that '[a]ll lawyers were observed to operate in a default mode, whereby they assumed that clients would plead guilty, and thus helped ensure that they did just that'.[43] They did so through subtle encouragement, resorting to more forceful language should that fail.

There are others who disagree with this assessment of criminal defence lawyers. Tague highlights that it is not in a barrister's self-interest to persuade their client to plead guilty. Rather, going to trial would be in their interest, as what matters to a barrister is demonstrating their advocacy skills; testing the prosecution's case in trial is where these skills can shine.[44] As Tague notes, demonstrating these skills and not settling for a guilty plea will help the advocate's career trajectory: '[T]he barrister's ability to persuade jurors and judges is on sale. He wants to burnish a reputation for advocacy, not for adeptness in negotiating guilty pleas or bludgeoning defendants to plead guilty.'[45] Unlike legal-aid lawyers in the United States, who are appointed by judges or paid on a salary, English barristers are instructed by solicitors; a barrister's failure to impress their instructing solicitor with their advocacy skills may risk losing the solicitor as a source for future briefs.[46] Moreover, each solicitor likely has a personal list of known barristers who they often turn to. Hence, a barrister must develop a reputation as a capable advocate to attract briefs, especially in more lucrative cases.[47] Hong Kong also maintains a split

42 D. Newman, *Legal Aid Lawyers and the Quest for Justice* (Oxford: Hart, 2013).

43 Ibid., p. 112.

44 P. W. Tague, 'Guilty pleas and barristers' incentives: lessons from England' (2007) 20 *The Georgetown Journal of Legal Ethics*, 287–320.

45 Ibid., 296.

46 The barrister professions in England and Hong Kong are both referred to as 'referral professions', save for certain circumstances, as a lay client cannot directly instruct a barrister. Instead, clients instruct a solicitor, who in turn instructs barristers on behalf of their clients. The rationale for this arrangement is that this allows the barrister to divert all their energy towards case preparation and remain objective by maintaining some distance from the client.

47 Tague, 'Guilty pleas and barristers' incentives', 303. For a similar view of barristers in Australia, see P. W. Tague, 'Guilty pleas or trials: which does the barrister prefer?' (2008) 32 *Melbourne University Law Review*, 242–74.

legal profession between solicitors and barristers, as well as the need for barristers to be instructed by solicitors.[48]

Unlike Tague, Alge casts doubt on the notion that it is always in the barrister's best financial incentive to opt for trial instead of guilty pleas. She notes that criminal defence barristers earn less compared with lawyers working in other areas of law; moreover, since barristers are self-employed,[49] they often take on a high number of cases at a time, perhaps to offset their typically lower earnings. Even though taking multiple cases may likely cause scheduling conflicts, a barrister will still do so knowing that many cases could end in a guilty plea before getting to trial.[50] Alge also points out that for legal-aid cases in England, the Criminal Legal Aid (Remuneration) Regulations 2013 structures barrister remunerations such that a barrister receives a basic fee per case and an 'uplift' for additional trial days, witnesses, and evidence beyond the amount set out in the basic fee.[51] Moreover, the Regulations divide the time between when a case is first listed for trial and the actual trial date into three equal periods, and specify that once the 'first third' is passed, the barrister is entitled to the cracked trial fee instead of the lower guilty plea fee. Therefore, it may be in the barrister's interest to have cases 'crack' early before they have done much preparation for trial. Doing so across multiple cases rather than focusing on a single case that goes to trial could give barristers a higher income.[52]

Empirical evidence nonetheless supports the idea that lawyers play a pivotal role in guilty plea decisions. In England and Wales, the Crown Court Study of 1993, one of the largest studies on the Crown Court system, took a snapshot of all except three Crown Courts over a two-week period to capture over 3,000 criminal cases. In particular, the questionnaires handed out to defendants asked: 'Who was the main

[48] Other jurisdictions with a split legal profession include Scotland, Australia, New Zealand, and South Africa. Jurisdictions with a unified legal profession include the United States and Canada.

[49] Generally, barristers only practice as sole proprietors and cannot enter into partnerships like solicitors can. This means that a barrister's income is derived from the individual cases that they advise and represent. Barristers must also pay for residence at chambers where they are 'tenants', in turn for access to facilities and administrative support. However, certain barristers may be employed at government institutions, such as the Crown Prosecution Service or the Armed Forces, or in the private sector.

[50] D. Alge, 'The effectiveness of incentives to reduce the risk of moral hazard in the defence barrister's role in plea bargaining' (2013) 16 *Legal Ethics*, 162–81, p. 171.

[51] The basic fee depends on the complexity of the case and the seniority of the barrister.

[52] Alge, 'The effectiveness of incentives', 172.

person to help them decide their plea?' Around 40 per cent of defendants responded that either their solicitor or barrister helped them to decide.[53] In Hong Kong, a study by Cheng *et al.* on 'cracked trials' in the Magistrates' Courts found that defendants represented by publicly funded lawyers (i.e., duty lawyers)[54] and defendants who self-represented (i.e., had no legal representation) were more likely to enter a late guilty plea than defendants represented by private lawyers.[55] However, another earlier study by Cheng that compared the likelihood of pleading guilty at the first opportunity in the Magistrates' Courts found no difference in plea outcomes between defendants represented by duty lawyers and defendants represented by private lawyers.[56]

Factors Affecting the Timing of Guilty Pleas: England and Wales

This study aims to investigate various factors, including defendants' demographic characteristics and earlier decisions in the criminal process, to identify which factors affect the timing of guilty pleas. For England and Wales, the CCSS provides valuable information in terms of case and defendant characteristics. Supplementary files to the CCSS also provide data on whether a defendant had previously made a confession; this data were extracted and included in the current dataset. A binary logistic regression was performed with the outcome variable being whether the defendant pleaded guilty at the first opportunity. The reference group for analysis was defendants who pleaded guilty at the first opportunity; therefore, the model tests the likelihood of not pleading guilty at the first opportunity, that is, pleading late. As previously noted, the decision for a defendant to plead at the first opportunity may occur anytime from before a plea hearing to during trial, depending on the circumstances of the case. For this reason, a defendant's decision to not plead guilty at

[53] M. Zander and P. Henderson, The Royal Commission on Criminal Justice: Crown Court Study (Research Study No. 19) (London: HMSO, 1993).

[54] In Hong Kong, duty lawyers represent defendants who appear in the Magistrates' Courts through the Duty Lawyer Scheme offered by the Duty Lawyer Service, which is operated by the Law Society of Hong Kong and the Hong Kong Bar Association and subvented by the government. In the District Court and higher courts, legal aid covers legal representation for indigent defendants. An exception to these arrangements is committal proceedings in the Magistrates' Courts, which are covered by legal aid.

[55] K. K. Cheng *et al.*, 'Why do criminal trials "crack"? An empirical investigation of late guilty pleas in Hong Kong' (2018) 13 *Asian Journal of Comparative Law*, 1–25.

[56] K. K. Cheng, 'Pressures to plead guilty: factors affecting plea decisions in Hong Kong's magistrates' courts' (2013) 53 *British Journal of Criminology*, 257–75.

the first opportunity was used as the dependent variable to analyse whether a defendant pleaded early or late with respect to the stage when the guilty plea was made. However, the different stages of when the guilty plea was entered – namely, early, intermediate, or late – were included as independent variables in the regression model.[57] This regression omits defendants who made no pleas, as the CCSS dataset does not include such defendants.

Table 5.1 illustrates the regression results of the CCSS data on plea outcomes. Unsurprisingly, pleading guilty at the intermediate or late stage positively and strongly correlates with pleading guilty 'not at the first opportunity', as more often than not, the early stage is the first opportunity for a defendant to plead guilty. In addition, two types of offences were statistically significant. Defendants charged with taking indecent photographs of children (IPC) were more likely to plead guilty at the first opportunity (i.e., at the early stage) compared to defendants charged with drug offences, the reference group used in the regression model. Conversely, defendants charged with sex offences were more likely than the reference group to not plead guilty at the first opportunity (i.e., enter a late guilty plea).

Among the demographic characteristics of defendants, age stood out as a significant predictor. In the model, the reference group was middle-aged defendants (ages 35–44), allowing for convenient comparisons between younger and older age groups. Strikingly, defendants in the two younger age groups (ages 18–24 and 25–34) were more likely to plead guilty at the first opportunity compared to defendants in the reference group, as were defendants in the eldest age group (ages 54 and above). As for other demographic characteristics, gender was not found to be significant. Existing illness was minimally significant predictor that was negatively associated with not pleading guilty at the first opportunity. However, given this small significance, interpreting the variable and drawing too many conclusions from it is not advised. Lastly, previous conviction was also found not to be a significant predictor; in other words, no statistically significant difference existed between defendants with previous convictions and defendants with a clean record regarding when they plead guilty.[58]

57 Early pleas are pleas entered at the Magistrates' Court prior to or at the plea and case management hearing (PCMH). Intermediate pleas are pleas entered after the PCMH but before trial. Late pleas are pleas entered on or after the day of trial.

58 It is important to emphasise again that the CCSS only records whether a defendant's previous convictions were considered by the sentencer when sentencing. There may be instances where a defendant has a previous record that was not considered when sentencing. The current analysis thus coded such cases as representing no previous offences.

Table 5.1 *Regression results for not pleading guilty at first opportunity: England and Wales*

Predictors	Odds ratio	95% CI
(Intercept)	0.45***	0.43–0.48
Timing of guilty plea (ref.: early)		
Intermediate	11.47***	10.80–12.18
Late	17.46***	16.61–18.36
Offence type (ref.: drugs)		
Arson	1.00	0.87–1.15
Assault	0.84	0.79–0.88
Burglary	1.03	0.97–1.09
Death	1.19	1.01–1.39
Driving	0.98	0.89–1.08
Fraud	1.22	1.00–1.49
Indecent photography of children (IPC)	0.73*	0.59–0.89
Other	1.08	1.01–1.16
Robbery	1.13	1.04–1.22
Sex	1.20*	1.11–1.30
Theft	0.97	0.91–1.03
Age group (years) (ref.: 35–44)		
18–24	0.90*	0.85–0.94
25–34	0.87*	0.84–0.93
45–54	0.94	0.89–1.00
≥54	0.84*	0.77–0.92
Gender (ref.: male)		
Female	1.09	1.03–1.16
Previous offences (ref.: no)		
Yes	1.03	0.99–1.07
Existing illness (ref.: no)		
Yes	0.87+	0.83–0.95
Confession made (ref.: no)		
Yes	0.10***	0.09–0.10
Model statistics		
Total observations	30,995	
Nagelkerke's R^2	0.70	

$^{+}p < 0.1$, $^{*}p < 0.05$, $^{**}p < 0.01$, $^{***}p < 0.001$.

In sum, the regression model found confession to be a very significant variable on pleading guilty. Defendants who had indicated their guilt to the police were much more likely to plead guilty at the first opportunity than defendants who had not confessed. The model offers evidence demonstrating that earlier decisions in the criminal process, in this case whether the defendant made a confession to the police, are associated with subsequent decisions about when to plead guilty.

Factors Affecting the Timing of Guilty Pleas: Hong Kong

For the Hong Kong District Court dataset, more variables could be extracted and coded compared to the CCSS. First, no plea (i.e., conviction after trial) was also coded as a category in the dataset besides early and late pleas. Second, besides offence type, the Hong Kong dataset also contains information about the number of charges per defendant. Third, besides the demographic characteristics of age and gender, information about the defendant's race/ethnicity was also available. This variable was categorised into three groups: local Hong Kong Chinese, Mainland Chinese, and foreigners, with the first group serving as the reference. Fourth, besides information about whether the defendant had previously confessed to the police, there was also information available about the type of legal representative and prosecutor for each case; the latter variables can enhance understandings about how earlier decisions in the criminal process may affect plea decisions. Finally, the Hong Kong courts' 'Reason for Sentence' reports also list the judge making the sentencing decisions, allowing judges to be coded in the dataset as well.

Based on the combination of variables listed earlier, an ordinal mixed-effects model was run to determine which variables significantly correlated to a defendant's guilty-plea stage. Since the data included information on presiding judges for each case, a mixed-effects model allowed for including both fixed and random effects that are present in non-independent data. Comparison with ordinary logistic regression, a mixed-effects model could determine and isolate the effect the presiding judge has on the defendant's submission of a guilty plea. A significant F-statistic of 4.74 between the presiding judge and guilty plea stage indicated that the timing of the guilty plea is not independent of the judge, highlighting that this relationship should be included.

In the model below, guilty pleas are categorised into three stages: (1) early, (2) late, and (3) no plea, with the first stage being used as the reference category. An early plea refers to those pleas made at the earliest opportunity and/or at a defendant's plea hearing, while a late plea includes all those made after a defendant's plea hearing to those made during the last day of trial. No plea refers to convictions after trial. For offence types, drug offences were used as the reference category. Four types of offences – namely, assault, driving, fraud, and other offences – were found to positively associate with late guilty pleas and no pleas compared to the reference. In addition, the number of charges per defendant was negatively correlated with both late and no guilty pleas, meaning that the more charges a defendant faced, the more likely they would plead guilty earlier. This is not too surprising, since the more charges one faces, the higher the likely sentence; therefore, it may be beneficial to plead guilty early in hopes of securing the highest sentence discount.

Regarding the demographic characteristics of defendants, race/ethnicity was found to be statistically significant. Here, when compared with local Hong Kong Chinese defendants, the foreigner status of certain defendants was found to positively correlate with late guilty pleas and testing of the prosecution's case at trial. This is consistent with extant literature on race and guilty pleas, which has posited that because ethnic minorities or foreigners have stronger distrust of the criminal process and the informal plea-bargaining system, they would much rather take their chances and have their case heard in open court in a contested trial. This finding of ethnic minorities being less likely to plead guilty is not limited to BAME defendants in a Western context, but also extends to ethnic minorities and foreigners in an Asian context such as the Hong Kong legal system. On the other hand, no differences were found between Mainland Chinese defendants and local Hong Kong Chinese defendants regarding guilty plea decisions. Lastly, in terms of other variables, no differences were found based on the defendant's gender or on their conviction history (prior convicts compared to first-time offenders).

Variables measuring earlier decisions in the criminal process demonstrated interesting results. Once again, confession was found to be strongly significant. Like the finding for the CCSS dataset, defendants in Hong Kong who had previously confessed to the police were negatively associated with late guilty pleas and not pleading guilty at all; in other words, like English defendants, Hong Kong defendants who had confessed were more likely to enter an early guilty plea. As mentioned previously, the type of legal representation offered to defendants was also coded in the Hong Kong dataset; it was found to be significant. Defendants represented by legal-aid lawyers were negatively associated with late guilty pleas and not pleading guilty compared with defendants represented by private lawyers; in short, defendants who received legal aid were more likely to plead guilty earlier. This is consistent with extant literature in the English context that points to the influence of legal-aid lawyers on their clients to plead guilty. Finally, in cases prosecuted by a public prosecutor, defendants were found to be positively associated with entering late guilty pleas and going to trial compared with cases that were prosecuted by prosecutors on fiat.

Table 5.2 illustrates the regression results of the Hong Kong District Court data on the stage when the guilty plea is entered.

The regression results for both the CCSS and Hong Kong District Court datasets indicate that three factors are significant, namely young adult defendants, confessions, and legal-aid lawyers. The following sections more closely investigate why the three factors are significant.

Young Adult Defendants

Young adult defendants are not treated as a distinct group in the criminal justice system. Unlike for 'child' or 'adult', there is no legal definition for the term 'young adult'. However, an increasing number of works in criminology, sociology, psychology, and neuroscience underscore the need for treating young adults as a distinct group. The regression results shown in Table 5.2, in particular for the CCSS data, indicate that defendants in the younger age groups were more likely to plead guilty earlier compared to the middle-aged reference category. Although no clear definition for the age of a young adult exists, the term has often referred to individuals aged 18 to 25. Arnett argues that 'emerging adulthood' is the stage when an individual departs from adolescence and gradually progresses towards assuming the responsibilities of adulthood.[59] Changes in society, as Arnett notes, 'have made the late teens and early twenties not simply a brief period of transition into adult roles but a distinct period in the life course, characterised by change and exploration of possible life directions'.[60] Unlike in generations past, it is common nowadays for young adults to be studying, exploring their life paths, and delaying marriage; in this sense, emerging adulthood is also a social phenomenon.[61]

There has been some traction in recognising young adults as a distinct group in the criminal process. Existing research has noted how the

[59] J. J. Arnett, 'Emerging adulthood: a theory of development from the late teens through the twenties' (2000) 55 *American Psychologist*, 469–80.

[60] Ibid., 469.

[61] Ibid.

Table 5.2 *Regression results for guilty plea stage: Hong Kong*

	Odds ratio	**95% CI**
Fixed effects		
Offence type (ref.: drugs)		
Assault	3.53***	2.34–5.31
Burglary/Robbery	0.87	0.61–1.25
Driving	6.89***	4.26–11.13
Fraud	8.33***	5.70–12.18
Other	3.10**	2.10–4.57
Theft	0.46	0.28–0.76
No. of charges per defendant	0.73***	0.67–0.80
Age group (years) (ref.: 35–44)		
18–24	0.77	0.53–1.13
25–34	0.78	0.56–1.08
45–54	0.97	0.69–1.36
≥55	1.46	1.03–2.08
Gender (ref.: male)		
Female	0.76	0.53–1.08
Race/ethnicity (ref.: local Hong Kong)		
Foreigner	0.89	0.61–1.30
Mainland Chinese	0.13***	0.06–0.25
Previous offences (ref.: no)		
Yes	0.74	0.57–0.96
Existing illness (ref.: no)		
Mental illness	0.86	0.55–1.34
Physical illness	0.60	0.39–0.91
Confession made (ref.: no)		
Yes	0.16***	0.13–0.20
Legal representative (ref.: private lawyer)		
Legal aid	0.40**	0.30–0.55
Prosecution (ref.: on fiat)		
Public prosecutor	13.33***	9.87–17.99
Random effects and model statistics		
SD of judges	0.92	
ICC	0.21	
Groups	38	
Observations	1,035	
Nagelkerke's R^2	0.30	

$^{+}p < 0.1$, $^{*}p < 0.05$, $^{**}p < 0.01$, $^{***}p < 0.001$.

complexities of the criminal process bewilder young adults. Moreover, young adults are susceptible to the influence of others, particularly family members, while making legal decisions, including plea decisions.[62] A report issued by the Judicial Committee of the United Kingdom House of Commons, titled 'The Treatment of Young Adults in the Criminal Justice System',[63] officially called for young adults to be treated distinctly in the criminal process. Citing works in criminology, neurology, and psychology, the report emphasised that the typical adult male brain is not fully formed until he reaches his mid-twenties. Specifically, in psychological terms, young adults remain closer to children than adults.[64] Parts of the brain that regulate an individual's weighing of long-term gains and costs against short-term rewards are still developing;[65] this has consequences for both the decision and timing of pleading guilty. Moreover, such consequences are magnified in a system that incorporates a sliding scale of sentence discounts for guilty pleas, which seemingly rewards the short-term benefit of pleading guilty while disregarding the long-term consequences of a criminal conviction. This may explain why young adult defendants are more likely to plead guilty earlier. However, adverse consequences for pleading guilty appear regarding the ability of defendants to integrate into society. Young people typically stop committing crimes by their mid-twenties; yet convictions and a criminal record make it harder for these offenders to find stable employment and affordable accommodation, as well as desist from further crime.[66]

Challenging a Confession

In both datasets, confession was found to be a significant variable affecting an early guilty plea. As discussed earlier, although a confession

62 K. K. Cheng and B. P. Leung, 'Passing the threshold of one justice system to the next: challenges of emerging young adults in Hong Kong's adult criminal justice system' (2017) 62 *International Journal of Offender Therapy and Comparative Criminology*, 2650–68; J. Thomas and B. Estep, *Young Adults in Court: Developing a Tailored Approach* (London: T2A Alliance, 2015).

63 House of Commons Judicial Committee, *The Treatment of Young Adults in the Criminal Justice System, Seventh Report of Session 2016–17* (London: House of Commons, 2016).

64 Ibid., paragraph 8.

65 Ibid.

66 Ibid., paragraphs 14 and 24. For more on desistance from crime, see for example J. H. Laub and R. J. Sampson, 'Understanding desistance from crime' (2001) 28 *Crime and Justice*, 1–69; S. Maruna, *Making Good: How Ex-Convicts Reform and Rebuild Their Lives* (Washington, DC: American Psychological Association, 2001).

is not a guilty plea and can be challenged in court, it is nonetheless a powerful piece of evidence. Furthermore, challenging the admissibility of a confession is not always easy. In both England and Wales and in Hong Kong, as well as in other similar common law jurisdictions, the admissibility of confessions is addressed during a *voir dire*, essentially a mini-trial within the larger trial.[67] For England and Wales, section 76 of the PACE Act states that in any proceedings where the prosecution gives evidence that the defendant has made a confession, the court may exclude this evidence if the confession is found to have been obtained 'by oppression'[68] or 'in consequence of anything said or done which was likely, in the circumstances existing at the time, to render unreliable any confession'.[69] The prosecution assumes the burden of proving to the court beyond a reasonable doubt that the confession was not obtained by oppression or is unreliable.[70]

Here, the meaning of 'oppression' is its ordinary dictionary meaning, 'the exercise of authority or power in a burdensome, harsh, or wrongful manner; unjust or cruel treatment of subjects, inferiors, etc., or the imposition of unreasonable or unjust burdens'.[71] For instance, several long police interviews where police shouted at the suspect what they wanted him to say, despite repeated denials by the suspect about his involvement, were held to be oppressive.[72] On the other hand, 'unreliable' means 'cannot be relied upon as being the truth'.[73] Determining whether a confession is unreliable is an objective test, which considers everything that police had said and done, in addition to asking whether what was said and done was likely in the circumstances, to render the consequent confession unreliable.[74] The test is fact- and defendant-specific, as '[t]he focus must be concentrated on the reliability of the

67 In Hong Kong, the procedure is known as the 'alternative procedure' when the case is before a judge sitting alone. Unlike a *voir dire*, where the jury is typically removed from the court while the judge deals with the special issue of admissibility, under the alternative procedure, the presiding judge will simultaneously deal with the special issue of admissibility and the general issue of guilt or innocence. The judge will also give a ruling on admissibility before the trial continues.

68 Section 76(2)(a) of the Police and Criminal Evidence (PACE) Act 1984.

69 Section 76(2)(b) of the PACE Act 1984.

70 Section 76(2) of the PACE Act 1984.

71 *R* v. *Fulling* (1987) 85 Cr App R 136 at 142.

72 *R* v. *Paris* (1993) 97 Cr App R 99. In this case, the police interview lasted 13 hours and officers shouted at the suspect, despite the suspect denying involvement over 300 times.

73 *R* v. *Crampton* (1991) 92 Cr App R 369 at 372.

74 *R* v. *Barry* (1992) 95 Cr App R 384.

confession made by the individual defendant, given the circumstances as they existed when the confession was made'.[75]

Under section 78 of the PACE Act, admissibility of a confession can also be challenged on unfairness, where

> the court may refuse to allow evidence on which the prosecution proposes to rely to be given if it appears to the court that, having regard to all the circumstances, including the circumstances in which the evidence was obtained, the admission of the evidence would have such an adverse effect on the fairness of the proceedings that the court ought not to admit it.

The court has to examine the circumstances in which the police interview occurred, as well as balance the interests of both the defence and the prosecution when determining whether admitting the evidence would have an adverse effect on the fairness of the proceedings.[76] Moreover, under common law, the trial judge has the discretion to exclude evidence in order to protect the defendant from an unfair trial.[77]

While Hong Kong does not have a statutory equivalent of the PACE Act, Hong Kong law regarding admissibility of confessions is also based on common law. Under such law, the court can exclude a confession if it determines that the confession was made involuntarily, as Lord Summer stated in the classic case of *Ibrahim* in the Privy Council:

> It has long been established as a positive rule of English criminal law, that no statement by an accused is admissible in evidence against him unless it is shewn by the prosecution to have been a voluntary statement, in the sense that it has not been obtained from him either by fear of prejudice or hope of advantage exercised or held out by a person in authority.[78]

The Hong Kong Court of Final Appeal affirmed this principle whereby the prosecution must establish that the confession was made voluntarily and not by 'oppression'.[79] Moreover, even when a confession is found to be voluntary, a judge can still exercise their discretion under common

[75] *R* v. *Wahab* [2003] 1 Cr App R 15, paragraph 40; [2002] EWCA Crim 1570.

[76] *R* v. *Hughes* [1988] Crim LR 519. There is no definitive case law that sets out the scope of section 78 of the PACE Act 1984. It has been drafted broadly to allow for a variety of cases that cannot be anticipated beforehand.

[77] *Scott* v. *R* (1989) 89 Cr App R 153. This power has been retained under section 82(3) of the PACE Act 1984.

[78] *Ibrahim* v. *R* [1914] AC 599 at 609.

[79] The House of Lords added mention of 'oppression' in *DPP* v. *Ping Lin* [1976] AC 574; this principle is affirmed in Hong Kong in *Secretary for Justice* v. *Lam Tat Ming* [2000] 2 HKLRD 431.

law to exclude it to ensure that the parties receive a fair trial.[80] Nevertheless, this discretion should be seldom exercised, since in instances of considering whether to exclude evidence from the jury, the judge assumes the role of weighing the evidence. Indeed, what is considered an unfair confession would already likely be excluded as an involuntary one.[81] The exclusion of a confession because of a breach of statues – namely the PACE Act or a Code of Practice dealing with police questioning and interviews for England and Wales, or the Rules and Directions for the Questioning of Suspects and the Taking of Statements for Hong Kong[82] – may be a factor contributing to excluding the confession, although it does not automatically lead to an exclusion. Should the defence successfully challenge the admissibility of a confession in a *voir dire* or alternative procedure, the trial proceeds without using it as evidence. Should the challenge fail, the prosecution can continue to put the confession forward in trial.

Despite the defence being able to challenge confessions, Hong Kong defence lawyers stressed in interviews that in reality, confessions are rather difficult to challenge. As one barrister explained:

> We call this 'fighting a confession'. They mainly occur after the arrest by the police. Police are experienced witnesses and indeed would hold no grudges against the defendant? And there are no prior complaints. So, it is hard to fight it. If the court accepts it, there is a lot of weight on it . . . Of course, every case is different but, in most cases, to have the court accept that the police did something inappropriate is very difficult.[83]

Another criminal defence lawyer explained that disparities in power exist between trained police officers and the defendant. This puts pressure on defendants in police interviews and subsequently affects the difficulty of challenging a confession in court:

> Unless there's evidence of physical abuse or it's videotaped, it's very difficult [to challenge the confession]. Any sensible lawyer, if they get to the police station, would advise their clients to say nothing. Most people are convicted because of statements made to the police . . . Cops are ruthless and some of them are good interrogators . . . they are

[80] *Noor Mohammed* v. *R* [1949] AC 182.

[81] *R* v. *Sang* [1980] AC 402; *R* v. *Lam Yip-ying* [1984] HKLR 419.

[82] The Secretary for Security issued these 'Rules and Directions' in 1992, replacing the Judges' Rules of 1912, to apply to all law enforcement agencies.

[83] K. K. Cheng, 'The guilty plea process in the Hong Kong magistrates' courts', Unpublished PhD thesis, 2013b, p. 175.

> trained ... It's easy for the police. It's all admissible because they are all given caution. The pressure is on these people [defendants].[84]

Given the difficulties in getting a confession to be excluded as evidence, in addition to how powerful a confession can be in supporting conviction, defendants who have confessed likely feel pressure to plead guilty earlier so they can receive a lower sentence and not risk trial. Reiterating the significance of how earlier stages in the criminal process affect subsequent stages, Bottoms and McClean point out, '[The police] effectively control the early stages of the criminal justice process; and through this early control – especially in its influence on pleas of guilty – they are able ... to influence powerfully the remainder of the criminal justice system.'[85] The extensive literature on confessions consistently underscores how police interviews or interrogation techniques are designed to enhance the chances of obtaining a confession, even false confessions.[86] In this way, the pressure to confess leads directly to the pressure to plead guilty.

Publicly Funded Lawyers

The results from the Hong Kong District Court dataset reveal that defendants represented by legal-aid lawyers are more likely to plead guilty earlier compared to defendants with private representation. This coincides with previous findings for England and Wales, where legal-aid lawyers were found to hold guilt-presumptive views of indigent defendants and thus pressure them into pleading guilty. Unfortunately, the CCSS did not record the type of legal representation each defendant received, rendering this important variable unexaminable in the English context. Conversely, in the Hong Kong context, a study by Cheng *et al.* offers insights about the experiences of defendants and their publicly funded lawyers through interviews.[87] They found that despite being in

[84] Ibid., pp. 176–7.

[85] A. E. Bottoms and J. D. McClean, *Defendants in the Criminal Process* (London: Routledge & Kegan Paul, 1976).

[86] See for example, S. M. Kassin and G. H. Gudjonsson, 'The psychology of confessions: a review of the literature and issues' (2004) 5 *Psychological Science in the Public Interest*, 33–67.

[87] K. K. Cheng, W. H. Chui, and R. Ong, 'Providing justice for low-income youths: publicly funded lawyers and youth clients in Hong Kong' (2015) 24(4) *Social & Legal Studies*, 577–93. While this study focused on youth defendants in the context of duty lawyers, their perceptions offer insights relevant to the findings for the current study.

lawyer–client relationships, both sides mistrusted each other. One barrister said this about indigent defendants:

> They would cooperate to the extent that they will try to find out what they need to say so that they won't be removed from their status quo. They will have made up a story by the time they see the lawyer . . . They will come up with stories which are seemingly believable but it's quite clear that it has been made up sometimes; they will cooperate so that they can stay out of custody.[88]

On the other hand, defendants are not fully forthright with their legal representatives because they believe that government-funded lawyers work for the government. Instead of viewing the lawyers as legal defenders who are on their side, defendants regarded them as siding with the police and the prosecution. Even when their legal representatives were advising them, defendants regarded it as pressure. One defendant remarked:

> The lawyer treated me as a criminal and examined me harshly, and also interrogated me about some facts that was already there [written in the police report] . . . For example, reading that my boss said I didn't show up to work a lot, she would interrogate me by saying 'Why do you always not show up for work?' I didn't know how to answer her questions. It seemed that she was helping others to scold me . . . I felt like she was acting like a policewoman in examining a criminal.[89]

Nevertheless, one should not simply conclude that all legal-aid and publicly funded lawyers hold guilt-presumptive views and persuade their clients to plead guilty. Furthermore, defendants often already have preconceived notions about publicly funded lawyers, who are considered advocates who are less desirable compared with privately retained lawyers, even though the former are in private practice and are simply instructed by the Director of Legal Aid or the Duty Lawyer Service to serve as legal-aid or duty lawyers. Defendants believe that if they were to contest the prosecution's case, they would try to engage a private lawyer. Speaking about duty lawyers in the Magistrates' Courts under another study involving adult defendants, one defendant stated,

> I think the duty lawyer was not 'qualified'. They just wanted to get a fixed pay. Some might be very good, but some were not. The duty lawyer would be more

[88] Ibid., p. 585.
[89] Ibid.

> helpful if you pleaded guilty and planned to make a mitigation plea. However, if you would like to get acquitted, it's better to get a private lawyer.[90]

Conversely, when defendants have no intention of challenging their case, they will seek out a public defender who can at least assist them in plea mitigation, in hopes that they can receive a more lenient sentence. Therefore, the choice of lawyers is shaped by the defendant's intention to plead guilty, as well as the advice lawyers provide to the defendant.[91]

Pretrial Detention

Pretrial detention is another factor worth discussing. Regrettably, both the CCSS and Hong Kong District Court datasets did not capture this variable. Extant literature nonetheless points to pretrial detention as a key preceding decision that influences plea decisions. In England and Wales, defendants have a general right to bail,[92] with exclusions applying to offences including murder,[93] manslaughter, serious sexual offences,[94] and class A drug use.[95] The court may also make other exceptions, denying bail if there are substantial grounds for believing that the defendant poses a real risk, including

- the belief that the defendant will fail to surrender in court, commit an offence whilst on bail, or interfere with witnesses or otherwise obstruct the course of justice;[96]
- the belief that the defendant will engage in conduct that will or likely cause physical or mental injury to their spouses, civil partners, relatives, cohabitants, or intimate partners of a significant duration; or cause these individuals[97] to fear physical or mental injury;[98] and
- the defendant being found on bail on the date of the offence.[99]

[90] Cheng *et al.*, 'Why do criminal trials "crack"?', 19–20.

[91] Of course, the defendants themselves must still qualify for legal aid. In Hong Kong, as in England and Wales, defendants may only receive legal aid by passing a means test and a merits test. Defendants who are keen to contest their case may try their utmost to hire a private lawyer, such as through asking friends and family.

[92] Section 4 of the Bail Act 1976.

[93] Section 115(1) of the Coroners and Justice Act 2009.

[94] Section 259(2) of the Criminal Justice and Public Order Act 1994.

[95] Schedule 1 of the Bail Act 1976, part I, paragraph 6.

[96] Ibid., paragraph 2.

[97] These individuals are referred to as 'associated persons' as defined under section 62 of the Family Law Act 1996.

[98] Schedule 1 of the Bail Act 1976, part I, paragraph 2ZA.

[99] Ibid., paragraph 2A.

When deciding on bail, the court shall consider circumstances as they appear relevant, such as the nature and seriousness of the offence; the character, antecedents, associations, and community ties of the defendant; and the defendant's record of fulfilling obligations to previous grants of bail.[100] If the conditions for bail, such as reporting to a police station or sureties, are seen as insufficient to mitigate the risks that the defendant may pose, then the defendant will be denied bail.[101]

In Hong Kong, defendants also have a general right to bail. The prosecution assumes the burden of satisfying the court that bail should be denied in a particular case.[102] The court may also deny bail if it believes that there are substantial grounds for believing that should the defendant be granted bail – with or without conditions[103] – they would not surrender to custody as the court may appoint, commit a criminal offence while on bail, interfere with a witness, or otherwise pervert or obstruct the course of justice.[104] In making this decision, the court has to consider matters such as the nature and seriousness of the offence, the background and demeanour of the defendant, their ties to the community, their financial position, and their home environment.[105]

As mentioned before, existing studies demonstrate that a relationship exists between pretrial detention and guilty pleas. In their study, Kellough and Wortley observed over 1,800 criminal cases that appeared in two Toronto bail courts between 1993 and 1994. All cases were followed from initial observation until final disposition and quantitatively coded for statistical analyses.[106] The variables used as proxies for the risk of absconding included employment status, home address, and Canadian citizenship, whereas the variables used as proxies for the risk of

[100] Ibid., paragraph 9.

[101] Schedule 1, part IIA, paragraph 1 of the Bail Act 1976 states: 'If the court decides not to grant the defendant bail, it is the court's duty to consider, at each subsequent hearing while the defendant is a person to whom section 4 above applies and remains in custody, whether he ought to be granted bail.'

[102] Article 5 of the Hong Kong Bill of Rights Ordinance (Cap. 383) provides that: 'Everyone has the right to liberty and security of person. No one shall be subjected to arbitrary arrest or detention. No one shall be deprived of his liberty except on such grounds and in accordance with such procedures as are established by law.' See also section 9D(1) of the Criminal Procedure Ordinance (Cap. 221).

[103] For possible conditions, see Section 9D(3) of the Criminal Procedure Ordinance (Cap. 221).

[104] Section 9G of the Criminal Procedure Ordinance (Cap. 221).

[105] Ibid.

[106] Kellough and Wortley, 'Remand for plea'.

committing future offences whilst on bail included the number of concurrent charges and previous criminal convictions. Analyses also coded for whether the defendant was remanded in custody and other demographic characteristics. The outcome of interest was whether the defendant pleaded guilty. Logistic regressions were performed, which found a strong significance between pretrial detention and the likelihood of pleading guilty. After controlling for all the variables, defendants who were denied bail and remanded in custody were found to be 2.5 times more likely than defendants on bail to plead guilty. Subsequent interviews with defendants shed light on the reasons for pleading guilty. Defendants who were denied bail indicated that they wanted to avoid 'dead time', referring to the time spent remanded in custody that may not be counted when a sentence is finally imposed. Certain defendants also noted that they expected to receive a non-custodial sentence, and so by pleading guilty they could be freed. Even if they received a custodial sentence, a guilty plea (and conviction) would mean moving from the less than decent conditions of a detention centre to those of a correctional facility.[107]

In another Canadian qualitative study that interviewed 12 defendants and 12 defence lawyers, Euvrard and Leclerc found that in certain situations, pretrial detention was a source of pressure for defendants to plead guilty. Overcrowding in detention centres, in addition to the stress, anxiety, and uncertainty of being remanded in custody for lengthy periods, led defendants to plead guilty, even when some had maintained their innocence. Moreover, for defendants that had originally intended to plead guilty, being denied bail made them do so earlier. Defendant interviewees revealed that had they been granted bail, they would have asked their legal representatives to hold more firmly in any plea bargain with the prosecution.[108] Looking at the United States, Sacks and Ackerman analysed criminal cases collected from New Jersey in 2004 and found that defendants held in pretrial detention were more likely to have shorter case dispositions. Since virtually all cases in the United States are resolved through guilty pleas, the shorter durations meant that defendants had pleaded guilty earlier.[109]

[107] Ibid., 199.

[108] E. Euvrard and C. Leclerc, 'Pre-trial detention and guilty pleas: inducement or coercion?' (2017) 19(5) *Punishment & Society*, 525–42.

[109] M. Sacks and A. R. Ackerman, 'Pretrial detention and guilty pleas: if they can't afford bail they must be guilty' (2012) 25 *Criminal Justice Studies*, 265–78.

In the Hong Kong context, Cheng and Leung's study on the experiences and perceptions of 34 detainees also confirmed the harsh conditions of detention centres. Being remanded in custody was made difficult not only by the harsh environment of detention centres, such as overcrowding and poor hygiene, but also the stress of confinement and the uncertainty regarding criminal cases. Detainees expressed that pretrial detention was worse than prison and that they would much rather spend their time in custody at a prison.[110] One interviewee explained that prisons offered more structured activities and engagement compared to the idleness of detention centres:

> It is a very tedious and dull life in remand. I was asked to sit there all day long. After the judgment was announced, I would be transferred to prison where I got something to do. For example, some 'jobs' or playing ball games. On the contrary, the life in remand was very boring and made me feel very fretful.[111]

Receiving a sentence brings finality and, in many ways, leads to peace of mind. As another defendant stated,

> After knowing the result [of my sentence], I felt more settled and at least I knew in mind how long I would have to live without freedom . . . Unlike pre-trial detention when most efforts are dedicated in handling the case, a person could concentrate on his own personal issues in prison.[112]

One of the quickest ways to bring about this sense of finality is by pleading quickly soon. The study by Cheng *et al.* on late guilty pleas in Hong Kong's Magistrates' Courts found that defendants held in pretrial detention were more likely to enter a late guilty plea compared with defendants on bail. Supplementary interviews with defendants revealed that prolonged detention in remand was one reason why defendants changed their pleas from an initial not guilty plea to a guilty plea.[113] One defendant said,

> I pleaded not guilty at the first court session. After being sent to [the remand centre], the government lawyer came to ask me to plead guilty. He told me that it's possible for me to receive a shorter punishment. I realized that I had already lost my freedom for more than one month.

110 K. K. Cheng and B. P. Leung, 'The punitive nature of pre-trial detention: perspectives of detainees in Hong Kong' (2018) 58 *The Howard Journal of Crime and Justice*, 143–60.

111 Ibid., 154.

112 Ibid., 155.

113 Cheng *et al.*, 'Why do criminal trials "crack"?'

> I had to think if I wanted to continue to go for a trial or if I wanted to plead guilty in order to get a more lenient punishment.[114]

In sum, the interplay between pretrial detention, advice from publicly funded lawyers, and the sentence discount offered for guilty pleas affects the timing of guilty pleas.

Conclusion

Under a guilty plea process that features a sliding scale of sentence discounts, different factors may serve as potential pressures for defendants to plead guilty, and to do so early. Interestingly, the stages of the criminal process preceding plea taking have been found to significantly affect plea outcomes. Criminal suspects may feel pressure to confess to police; once they make a confession, they may feel pressure to plead guilty soon afterwards. Throughout the past half century, lawyers have also been found to be a source of pressure on defendants to plead guilty in England and Wales. Additionally, in present-day Hong Kong, indigent defendants represented by legal-aid lawyers were found to be more likely to plead guilty earlier. Furthermore, extant literature also points to pretrial detention as a source of pressure for remanded defendants to eventually plead guilty. Lastly, for young adult defendants, their lacking in psychological development may make them more susceptible to various pressures to plead guilty.

[114] Ibid., 20.

6

Trial and Late-Plea Penalties

When deciding whether to plead guilty, the question of sentencing outcomes inevitably arises. After all, the sliding scale of sentence discounts encourages guilty defendants to plead guilty as early as possible by offering greater sentence reductions for earlier pleas. Existing literature points to a plea-trial disparity in sentences, with scholars referring to this as a 'trial penalty' or a 'trial/jury tax', while courts and policymakers use the terms 'sentence discounts' or 'sentence reductions'. Nowadays, with the sliding scale of sentence discounts in effect, the question becomes not just one of a 'plea-trial disparity' for sentences, but also one of a 'early/late-plea disparity' and a 'late-plea penalty'. As discussed in Chapters 1 and 2, official discourse suggests that sentence discounts based on the timing of guilty pleas bring additional benefits to the criminal justice process. This chapter, which focuses on the crucial question of sentence outcomes, argues that contrary to what has been suggested, plea-trial and plea-timing disparities have negative consequences for the justice system, as well as that the sentence disparity should be conceptualised as a trial and late-plea penalty. This chapter begins by describing the debate surrounding the conceptualisation of the plea-trial sentence disparity as one between a trial penalty and a guilty plea discount. It then reviews existing studies that have measured the plea-trial disparity, highlighting how inadequate attention has been given to the issue in the jurisdictions of England and Wales and Hong Kong, as well as to the overall timing of guilty pleas. Thereafter, using the datasets from the Crown Court Sentencing Survey (CCSS) and the Hong Kong District Court compiled for this study, this chapter investigates the effects that the timing of guilty pleas may have on sentence outcomes. Interestingly, a late-plea penalty was found for England and Wales, whereas only a trial penalty was found for Hong Kong. The chapter concludes by discussing the implications of these results.

Guilty Plea Discount or Trial Penalty?

There is considerable debate on how to conceptualise the differentials in sentences for defendants who plead guilty and for defendants convicted after trial. Are they sentence discounts or trial penalties (also referred to as jury or trial taxes)? As Chapters 1 and 2 have illustrated, courts use the term 'sentence discounts' or 'sentence reductions'. The terms are based on the notion that defendants who save the court's time and resources by pleading guilty should be rewarded for admitting their guilt. On the other hand, the sentence differential could be viewed as a penalty for those defendants exercising their constitutional right to trial.[1] At face value, these two perceptions may simply seem like two sides of the same coin. Yet closer scrutiny reveals that how one conceptualises the sentence differential, whether as a discount or a penalty, depends on what one considers as the basis for sentencing – the outcome of trial or of a guilty plea.

If trial sentences are the standard, then lower sentences resulting from guilty pleas should be considered as sentence discounts. This perspective views trial sentences as the appropriate punishment and that, as the courts have reiterated, a lower sentence reflects a reward. Yet others have asserted that trial sentences should not be the basis of sentencing when most criminal cases are resolved through guilty pleas. In other words, because trials are not the norm, trial sentences should not be the baseline for calculating sentence outcomes. Instead, given that guilty pleas dominate in the adjudication of criminal cases, sentences resulting from guilty pleas, also known as plea sentences, should be the baseline. More punitive sentences that result from a trial therefore serve as a penalty for a defendant exercising their constitutional right to contest the state's case, hence the term 'trial penalty'. Following this logic, given that most guilty pleas are made at the first opportunity,[2] the penalty is not just for electing to go to trial, but also for not pleading guilty early enough.

Moreover, in the context of plea bargaining, prosecutors, defence lawyers, and judges know the 'going rates' of plea sentences, using those as benchmarks during plea bargaining.[3] Although plea bargaining may

[1] B. D. Johnson, 'Trials and tribulations: the trial tax and the process of punishment' (2019) 48 *Crime and Justice*, 313–63; S. Yan and S. D. Bushway, 'Plea discounts or trial penalties? Making sense of the trial-plea sentence disparities' (2018) 35 *Justice Quarterly*, 1226–49.

[2] This is certainly the case for the England and Wales and Hong Kong datasets for this book.

[3] P. F. Nardulli, J. Eisenstein, and R. B. Flemming, *The Tenor of Justice: Criminal Courts and the Guilty Plea Process* (Urbana: University of Illinois Press, 1988). This view is informed by the courtroom workgroup model, which posits that courtroom actors must work

not be as prolific in certain jurisdictions,[4] in those such as England and Wales and Hong Kong, where sentence bargaining is not permitted, prosecutors and defence lawyers can still expect estimates of sentence outcomes. Even for straight guilty pleas, defence lawyers can properly advise their clients what an expected sentence is based on their experiences, sentencing guidelines, and the sliding scale of sentence discounts. Although more recently, some scholars have adopted the more neutral term of a plea-trial disparity[5] to describe the differential between expected and actual sentence outcomes, the underlying intention is to impose – or at least give the appearance of imposing – a heavier sentence on defendants who take their chances at trial. Despite the rhetoric regarding the differential being a sentence discount that rewards the defendant for saving the court's time and resources, as this chapter shows, the actual effect is a sentence disparity, where defendants convicted by trial receive more severe sentences than defendants convicted by their own pleas. Furthermore, at least in England and Wales, defendants who do not plead at the first opportunity often receive more severe sentences. Given that most criminal cases are disposed of through *early* guilty pleas, any heavier sentence because of a delayed guilty plea should be regarded as imposing a late-plea penalty in addition to a potential trial penalty.

How sentence differentials are conceptualised also plays an important role in understanding the magnitude of the sentence disparity. This is because plea discounts underestimate the magnitude of trial penalties. Johnson acutely observes that '[o]ne implication is that sentencing systems, as in England and Wales, that provide for explicit plea discounts underestimate potential trial penalties. The standard 33 percent sentence plea discount in the English system, conceptualised as a trial tax, becomes 50 percent'.[6] With a sliding scale of sentence discounts, the question is

together to ensure the shared objective of processing cases quickly. These actors include prosecutors, defence lawyers, judges, and even court clerks and court bailiffs, along with defendants themselves to a lesser extent.

4 See Chapter 3.

5 C. Tata and J. Gormley, 'To plead or not to plead? "Guilt" is the question: rethinking sentencing and plea-decision making in Anglo American countries', in C. Spohn and P. K. Brennan (eds.), *Handbook on Sentencing Policies and Practices in the 21st Century* (New York: Routledge, 2020).

6 Johnson, 'Trials and tribulations', 323. Johnson also provides another illustration: 'Consider a case in which the expected sentence at trial is 10 years, and the expected sentence after a guilty plea is 5 years. Conceived of as a plea discount, the defendant receives a 50 percent reduction from the trial sentence; conceptualised as a trial penalty, he or she receives a 100 percent increase' (pp. 323–4).

not just whether a plea-trial sentence disparity exists, but also whether a late-plea penalty exists.

Existing Studies Measuring Trial Penalty

Most existing empirical studies have pointed to the existence of a trial penalty; however, the research context of these studies is mainly limited to the United States. Analysing sentencing data for serious violent offences from county criminal courts in Pennsylvania between 1997 and 2000, Ulmer and Bradley found a significant trial penalty.[7] Controlling for legally relevant variables, including offence severity[8] and offence type;[9] defendant characteristics such as race/ethnicity, gender, and age; and court caseloads, they discovered that the mode of conviction, whether by guilty plea, bench trial (trial by judge), or jury trial, significantly correlates with both likelihood of incarceration and sentence length in terms of imprisonment duration in months. The likelihood of incarceration was more than twice as likely for a guilty plea and 2.7 times more likely from a jury trial.[10] Regarding sentence length, defendants convicted through bench trials faced a 22 per cent longer sentence compared with those who pleaded guilty, whereas those convicted by a jury faced a significant 57 per cent longer sentence compared with those who pleaded guilty.[11] Similarly, through examining sentencing statistics for Florida between 1998 and 2006, Lehmann found that after controlling for case severity and other defendant characteristics, defendants convicted after trial were more likely to receive a custodial sentence than community supervision compared with defendants who pleaded guilty. A conviction by trial was also found to positively correlate with imprisonment sentence length.[12]

Evidence for a trial penalty is also present at the federal level. Comparing differences in sentencing outcomes between defendants who pleaded guilty and defendants convicted by trial in the US District

[7] J. T. Ulmer and M. S. Bradley, 'Variations in trial penalties among serious violent offences' (2006) 44 *Criminology*, 631–70.

[8] Offence severity was measured by scores based on Pennsylvania sentencing guidelines.

[9] The serious violent offences measured in this study included homicide, rape and involuntary deviant sexual intercourse, aggravated assault, and robbery.

[10] Ulmer and Bradley, 'Variations in trial penalties', 650.

[11] Ibid., 652.

[12] P. S. Lehmann, 'Trial penalties under Florida's sentencing guidelines: the moderating role of case seriousness' (2020) 67 *Crime & Delinquency*, 1728–64.

Courts, Ulmer, Eisenstein, and Johnson found that sentence lengths are much longer for the latter. Even when controlling for relevant departures from the US federal sentencing guidelines, such as substantial assistance departures and acceptance of responsibility,[13] in addition to other case details and defendants' demographic characteristics, sentence lengths were still longer for defendants found guilty post-trial compared with defendants convicted by guilty pleas.[14] Using Sentencing Commission data that compared different types of offences, a report by the National Association of Criminal Defense Lawyers found that across virtually all offences types, trial sentences were higher on average compared with sentences resulting from guilty pleas.[15] In a review of existing sentencing studies in the United States, Johnson concluded that defendants convicted post-trial are generally two to six times more likely to be incarcerated compared with defendants who pleaded guilty and receive prison terms that are 15–60 per cent longer.[16]

Other studies in the United States had mixed conclusions regarding evidence for a trial penalty. For example, King and colleagues examined sentencing data for five states with sentencing guidelines: Kansas, Maryland, Minnesota, Pennsylvania, and Washington.[17] They discovered that conclusive evidence of lengthier jury trials for defendants who do not plead, or of sentences given from the bench (i.e., by the judge alone without a jury), resulting in longer sentences was only present for two of the five states surveyed.[18] In Maryland, for instance, defendants convicted of heroin distribution by jury faced an average sentence that was

[13] Downward departures or reductions because of substantial assistance or acceptance of responsibility only apply where the defendant pleads guilty. See sections 5K1.1 and 3E1.1, respectively, of the *United States Sentencing Commission's Guidelines Manual* (Washington, DC: United States Sentencing Commission, 2018).

[14] J. T. Ulmer, J. Eisenstein, and B. D. Johnson, 'Trial penalties in federal sentencing: extra-guidelines factors and district variation' (2010) 27 *Justice Quarterly*, 560–92.

[15] National Association of Criminal Defense Lawyers, *The Trial Penalty: The Sixth Amendment Right to Trial on the Verge of Extinction and How to Save It* (Washington, DC: National Association of Criminal Defense Lawyers, 2018). Out of 32 offences measured, exceptions in which the average plea sentence was higher than the trial sentences (both measured in years) were for drugs – communication facilities and drugs – simple possession. Both sentence lengths were the same for forgery/counterfeiting. See figure 1, pp. 20–1.

[16] Johnson, 'Trials and tribulations'.

[17] N. J. King, D. A. Soulé, S. Steen, and R. R. Weidner, 'When process affects punishment: differences in sentences after guilty plea, bench trial, and jury trial in five guidelines states' (2005) 105 *Columbia Law Review*, 959–1009.

[18] Maryland and Pennsylvania.

350 per cent longer than defendants who had pleaded guilty, while defendants convicted of heroin distribution by a judge alone resulted in an average sentence that was 150 per cent longer than their counterparts who had pleaded guilty.[19] Yet for various offences in the other states, no discernible patterns were observed for differences between jury trials, bench trials, and guilty pleas.[20]

Perhaps the most striking study is the one by Abrams, who challenged conventional wisdom regarding a trial penalty. According to his study of Cook County state courts in Illinois, where criminal cases from the city of Chicago made up the bulk of his sample, defendants who opted for trial fared *better* in sentences compared with those who pleaded guilty; in other words, a 'plea penalty' existed.[21] Abrams asserted that previous empirical studies were mistaken in simply comparing sentence lengths between defendants who pleaded guilty and defendants convicted after electing for trial. The biggest problem, he argued, is that those studies only analysed cases with sentences that were carried out; they did not account for cases of acquittal. As Abrams explains, the 'trial penalty' as previous studies have measured it is based on the simple notion that defendants who choose trial receive a longer sentence compared to pleading guilty. Yet he asserts that what is missing is the incorporation of defendant choice, which 'would imply that defendants choose pleas at a high rate because they lead to a lower expected sentence than do trials'.[22]

Using the American context where plea bargaining is dominant, Abrams elaborates on what he terms 'conditional expected sentences' and 'unconditional expected sentences'.[23] The conditional expected sentence is the measure of the average trial sentence length for imprisonment that excludes any prison sentences of length zero, such as those that result in an acquittal or a non-custodial sentence. This is what scholars have typically used as the outcome measure for trial penalty studies. Conversely, the unconditional expected sentence is the measure that includes the likelihood of trial sentences resulting in a non-custodial sentence. Thus, we can think of the unconditional expected sentence as the trial sentence length multiplied by the odds of conviction. This

[19] King *et al.*, 'When process affects punishment', 973.

[20] Ibid., 974–5.

[21] D. S. Abrams, 'Is pleading guilty really a bargain?' (2011) 8 *Journal of Empirical Legal Studies*, 200–21.

[22] Ibid., 202.

[23] D. S. Abrams, 'Putting the trial penalty on trial' (2013) 51 *Duquesne Law Review*, 777–85, pp. 778–9.

outcome is what Abrams contends should be used in measuring any potential trial penalties. He explains:

> A defendant who has been found guilty and wishes to have the best guess of the likely sentence he will receive will be interested in the conditional expected sentence. But the defendant who has been offered a plea deal, but has yet to be found guilty should be interested in the unconditional expected sentence when trying to determine whether or not to accept the sentence proffered by the prosecutor.[24]

Since a defendant who is offered a plea deal has yet to be found guilty, they should only elect for trial if the sentence offered is lower than the unconditional expected sentence, which includes chances for acquittal or a non-custodial sentence. Abram's analyses of the Cook County dataset include cases of sentences with length zero, that is, non-custodial sentences. When comparing plea and trial outcomes in the dataset, Abrams concluded that the average sentence resulting from a plea is 2.4 years, 1.1 years *longer* than sentences resulting from trials.[25]

Offering a thorough critique of Abrams' study,[26] Kim cautions against interpreting Abrams' findings as indicating the absence of any trial penalty because of his terminology. Abrams' understanding of 'trial sentence' – the 'unconditional expected sentence' – is one where the trial sentence length is multiplied by the odds of conviction, equivalent to the conventional understanding of 'trial sentence' used in existing literature subtracted by the defendant's odds of conviction. On the other hand, the 'trial penalty' in Abrams' study is the trial sentence length multiplied by the odds of conviction subtracting the plea sentence. This differs from the conventional sense of 'trial penalty', which is just the trial sentence length subtracted by the plea sentence length. Following Abrams' definitions, Kim points out,

> [The trial penalty] can actually be a negative *even when the conventional trial penalty is positive*. Indeed, the Abrams Trial Penalty will *always* be negative, unless the conventional trial penalty is both positive and *larger*, as a percentage of the final trial sentence, than the expected odds of acquittal.[27]

[24] Ibid., 779.

[25] Ibid., 780. The results were similar for Abrams' regression models, in which control variables included the number of charges per defendant and defendants' characteristics.

[26] A. C. Kim, 'Underestimating the trial penalty: an empirical analysis of the federal trial penalty and critique of the Abrams study' (2015) 84 *Mississippi Law Review*, 1195–256.

[27] Ibid., 1217–18.

Kim further notes that while such terminology may make sense from an economist's viewpoint,[28] it does not reflect a proper understanding of the criminal justice system.

Kim notes that the reason why conventional measurements of the trial penalty exclude acquitted or 'no punishment' sentences is that because under the eyes of the law, acquitted defendants deserve no punishment.[29] This exclusion of acquittals reflects '[the] fact that many defendants are acquitted is a testament to the fact that our system requires proof of guilt beyond a reasonable doubt or admission of guilt through a guilty plea'.[30] Moreover, Kim argues Abrams has a (false) built-in assumption that the expected odds of acquittal for defendants who stand trial are the same as for defendants who pleaded guilty had they gone to trial.[31] In sum, Abrams did not measure a trial penalty, but rather addressed the narrower question of whether the risk-adverse defendant experiences any rational incentives to plead guilty rather than go to trial.[32] Reanalysing Abrams' conclusion to measure the trial penalty is nonetheless simple; it is done by taking Abrams' 'unconditional expected' measure of the trial sentence and dividing it by the odds of acquittal. Applying this to Abrams' Cook County dataset, the average sentence for defendants convicted post-trial is 2.72 years, over four months *longer* than those given to defendants who pleaded guilty. This differential supports the notion that a trial penalty indeed exists.[33]

Some scholars have also paid attention to the issue of time to conviction regarding plea-trial differences in sentencing. For instance,

[28] Ibid., 1219.

[29] Ibid., 1218.

[30] Ibid.

[31] Ibid., 1229. Kim claims that Abrams' assumption is false because many defendants who do not plead guilty may have already assessed that their chances of acquittal are higher during trial. Therefore, it is likely that defendants who go to trial have higher odds of acquittal than defendants who plead guilty.

[32] Ibid., 1228.

[33] Ibid., 1220. In fact, Abrams acknowledges that if he only included non-zero sentences, the average sentence length is indeed longer for defendants who go to trial and are convicted than for defendants who plead guilty. See 'Putting the trial penalty on trial', 781. Kim notes other methodological problems with Abrams' study, such as using sentence length as the outcome measure of his linear regressions as opposed to logged sentence length, which may skew their results. Additionally, Abrams' models included no variable measuring the severity of crimes, the closest indicator being the number of charges per defendant. As crimes that generally go to trial are more serious than crimes for which defendants plead guilty, this lack leads to the problems of specification error and omitted variable bias.

Bradley-Engen and colleagues investigated how the duration between indictment and conviction, as well as the mode of conviction (plea or trial), affects sentencing in the United States; however, their study was limited to only severe crimes of terrorism that were sentenced in federal courts.[34] They discovered a significant relationship between the time to conviction and sentence length, where every 1 per cent increase in the time from indictment to conviction led to approximately a 3 per cent increase in sentence length. Furthermore, consistent with a trial penalty, defendants convicted post-trial received longer sentences than defendants who pleaded guilty.[35] However, the study also found that just among defendants who pleaded guilty, although some who pleaded later did receive lengthier sentences, the differences with those who pleaded early were not substantial.[36]

In sum, existing empirical studies on trial penalties have largely focused only on the United States, whereas other common law jurisdictions remain unexamined. These studies have also predominately focused on plea-trial differences without measuring the timing of guilty pleas. Regarding analyses of common law jurisdictions, although their primary aim was not to study plea-trial differences regarding sentences, Pina-Sánchez and colleagues found that the stage when a defendant enters a guilty plea significantly affects sentence outcomes when they analysed earlier data for the Crown Court in England and Wales.[37] Using the datasets for the CCSS and the Hong Kong District Court, this study can also further investigate the potential impacts that late guilty pleas may have on sentence outcomes.

Late-Plea Penalty: England and Wales

This study seeks to examine the relationship between the stage when guilty pleas are entered and sentencing outcomes in England and Wales and in Hong Kong. Two outcomes are examined: whether the defendant receives an immediate prison sentence and, if the defendant is imprisoned, the sentence length. For the CCSS, only ranges of sentence lengths, from up to three months to indeterminate, are reported. For the

[34] M. S. Bradley-Engen *et al.*, 'The time penalty: Examining the relationship between time to conviction and trial vs. plea disparities in sentencing' (2012) 29 *Justice Quarterly*, 829–57.

[35] Ibid., 846.

[36] Ibid., 847.

[37] J. Pina-Sánchez, I. Brunton-Smith, and G. Li, 'Mind the step: a more insightful and robust analysis of the sentencing process in England and Wales under the new sentencing guidelines' (2020) 20 *Criminology & Criminal Justice*, 268–301.

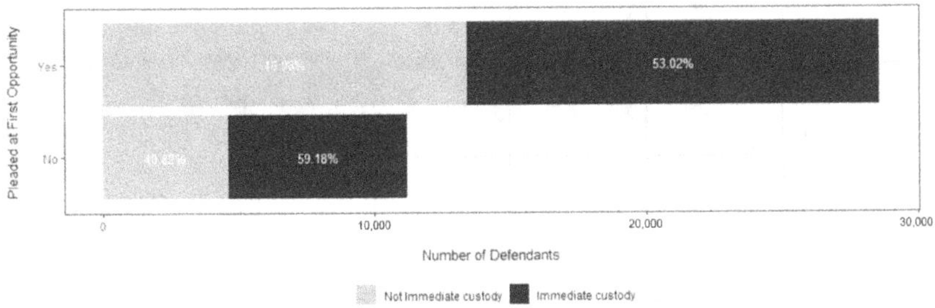

Figure 6.1 Pleading guilty at first opportunity compared to immediate custody: England and Wales

Hong Kong District Court cases, exact sentence lengths (measured in months) were available from Reasons for Sentence reports.

For the CCSS sample, 22,621 convicted defendants (54.53 per cent) received an immediate imprisonment sentence, while 18,860 (45.47 per cent) did not.[38] Here immediate imprisonment refers to all sentences that immediately send defendants to prison. Sentences that do not result in immediate imprisonment include hospital orders, probation orders, and rehabilitation centre orders. Figure 6.1 illustrates the relationship between defendants who pleaded guilty at the first opportunity and defendants who did not in terms of whether they received an immediate imprisonment sentence. As the chart illustrates, only a marginal difference in likelihood exists between whether a defendant pleads guilty at the first opportunity and whether they receive an immediate imprisonment sentence. Among defendants who pleaded guilty at the first opportunity, approximately 53.02 per cent were sentenced to immediate imprisonment, compared to 59.18 per cent of defendants who did not plead guilty at the first opportunity.

[38] Murder was not included in the sample as being the most serious offence, the corresponding sentence is life imprisonment. Moreover, the determination of the level of sentence discounts applicable to guilty pleas for murder differs from that for other offences. As the Sentencing Guidelines Council's *Reduction on Sentence for a Guilty Plea: Definitive Guidelines* (2007) report explains, 'Given this difference, the special characteristic of the offence of murder and the unique statutory provision of starting points, careful consideration will need to be given to the extent of any reduction and to the need to ensure that the minimum term properly reflects the seriousness of the offence. Whilst the general principles continue to apply (both that a guilty plea should be encouraged and that the extent of any reduction should reduce if the indication of plea is later than the first reasonable opportunity), the process of determining the level of reduction will be different' at paragraph 6.5.

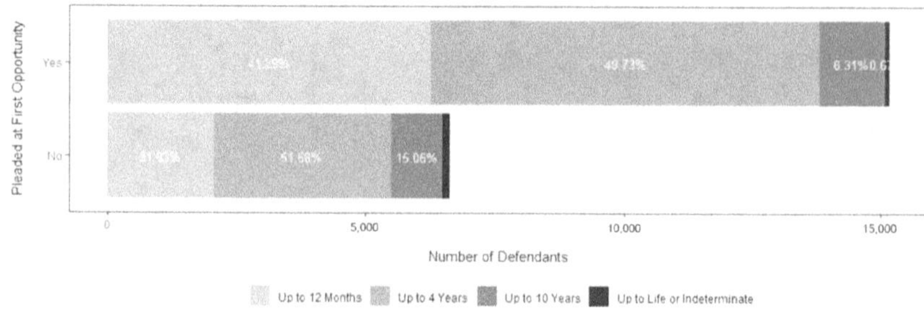

Figure 6.2 Pleading guilty at first opportunity compared to sentence length: England and Wales

Turning to sentence length, Figure 6.2 illustrates the relationship between whether a defendant pleaded guilty at the first opportunity and the duration of imprisonment they are sentenced to, the latter being categorised into four ranges, from up to 12 months to life. Here, some notable differences are observed. Among defendants that pleaded guilty at the first opportunity, a significant proportion (41.29 per cent) received a sentence of up to 12 months' imprisonment and almost half (49.73 per cent) received a sentence of up to four years' imprisonment. Most defendants who pleaded guilty at the first opportunity received prison terms on the shorter end. By contrast, among defendants who did not plead guilty at the first opportunity, slightly more than half (51.68 per cent) received prison terms between 12 months and 4 years; a smaller proportion (31.03 per cent) received prison terms of up to 12 months compared to defendants who pleaded guilty at the first opportunity, while a larger proportion (15.06 per cent) received prison terms of up to 10 years (compared to 8.31 per cent for the former group).

However, descriptive statistics only tell part of the story, and one criticism against a side-by-side comparison of plea timings and sentence outcomes is that it does not consider different offence types. This can be explored by creating multivariate models. For the CCSS dataset, a binary logistic regression model was run to determine variables significantly correlated with a judge's decision to serve an imprisonment sentence, controlling for case and defendant characteristics. Independent variables for the model included the offence type as per CCSS categories,[39] the

[39] The only exception is robbery. Because of case numbers being too few, cases for other types of robbery were consolidated into a single 'robbery' category.

defendant's age and gender, the defendant's criminal history, any record of the defendant's existing illnesses, and whether a confession was made. Sentences that did not result in immediate custody were used as the reference group for the outcome variable.

The model sought to reveal the relationship between whether a defendant pleaded guilty at the first available opportunity and whether an immediate imprisonment sentence was imposed. Consequently, the model included a dummy variable for whether a defendant submitted a guilty plea at the first opportunity. Since this first opportunity may differ based on the type of case, the CCSS records both the stage when the guilty plea was entered and whether the indicated plea was made at the first opportunity. The model hence included an interaction term between the stage when the guilty plea was entered and whether the plea was made at the first opportunity. Lastly, the CCSS data did not provide a variable for defendants who did not plead guilty; consequently, the model presented can only test whether a late-plea penalty exists. Table 6.1 illustrates the regression results for immediate imprisonment for the CCSS sample.

When looked at independently, the effect of pleading guilty at the first opportunity on immediate imprisonment was inconclusive, as was the stage when the guilty plea was entered. As an independent factor, whether a defendant pleaded guilty at the first opportunity did not significantly influence the likelihood of receiving an immediate imprisonment sentence. In addition, contrary to expectations, defendants who entered a guilty plea at the intermediate or late stage were less likely to receive an immediate imprisonment sentence compared with those who entered guilty pleas at an early stage. However, as explained earlier, the stage when a defendant can enter a guilty plea differs depending on the circumstances of the case. In other words, the first opportunity for a defendant to plead guilty is not always at the early plea stage. The results of the interaction terms provide a more nuanced understanding of the effect and relationship between whether a defendant pleads at the first opportunity and the guilty plea stages. Defendants who did not plead guilty at the first opportunity but at an intermediate stage were significantly more likely to be imprisoned than defendants who pleaded guilty at the first opportunity and at an early stage. This likelihood is even greater for defendants who did not enter guilty pleas at the first opportunity but did so at the late stage. The results indicate that for defendants who did not plead guilty at the first opportunity, the later the plea is entered, the more likely they would receive an immediate imprisonment sentence.

Table 6.1 *Regression results for guilty pleas and immediate imprisonment: England and Wales*

Predictors	Odds ratio	95% CI
(Intercept)	0.59**	0.56–0.63
Guilty plea at first opportunity (ref.: yes)		
No	1.03	0.99–1.07
Timing of guilty plea (ref.: early)		
Intermediate	0.67**	0.64–0.70
Late	0.48***	0.46–0.50
Offence type (ref.: drugs)		
Arson	1.45***	1.30–1.62
Assault	0.73***	0.70–0.76
Burglary	1.84***	1.75–1.93
Death	2.12***	1.84–2.44
Driving	0.78***	0.73–0.84
Fraud	0.72*	0.61–0.84
Indecent photographs of children (IPC)	0.44***	0.40–0.50
Other	1.05	1.00–1.11
Robbery	4.81***	4.44–5.21
Sex	1.80***	1.68–1.93
Theft	0.89**	0.85–0.92
Age group (ref.: 35–44)		
18–24	0.86***	0.82–0.89
25–34	0.95	0.91–0.99
45–54	0.89*	0.84–0.93
≥54	0.84*	0.79–0.90
Gender (ref.: male)		
Female	0.51***	0.49–0.53
Previous offences (ref.: no)		
Yes	3.00***	2.92–3.10
Existing illness (ref.: no)		
Yes	0.38***	0.36–0.39
Confession made (ref.: no)		
Yes	0.54***	0.52–0.55
Interaction terms and model statistics		
First opportunity: no * guilty plea: intermediate	1.42**	1.25–1.62
First opportunity: no * guilty plea: late	1.54***	1.39–1.70
Observations	30,914	
Nagelkerke's R^2	0.77	

$^{+}p < 0.1$, $^{*}p < 0.05$, $^{**}p < 0.01$, $^{***}p < 0.001$.

Regarding different offence types, compared with the reference category of drug offences, defendants convicted of arson, burglary, offences causing death, robbery, and sex offences were more likely to receive an immediate imprisonment sentence. Conversely, defendants convicted of assault, driving offences, taking indecent photographs of children, and theft were less likely to be imprisoned compared with their drug offender counterparts.

In terms of demographic characteristics, defendants aged 18–24 and older defendants (two age groups, 45–54 and over 54) were less likely to be imprisoned than the reference group of middle-aged defendants (aged 34–44). In particular, the odds ratio for the youngest age group of 18–24 was found to be the most statistically significant regarding not receiving an immediate imprisonment sentence. This may be because young adult offenders under 21 in England and Wales have traditionally separate custodial institutions just for them. Such an arrangement is based on the idea that younger offenders should not be influenced by older, more experienced offenders in penal institutions. Nevertheless, a separate sentencing regime for young adult offenders does not exist.[40] Although sentencing guidelines do not treat younger adult offenders separately, they require the sentencing judge to consider the age and maturity of the offender where it affects their individual responsibility, as well as the effect of a sentence on them.[41] Moreover, the courts recognise both young and old age as mitigating factors.[42]

[40] Chapter 3 of the Sentencing Act 2020 stipulates a limited number of separate sentencing provisions for young adult offenders, such as detention in a Young Offender Institution, which applies to a convicted offender aged 18–21. Moreover, there have been increasing calls for young adult offenders to be treated differently throughout the criminal justice process and during sentencing. See also House of Commons Justice Committee, *Young Adults in the Criminal Justice System: Eighth Report of Session 2017–19* (London: House of Commons, 2018); Howard League for Penal Reform, *Judging Maturity: Exploring the Role of Maturity in the Sentencing of Young Adults* (London: Howard League for Penal Reform, 2017).

[41] See for example, Sentencing Council, *General Guideline: Overarching Principles* (London: Sentencing Council, 2019). The guidelines state that age and/or lack of maturity is an important factor for reducing the severity of punishment or reflecting personal mitigation. As young adults are still developing neurologically, they may be less able to evaluate the consequences of their actions, susceptible to peer pressure, more impulsive, and more prone to risk-taking. Furthermore, an immature offender may find it more difficult to cope with custody and be more susceptible to self-harm while in custody. Lastly, the guidelines note that many young people stop committing crimes or begin the process of ceasing to commit crimes in their late teens and early twenties.

[42] For young adults and sentencing, see for example *R* v. *Balogun* [2018] EWCA Crim 2933 at paragraph 41, where the court stated, 'In accordance with the principles which we have summarised, the fact that the appellant had attained the age of 18 before he

Looking at other predictors, gender was found to be significant in that female defendants were less likely to be immediately imprisoned, which aligns with previous findings.[43] Defendants with existing mental or physical illnesses were also less likely to be imprisoned. This reflects the fact that physical disabilities, serious medical conditions, mental disorders, and learning disabilities are recognised as mitigating factors that the sentencer should consider.[44] Similarly, defendants who confessed their crimes were less likely to receive an immediate imprisonment sentence, as cooperating with the investigation and early admissions are recognised as mitigating factors in sentencing.[45] Lastly, defendants with past criminal records were unsurprisingly more likely to receive an immediate imprisonment sentence compared with first-time offenders.[46]

To determine the presence of an early/late-plea disparity, a proportional odds ordinal logistic regression[47] with maximum likelihood

committed the offences does not of itself mean that the factors relevant to the sentencing of a young offender had necessarily ceased to have any relevance. He had not been invested overnight with all the understanding and self-control of a fully mature adult.' For old age and sentencing, see for example *Clarke and Cooper* [2017] EWCA Crim 393, where the court stated, 'By the time very old offenders of this sort fall to be sentenced, the question of rehabilitation is unlikely to be significant. Nor is the question of dangerousness. The court's focus will be on finding the appropriate sentence for the offending, where harm done and culpability of the offender are the primary considerations subject to balance for mitigation including guilty plea. It is clear that old age is a material mitigating consideration. Frequently it will be combined with considerations of ill health. The focus of the court will be on the extent to which a custodial sentence will be more onerous, compared to a younger, fitter offender. Old age and extreme age are both relevant aspects of that consideration even in the absence of specific health considerations' at paragraph 21.

43 A. Ashworth, *Sentencing and Criminal Justice*, 6th ed. (Cambridge: Cambridge University Press, 2015), chapter 7. In criminology, the chivalry hypothesis posits that female defendants are treated more leniently compared with their male counterparts based on gender stereotypes that consider women to be weak and in need of protection. See for example, E. F. Mould, 'Chivalry and paternalism: disparities of treatment in the criminal justice system' (1978) 3 *The Western Political Quarterly*, 416–30.

44 Sentencing Council, *General Guideline: Overarching Principles.*

45 Ibid.

46 Section 65(2) of the Sentencing Act 2020 states,

> The court must treat as an aggravating factor each relevant previous conviction that it considers can reasonably be so treated, having regard in particular to – (a) the nature of the offence to which the relevant previous conviction relates and its relevance to the current offence, and
> (b) the time that has elapsed since the relevant previous conviction.

47 Key assumptions for ordinal models, such as the assumptions of proportional odds and no multicollinearity, were met and confirmed using RStudio v4.0.3.

estimations was run to determine the factors that affect the length of a defendant's prison term.[48] Table 6.2 presents the regression results for sentence length using the CCSS sample. As expected, whether the defendant pleaded guilty at the first opportunity was found to be statistically significant with respect to sentence length. Defendants who did not plead guilty at the first opportunity were more likely to receive longer imprisonment terms than those who pleaded guilty early. This further bolsters the notion that a late guilty plea penalty exists in England and Wales. In terms of the stage when the guilty plea is entered, taken as an independent factor, defendants who pleaded guilty later received shorter sentence lengths. However, reviewing the results of its interaction with pleading guilty at the first opportunity underscores that for pleas made after the first opportunity, the later the guilty plea is entered, the longer the sentence length. Therefore, both pleading guilty at first opportunity and guilty plea stage demonstrated significance.

Trial Penalty: Hong Kong

Turning to the Hong Kong District Court sample, the stage when guilty pleas are entered was also compared with sentence outcomes in terms of whether an immediate imprisonment sentence was imposed and the sentence length (in months). As with the CCSS analyses earlier, immediate imprisonment sentences refer to all sentences that immediately send defendants to prison. Suspended imprisonment sentences as well as hospital orders, probation orders, and community service orders were used as the reference group. In the overall sample, 1,448 convicted defendants (94.46 per cent) received an immediate imprisonment sentence, while only 85 defendants (5.54 per cent) did not. In terms of the stages when guilty pleas are entered, the Hong Kong data provided for whether the defendant made a guilty plea early (i.e., at the first opportunity), late, or not and thus was ultimately convicted after trial. Figure 6.3 illustrates the relationship between guilty plea stages and sentencing outcomes in terms of an immediate imprisonment sentence

[48] Ulmer and Bradley, 'Variations in trial penalties', 651 notes that it is typical and recommended for sentence length analyses to include a Heckman two-step correction, which accounts for selection bias generated from incarceration decisions. See also S. Bushway, B. D. Johnson, and L. A. Slocum, 'Is the magic still there? The use of the Heckman two-step correction for selection bias in criminology' (2007) 23 *Journal of Quantitative Criminology*, 151–78.

Table 6.2 *Regression results for guilty pleas and sentence length: England and Wales*

Predictors	Odds ratio	95% CI
(Intercept)	1.14***	1.05–1.23
Guilty plea at first opportunity (ref.: yes)		
No	1.20***	1.11–1.29
Timing of guilty plea (ref.: early)		
Intermediate	0.83***	0.76–0.89
Late	0.65*	0.56–0.72
Offence type (ref.: drugs)		
Arson	0.85	0.67–1.08
Assault	0.31***	0.23–0.41
Burglary	0.73***	0.66–0.81
Death	1.91***	1.46–2.52
Driving	0.16***	0.14–0.20
Fraud	0.20***	0.13–0.30
IPC	0.36***	0.25–0.51
Other	0.15***	0.13–0.16
Robbery	2.25***	2.00–2.53
Sex	1.51***	1.31–1.73
Theft	0.16***	0.14–0.18
Age group (ref.: 35–44)		
18–24	0.78***	0.67–0.89
25–34	0.94+	0.85–1.04
45–54	1.20**	1.00–1.40
≥54	1.26**	1.01–1.56
Gender (ref.: male)		
Female	0.79***	0.40–1.58
Previous offences (ref.: no)		
Yes	2.97***	1.77–4.91
Existing illness (ref.: no)		
Yes	1.01	0.47–2.21
Confession made (ref.: no)		
Yes	0.64***	0.59–0.69
Interaction terms and model statistics		
First opportunity: no * guilty plea: intermediate	1.66**	1.22–2.28
First opportunity: no * guilty plea: late	1.75***	1.36–2.26
Observations	16,983	
Nagelkerke's R^2	0.59	

$^{+}p < 0.1$, $^{*}p < 0.05$, $^{**}p < 0.01$, $^{***}p < 0.001$.

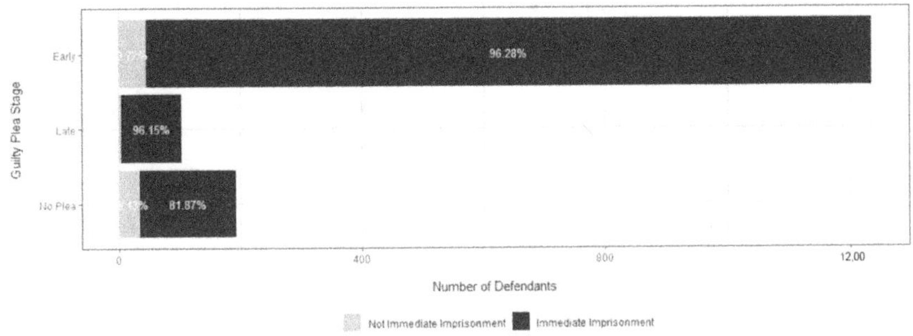

Figure 6.3 Guilty plea stage compared to immediate imprisonment: Hong Kong

for the Hong Kong District Court dataset. As the chart illustrates, no significant differences exist between early, late, and no pleas in terms of whether immediate imprisonment was imposed. For all plea stage groups, an overwhelming majority of defendants, ranging from 82 per cent to 96 per cent, received an immediate imprisonment sentence.

Figure 6.4 illustrates the relationship between guilty plea stage and sentence length, the latter being categorised into three ranges – up to two years, up to four years, and up to seven years, the last being the maximum length of imprisonment the District Court can impose. Again, some notable differences are observed here. The chart shows that a significant proportion of defendants (16.27 per cent) who did not plead guilty received prison terms in the highest range of four to seven years. By contrast, smaller proportions of defendants who pleaded guilty early (5.93 per cent) or late (11 per cent) received prison terms in the highest range. The mean sentence lengths following early guilty pleas, late guilty pleas, and convictions post-trial without a guilty plea were 28.65, 29.12, and 31.92 months, respectively; the average sentence length increases when moving from early pleas to late pleas to no plea. Moreover, defendants who pleaded not guilty (and were convicted post-trial) received sentences that were 11 per cent longer on average than defendants who pleaded guilty at the first opportunity.

Multivariate models were run to determine the effects that the timing of guilty pleas may have on sentence outcomes for the Hong Kong dataset, controlling for the case and defendant characteristics. The first set of models tested whether the guilty plea stage, including no plea (conviction post-trial), affects whether the defendant receives an immediate imprisonment sentence. Two mixed effects logistic regression

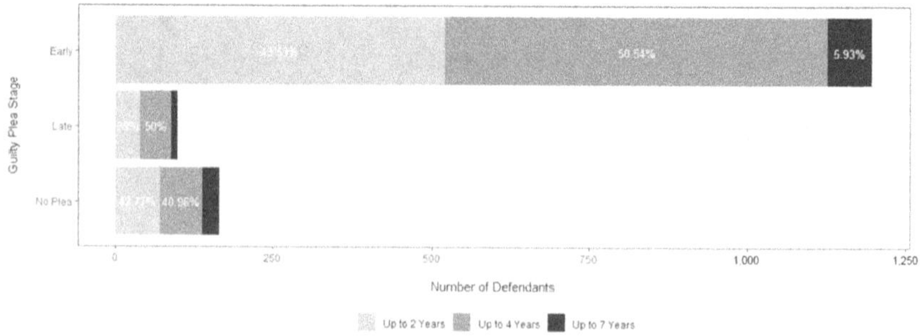

Figure 6.4 Guilty plea stage compared to sentence length: Hong Kong

models were run to determine variables significantly correlated with a judge's decision to serve an immediate imprisonment sentence. A significant F-statistic of 1.70 confirmed that there is some variation among judges' sentencing of defendants. Unlike the CCSS models, in addition to the offence type and defendant's background, the Hong Kong District Court models could code for and incorporate additional variables, including legal representation and prosecution type. Table 6.3 presents the results of the first set of two models, which differ in the guilty plea categories included. The first model included only defendants who pleaded guilty and omitted defendants who did not plea and were convicted after trial, while the second model included all defendants in the sample.

The most interesting result is that the guilty plea stage did not influence whether the defendant was sentenced to immediate imprisonment. This remains the same when the 'no pleas' category was incorporated into the model. This result differs from the results for the CCSS sample, where English Crown Court judges were more likely to impose immediate imprisonment for defendants who did not plead at the first opportunity and for those who pleaded late. Conversely, prosecution type was a significant variable. In both models, cases handled by public prosecutors were found to correlate with a lower likelihood of immediate imprisonment compared with prosecutors on fiat.

Another significant variable was age, given that the youngest defendants (aged 18–24) were less likely to receive an immediate imprisonment sentence compared with middle-aged defendants (aged 35–44). The results for age are consistent with established case law, since the 'age of an offender, whether youth or advanced age, is always a mitigating

Table 6.3 *Regressions on guilty plea stage and immediate imprisonment sentence: Hong Kong*

	Model 1 - Defendants who pleaded guilty		**Model 2 - All defendants**	
Fixed effects	**Odds ratio**	**95% CI**	**Odds ratio**	**95% CI**
(Intercept)	2.86	1.26–6.47	4.05	1.79–9.21
Guilty plea stage (ref.: early)				
Late	0.71	0.30–1.72	1.15	0.47–2.83
No plea	–	–	0.74	0.31–1.79
Offence type (ref.: drugs)				
Assault	0.28*	0.15–0.53	0.35	0.16–0.73
Burglary/robbery	0.39	0.21–0.74	0.34	0.17–0.70
Driving	0.25	0.06–1.01	0.24	0.08–0.73
Fraud	0.15*	0.07–0.34	0.10**	0.05–0.23
Other	–	–	0.79	0.24–2.59
Theft	0.38	0.18–0.80	0.72	0.27–1.91
No. of charges per defendant	1.01	0.94–1.08	1.00	0.93–1.07
Age group (ref.: 35–44)				
18–24	0.15***	0.09–0.26	0.14**	0.08–0.26
25–34	1.70	0.81–3.56	2.46	1.00–6.05
45–54	4.14	1.34–12.81	2.46	0.97–6.23
55+	–	–	1.45	0.58–3.60
Gender (ref.: male)				
Female	1.06	0.50–2.25	0.66	0.33–1.32
Race/ethnicity (ref.: local Hong Kong)				
Foreigner	4.81	1.52–15.18	7.85$^+$	2.64–23.33
Mainland Chinese	1.43	0.46–4.44	3.71	1.23–11.13
Previous offences (ref.: no)				
Yes	1.99	1.27–3.13	1.79	1.08–2.94
Existing illness (ref.: no)				
Mental illness	0.32$^+$	0.17–0.59	0.34	0.18–0.65
Physical illness	–	–	1.73	0.52–5.81
Confession made (ref.: no)				
Yes	0.20	0.07–0.61	0.40	0.18–0.88
Legal representative (ref.: private lawyer)				
Legal aid	2.18	1.27–3.74	2.56$^+$	1.46–4.48
Prosecution (ref.: on fiat)				
Public prosecutor	0.46$^+$	0.30–0.70	0.22**	0.13–0.37

Table 6.3 (*cont.*)

	Model 1 - Defendants who pleaded guilty		Model 2 - All defendants	
Fixed effects	**Odds ratio**	**95% CI**	**Odds ratio**	**95% CI**
Random effects and model statistics				
SD of judges	0.40		0.16	
ICC	0.05		0.08	
Groups	38		38	
Observations	983		1,066	
Nagelkerke's R^2	0.97		0.45	

$^+p < 0.1$, $^*p < 0.05$, $^{**}p < 0.01$, $^{***}p < 0.001$.

factor'.[49] While determining whether to impose a custodial sentence involves competing aggravating and mitigating factors, the Hong Kong courts have noted that great care must be exercised when sentencing younger offenders to prison. Indeed, local courts have determined their principle of practice to be that 'no young person should be sentenced to imprisonment if he or she can be dealt with in another way'.[50] This principle promotes the prospect of rehabilitation for younger offenders,[51] despite the fact that all defendants who appear in the District Court are

[49] *Secretary for Justice* v. *Wong Chi-fung and Others* [2018] HKCFA 4; [2018] 2 HKC 50 at 84. Section 109A(1) of the Criminal Procedure Ordinance (Cap. 221) states, 'No court shall sentence a person of or over 16 and under 21 years of age to imprisonment unless the court is of the opinion that no other method of dealing with such person is appropriate; and for the purpose of determining whether any other method of dealing with any such person is appropriate the court shall obtain and consider information about the circumstances, and shall take into account any information before the court which is relevant to the character of such person and his physical and mental condition.'

[50] *HKSAR* v. *Wu Yee-ki* [2006] HKCU 1100 CACC 513/2005 (30 June 2006, unreported). See also *Secretary for Justice* v. *Chau Tsz-tim and Ho Wan-chiu* [2015] 2 HKC 88 at 93.

[51] Some scholars have asserted that Hong Kong has maintained the 'rehabilitative ideal' even though rehabilitation has lost much of its appeal in Western countries in the past few decades. See for example M. Adorjan and W. H. Chui, 'Making sense of going straight: personal accounts of male ex-prisoners in Hong Kong' (2012) 52 *British Journal of Criminology*, 577–90; W. H. Chui, 'Theoretical underpinnings of community-based sentences and custody for young offenders in Hong Kong' (2001) 31 *Hong Kong Law Journal*, 266–82.

considered adults,[52] and that cases heard in the District Court are considered more serious than those heard in the Magistrates' Courts.[53] Nevertheless, the regression results reflect the fact that younger offenders often benefit from not being likely to receive immediate imprisonment sentences.

The second set of mixed effects models tested sentence length as their outcome to analyse whether any plea-trial differences and early/late plea differences existed with respect to imprisonment length. As with the first set, this set of models differed in the guilty plea categories they included. Model 3 only included defendants who pleaded guilty at any stage, while Model 4 included defendants who did not plead. Table 6.4 presents the results for the logged sentence length models.

For Model 3, which only included early and late guilty pleas, no significant difference was found between both stages in terms of sentence length. This was somewhat contrary to expectations, given how the sliding scale of sentence discounts in Hong Kong explicitly stipulates a lesser sentence reduction for late pleas compared with early pleas. However, under Model 4, which included the 'no pleas' category, defendants who did not plead guilty and were convicted after trial were found to have approximately 20 per cent higher sentence lengths compared to those defendants who pleaded guilty early. Taken together, these results show that a trial penalty exists in Hong Kong, yet unlike in England and Wales, a late-plea penalty is not apparent.

Compared with the reference category of drug offences, all other offence types were more likely associated with a shorter sentence length,[54] meaning that defendants convicted of non-drug offences, whether through their own plea or post-trial, were more likely to receive a shorter prison term. One reason may be that drug offences are serious and prevalent in Hong Kong, therefore warranting harsher sentencing.[55]

[52] Section 2 of the Juvenile Offenders Ordinance (Cap. 226) defines a 'young person' as 'a person who is, in the opinion of the court having cognisance of any case in relation to such person, 14 years of age or upwards and under the age of 16 years'. Section 3 of the Interpretation and General Clauses Ordinance (Cap. 1) defines an 'adult' under Hong Kong law as 'a person who has attained the age of 18 years'.

[53] Some argue that the seriousness of the offence ought to lead to an immediate custodial sentence despite the young age of the convicted offender. The sentencing judge would have to determine a sentence based on competing objectives of rehabilitation, deterrence, and serving the public interest. See *HKSAR* v. *Law Ka-kit* [2003] 2 HKC 178.

[54] Drug offences was used as the reference category, as it was the most frequent in the sample.

[55] The prevalence of the offence is a factor that may warrant a harsher sentence. Section 27 of the Organized and Serious Crimes Ordinance (Cap. 455) allows the prosecution to

Table 6.4 *Guilty plea stage and sentence length: Hong Kong*

	Model 3 – Defendants who pleaded guilty		**Model 4 – All defendants**	
Predictors	**B**	**SE**	**B**	**SE**
(Intercept)	3.29***	0.07	3.30***	0.07
Guilty plea stage (ref.: early)				
Late	0.03	0.06	0.04	0.06
No plea	–	–	0.19**	0.06
Offence type (ref.: drugs)				
Assault	−0.47***	0.06	−0.46***	0.06
Burglary/robbery	−0.30***	0.09	−0.30***	0.04
Driving	−0.98***	0.04	−1.05***	0.08
Fraud	−0.29***	0.06	−0.31***	0.06
Other	−0.51***	0.05	−0.46***	0.05
Theft	−0.52***	0.05	−0.53***	0.05
No. of charges per defendant	0.04***	0.01	0.04***	0.01
Age group (years) (ref.: 35–44)				
18–24	0.09	0.04	0.02*	0.05
25–34	−0.02	0.04	−0.02	0.05
45–54	−0.03	0.04	−0.05	0.04
≥55	0.01	0.05	−0.01	0.04
Gender (ref.: male)				
Female	−0.03	0.04	−0.01	0.05
Race/ethnicity (ref.: local Hong Kong)				
Foreigner	−0.02	0.05	−0.17*	0.05
Mainland Chinese	0.06	0.06	−0.06	0.06
Previous offences (ref.: no)				
Yes	0.07*	0.03	0.08*	0.03
Existing illness (ref.: no)				
Mental illness	−0.08	0.07	−0.09	0.07
Physical illness	−0.07	0.05	−0.06	0.05
Confession made (ref.: no)				
Yes	0.05	0.04	0.05	0.03
Legal representative (ref.: private lawyer)				
Legal aid	0.07	0.05	0.06	0.04
Prosecution (ref.: on fiat)				
Public prosecutor	0.06*	0.03	0.05⁺	0.04
SD of judges	0.08		0.09	
ICC	0.17		0.20	
Groups	38		38	

Table 6.4 (*cont.*)

	Model 3 - Defendants who pleaded guilty		Model 4 - All defendants	
Predictors	**B**	**SE**	**B**	**SE**
Observations	963		1,038	
Nagelkerke's R^2	0.92		0.87	

$^{+}p < 0.1$, $^{*}p < 0.05$, $^{**}p < 0.01$, $^{***}p < 0.001$.

Moreover, the number of charges a defendant has is positively correlated with sentence length; this is expected, since more charges would likely lead to a longer sentence, even when considering the totality principle. Likewise, having a previous criminal record correlated with receiving a longer prison term; this is again coherent with expectations, since a prior criminal record often serves as an aggravating factor in sentencing.[56]

In terms of age, for Model 4, convicted defendants in the youngest age group (18–24) were marginally more likely to receive longer imprisonment sentences compared to the reference group (35–44). Taking this result together with previous findings illustrates a phenomenon of young adult defendants who are sentenced to imprisonment receiving longer prison terms by approximately 2 per cent, even as young adult

'furnish information to the court' regarding 'the prevalence of that specified offence', and the court may 'pass a sentence on the person for that offence that is more severe than the sentence it would, in the absence of such matter, have passed'. Trafficking in dangerous drugs, trafficking in purported dangerous drugs, and manufacturing a dangerous drug are listed as specified offences that fall under this Ordinance. For drug offences specifically, in *R* v. *Chiu Hung-wong* [1994] 1 HKCLR 184; [1993] HKCU 214, the court stated, 'However it is now clear that the legislative temper is for very much stiffer penalties and the incarceration of those in possession of dangerous drugs for a much longer period than that earlier sentencing norm and the emphasis has moved away from the prior aim of rehabilitation' at 188.

56 Not only would a defendant with a previous criminal record be unable to claim that they acted out of character, but their previous criminal history also serves to aggravate the sentence; see *R* v. *Lui Shu-tong* [1961] HKLR 129; [1961] HKCU 5. In *HKSAR* v. *Ngo Van Huy* [2005] 2 HKLRD 1; [2004] HKCU 1136, the court stated, 'Sentencing policy in Hong Kong (and, it should be noted, elsewhere in the world including the United Kingdom and Australia) recognises that where there are repeat offences of the same kind, a person's previous record is likely to be an aggravating feature where this demonstrates in particular either the need to impose a deterrent sentence on the particular accused (the previous ones not having apparently had this effect) or the need to protect society from criminals like him' at paragraph 8.

defendants are less likely to be imprisoned overall. A possible reason for this may be that in Hong Kong, imprisonment and rehabilitation are not considered mutually exclusive but rather complementary to one another. Jones and Vagg note, '[The Correctional Services Department][57] never resiled from the rehabilitative ideal of imprisonment even when it has become discredited in the "West." Indeed, CSD pursued it with even more vigour.'[58] Furthermore, contrary to previous models, cases with public prosecutors were associated with a lower likelihood of imprisonment; yet among cases where the court had imposed immediate imprisonment, those handled by public prosecutors were positively correlated with longer prison terms by about 6 per cent compared with cases handled by prosecutors on fiat. This is an interesting finding that merits further exploration.[59]

Adverse Impacts

By adjusting a sentence based on whether and when the defendant pleads guilty, one can argue that the sentence no longer justly reflects the criminality of the offence(s) for which the defendant is convicted. In accordance with the classical sentencing principle of retribution,

[57] The Correctional Services Department (CSD) is responsible for operating correctional institutions in Hong Kong, including minimum-, medium-, and maximum-security prisons, as well as detention centres. In 1998, a Rehabilitation Division was created within the CSD that focuses on rehabilitation services for offenders. The division includes separate units responsible for pre-sentence assessments, welfare and counselling, education, industrial and vocational training, and psychological services.

[58] C. Jones and J. Vaggs, *Criminal Justice in Hong Kong* (Oxford: Routledge, 2007), p. 597.

[59] Paragraph 21.1 of The Prosecution Code (Hong Kong: Department of Justice, 2013) provides that:

> A prosecutor has an active role to play in the sentencing process by assisting the court to impose the appropriate penalty and to avoid appealable error; but a prosecutor should not attempt by advocacy to influence the court in relation to the quantum of sentence. A prosecutor should:
> adequately (fully and accurately) present the relevant facts;
> assist the court to avoid proceeding on any error of fact or law;
> respond helpfully to any request by the court for relevant information;
> fairly evaluate and, if necessary, test the opposing case and correct any apparent legal or factual error made by the defense in submissions;
> provide information from previous relevant court decisions and official statistics;
> where appropriate, make submissions on the type of sentence, but not quantum beyond providing a range supported by previous cases.

sentences should reflect the severity of the crime and the culpability of the offender, as well as be proportionate to the wrongdoing.[60] However, the sliding scale of sentence discounts introduces the additional element of the timing of a guilty plea (assuming one is made). Bagaric and Brebner observe, 'The guilty plea discount remains one of the most controversial aspects of sentencing. There is no *obvious* principled criminological basis for punishing offenders less severely than those who elect to proceed to trial.'[61] For instance, if two defendants of similar backgrounds and circumstances are charged with exactly identical offences, yet one defendant pleads guilty, whereas the other does not and is ultimately convicted after trial, the latter would receive a more severe sentence compared with the former who pleaded guilty. This plea-trial disparity in sentencing, along with the early/late-plea disparity as illustrated earlier for the case of England and Wales, therefore renders sentences as not accurately reflecting the criminality of the offence and the moral failings of the offender. Instead, sentences become largely dependent on whether and when the defendant pleads guilty.

Such sentencing disparities also conflict with established judicial principles that extra punishment should not be imposed on defendants who plead not guilty. For example, in the Hong Kong case of *Lui Koon-man and others*,[62] the defendants' sentences were overturned because the appeal judge deemed that the more severe sentences the magistrate had imposed were responses to the defendants' not guilty pleas. In this case, around 600 men, many of them wearing white gloves, had arrived at a construction site one evening to shout foul language and wave wooden planks. Police had confronted them, and after they refused to heed dispersal warnings, some were arrested for unlawful assembly. It was later revealed that the group went to the construction site as a show of force to rival triad groups in order to gain control over the site, with the white gloves being a form of identification. Of the over 100 defendants who were charged, only three did not plead guilty, two being appeal applicants of the case. Whereas the vast majority of defendants, who had pleaded guilty, received a fine and a one-year bind over order, the three

60 A. von Hirsh, 'Proportionality in the philosophy of punishment' (1992) 16 *Crime and Justice*, 55–98.

61 M. Bagaric and J. Brebner, 'The solution to the dilemma presented by the guilty plea discount: the qualified guilty plea – "I'm pleading guilty only because of the discount"' (2002) 30 *International Journal of the Sociology of Law*, 51–74, p. 51.

62 *R* v. *Lui Koon-man and Others* [1991] HKEC 394.

defendants went to trial, were convicted, and were sentenced to three months' imprisonment and heftier fines. Regarding this, the appeal judge stated,

> In my judgment, what appears to have happened here is that these three have been punished for their plea of not guilty. It must be remembered that it is the right of every person before a court to plead not guilty; he disentitles himself to the credit which a plea of guilty brings, but he must not be punished, nor appear to be so, for pleading not guilty. The disparity between the sentences passed on those who pleaded guilty and not guilty is most severe, and in my judgment, when it is recognised that the three who were sentenced played no part at all in the disorder other than for being present, the sentence which was passed gives the appearance of a punishment.[63]

In the case of *Cameron*,[64] the High Court of Australia attempted to reconcile this apparent paradox in judicial principles by stating the following:

> Although a plea of guilty may be taken into account in mitigation, a convicted person may not be penalised for having insisted on his or her right to trial. The distinction between allowing a reduction for a plea of guilty and not penalising a convicted person for not pleading guilty is not without its subtleties, but it is, nonetheless, a real distinction, albeit one the rationale for which may need some refinement in expression if the distinction is to be seen as non-discriminatory.[65]

The distinction the court mentions is between conceptualisations of whether the plea-trial disparity is a trial penalty or a sentence discount, as discussed previously, with the court obviously preferring the latter interpretation. Yet such an argument has been criticised as 'no more than an appeal to confusion by invoking the perennial glass is half empty or half full subterfuge'.[66] Bagaric and Brebner point out that 'to get to the crux of the matter at hand, all that needs to be asked is: Do offenders who plead not guilty (and) who commit *identical* offences to offenders who plead guilty receive *harsher* sentences?'[67] The answer to this straightforward question is yes.

[63] Ibid., paragraph 7.

[64] *Cameron* v. *R* (2002) 187 ALR 65.

[65] Ibid., paragraph 12.

[66] Bagaric and Brebner, 'The solution to the dilemma', 58.

[67] Ibid.

Another adverse impact of sentencing disparities is that both the trial and late-plea penalties give prosecutors enormous leverage in securing pleas, especially in plea bargaining. Defendants and prosecutors do not occupy equal positions of power. Faced with sentence differentials, defendants are often pressured into accepting a plea deal – and sooner rather than later – or otherwise face a heavier sentence. Prosecutors are already some of the most powerful actors in the criminal justice system; the prospect of using the plea-trial and early/late-plea disparities to their advantage gives them additional ammunition in securing early guilty pleas. Besides prosecutors in plea bargaining, defence lawyers who want to 'encourage' their clients to plead guilty, and to do so as soon as possible, can simply point to the sliding scale of sentence discounts.[68] These differences between sentences resulting from pleas and trials have prompted one commentator to remark: 'the legal profession must start to ask whether it amounts to institutionalised coercion.'[69]

Conclusion

Sentence outcomes are undoubtedly an important facet of the sliding scale of sentence discounts. While official discourse and court judgments may want to frame any sentence disparities as sentence discounts for guilty pleas, in effect, such disparities serve as penalties for defendants who do not plead guilty early enough. The statistical findings revealed that a late-plea penalty exists in England and Wales, where defendants who did not plead guilty at the first opportunity were more likely to be sent immediately to prison and receive longer prison terms compared with their counterparts who pleaded guilty at the first opportunity. In Hong Kong, a late-plea penalty is not apparent; instead, a trial penalty is apparent among cases that resulted in imprisonment. Defendants who elected to go to trial but ultimately lost at trial were more likely to face longer prison terms compared with defendants who pleaded guilty at the first opportunity. Why a late-plea penalty was not apparent among the Hong Kong cases will be explored in Chapter 7. Nevertheless, this chapter has presented evidence that defendants who do not plead guilty at the first opportunity likely face more severe sentences.

[68] See Chapter 4.

[69] C. McCoy, 'Plea bargaining as coercion' (2005) 50 *Criminal Law Quarterly*, 67–107, p. 91.

7

Consistency in Applying Sentence Discounts

Even though England and Wales and Hong Kong have adopted quantified sliding scales for sentence discounts, this does not mean that no judicial discretion is applicable in imposing sentences. Indeed, the sentencing guidelines for the sliding scale of sentence discounts in both jurisdictions have stipulated the ability to depart from recommended sentence reductions.[1] This chapter focuses on the consistency of applying the sentencing guidelines for sentence reductions in guilty pleas in England and Wales and in Hong Kong. Cross-tabulation of the stage when guilty pleas are entered and the corresponding sentence discounts are shown for both jurisdictions. In general, both English and Hong Kong courts strongly adhere to the recommended sentencing guidelines. Yet certain interesting results emerge when looking at instances of departures from such guidelines. Multivariate analyses using the sentence discount as the outcome reveal gender and confession to be significant factors for departing from guidelines, with female defendants and defendants who have confessed given a higher sentence discount. Analysing the sentence discount given for guilty pleas reveals sentencing leniency for certain factors that sentencing guidelines do not account for. Furthermore, when examining consistency in sentencing, sentencing outcomes should not be the sole focus; consequently, this chapter also discusses the courts' sentencing process. This discussion reveals that inconsistencies in *when* judges apply aggravating and mitigating factors, as well as the sentence discount for guilty pleas, may lead to inconsistencies in sentence outcomes.

[1] Although Chapter 6 argued that plea-trial and early or late-plea disparities should be respectively considered as trial and late-plea penalties instead of sentence discounts, the terms 'sentence discount' and 'sentence reductions' are still used here to reflect the terminology that the Sentencing Council and the English courts have adopted.

Applying Sentencing Guidelines

The role of the Sentencing Council in England and Wales is to issue sentencing guidelines to promote greater transparency and consistency in sentencing. At the same time, the Council affirms maintaining judicial independence.[2] Under Chapter 2 of the Sentencing Code, 'Every court – must, in sentencing an offender, follow any sentencing guidelines which are relevant to the offender's case . . . unless the court is satisfied that it would be contrary to the interests of justice to do so.'[3] This extract therefore demonstrates the primary duty of the courts to apply relevant sentence guidelines, according to them the ability to depart from the guidelines only if adherence runs contrary to the interests of justice; moreover, the courts would need to provide reasons for such departures.

English sentencing guidelines were not always so authoritative. For instance, the previous Criminal Justice Act 2003 only stated that '[e]very court must – in sentencing an offender, have regard to any guidelines which are relevant to the offender's case'.[4] The more stringent wording of 'must follow' replaced the laxer wording of 'have regard to' in the Coroners and Justice Act 2009,[5] which the Sentencing Act 2020 reiterates. This represented a fundamental change in the statutory duty imposed on the courts, from only considering the recommended sentencing guidelines[6] to strictly complying, as indicated by the wording 'must follow'.[7] Since being established in 2010, the Sentencing Council has issued various sentencing guidelines for the most common criminal offences. Where no specific guidelines for certain offences exist, the courts can refer to the general guidelines and overarching principles issued by the Council,[8] which include guidelines pertaining to sentence reductions for guilty pleas that apply to all offences.[9]

[2] Sentencing Council, 'About the Sentencing Council', available at www.sentencingcouncil .org.uk/sentencing-and-the-council/about-the-sentencing-council/.

[3] Section 59(1) of the Sentencing Act 2020.

[4] Section 172(1) of the Criminal Justice Act 2003.

[5] Section 125(1) of the Coroners and Justice Act 2009.

[6] Section 172 of the Criminal Justice Act 2003.

[7] See J. V. Roberts, 'Sentencing guidelines and judicial discretion: evolution of the duty of courts to comply in England and Wales' (2011) 51 *British Journal of Criminology*, 997–1013.

[8] Sentencing Council, *General Guideline: Overarching Principles* (London: Sentencing Council, 2019).

[9] Section 60(3) of the Sentencing Act 2020.

In *Lee Oosthuizen*, a Court of Appeal case about whether individual judges could disregard the definitive guidelines on sentence reductions for guilty pleas, Rose LJ held that 'Individual judges and indeed constitutions of this Court may, from time to time, disagree with some aspect of a guideline issued by the Sentencing Guidelines Council. But it is not open to them to disregard what the Council says.'[10] However, Ashworth points out that departing from sentencing guidelines may not be that difficult. The statutory duty in which the courts 'must follow' the sentencing guidelines does not pertain to the 'category range' of sentences applicable to a particular case, but the 'offence range' that has been set out for all forms of the offence in question. The 'offence range' includes the lowest sentence in the least serious category of the offence and the highest sentence in the most serious category,[11] whereas the 'category range' refers to smaller intervals within the offence range that correspond to various severity levels. Indeed, section 60(2) of the Sentencing Act 2020 states that '[t]he principal guidelines duty includes a duty to impose on the offender, in accordance with the offence-specific guidelines, a sentence which is within the *offence range*'.[12] (Emphasis added.)

Aside from the primary goal of promoting consistency in sentencing, sentencing guidelines also serve another utilitarian objective of 'achiev [ing] greater accuracy in projections of the number of prisoners'.[13] Changing political and public attitudes towards crime have led to a more punitive climate.[14] Consequently, because of legislative changes imposing increased sentences, the number of custodial sentences imposed by the courts has escalated.[15] In the 2007 'Carter review' about the mounting

[10] *R* v. *Lee Oosthuizen* [2005] EWCA Crim 1978; [2006] 1 Cr App R (S) 73 at paragraph 15.

[11] A. Ashworth, *Sentencing and Criminal Justice*, 6th ed. (Cambridge: Cambridge University Press, 2015), p. 31.

[12] Section 60(4) of the Sentencing Act 2020 states:

> If the offence-specific guidelines describe different seriousness categories—
> (a) the principal guidelines duty also includes a duty to decide which of the categories most resembles the offender's case in order to identify the sentencing starting point in the offence range, but
> (b) nothing in this section imposes on the court a separate duty to impose a sentence which is within the category range.

[13] A. Ashworth and J. V. Roberts, 'The origins and nature of the sentencing guidelines in England and Wales', in A. Ashworth and J. V. Roberts (eds.), *Sentencing Guidelines: Exploring the English Model* (Oxford: Oxford University Press, 2013), pp. 1–11, p. 1.

[14] L. Carter, *Securing the Future: Proposals for the Efficient and Sustainable Use of Custody in England and Wales* (London: Ministry of Justice, 2007), p. 6.

[15] Ibid., pp. 6–7.

prison population in England and Wales, Lord Carter proposed implementing a 'structured sentencing framework', where

> [s]ubsequent versions would draw on current sentencing practice but would be modified so far as necessary as to take account of:
>
> the principles of sentencing as set down in legislation . . .; and
>
> the total impact on prison places and other penal services to ensure that they would come within a published financial envelope as set out by government to Parliament.[16]

The idea was that adopting this sentencing framework, supervised by a sentencing commission, would allow for greater control over the factors affecting sentencing and thus lead to greater accuracy in predicting the size of the prison population.[17]

Unlike the United States (US), where a grid system for sentencing guidelines has been operated since the 1980s at the federal level and in certain states – notably Minnesota – English officials decided not to use the same approach;[18] instead, sentencing guidelines for England and Wales have been described as 'step-by-step decision trees'[19] (discussed under 'Sentencing Process'). Conversely, US sentencing guidelines are based on two-dimensional numerical sentencing grids. For instance, US federal sentencing guidelines provide a 'sentencing table', where the offence level (from 1 to 43) forms the vertical axis, while the criminal history category (from I to VI) as determined by criminal history points (from 0 to 13 or more) forms the horizontal axis. Sentence ranges measured in months of imprisonment correspond to the judge's determination of the offense level and criminal history.[20] However, in the seminal decision made in *Booker*,[21] the Supreme Court struck down the provisions that had made the sentencing guidelines mandatory, rendering them only advisory. Nevertheless, England and Wales and the United States represent the only two jurisdictions to have developed and implemented formal sentencing guidelines in the common law

16 Ibid., p. 33.

17 Ibid., p. 34.

18 J. V. Roberts, 'The evolution of sentencing guidelines in Minnesota and England and Wales' (2019) 48 *Crime and Justice*, 187–253.

19 Ibid., 187.

20 United States Sentencing Commission, *Guidelines Manual* (Washington, DC: United States Sentencing Commission, 2018), chapter 5. The guidelines also permit the imposition of non-custodial sentences such as probation.

21 *United States* v. *Booker*, 543 US 20 (2005). See also *Gall* v. *United States*, 552 US 38 (2007) and *Irizarry* v. *United States*, 553 US 708 (2008).

world, with the former's guidelines presumably being binding for the courts.[22]

As in other common law jurisdictions, sentencing guidelines for Hong Kong are set by the appellate courts.[23] Yet unlike in England and Wales, where sentencing guidelines are available for most common offences, in Hong Kong's sentencing system, guidelines are the exception rather than the norm.[24] This is because a firm belief persists that guidelines would be inappropriate for many types of offences where the circumstances of individual cases would vary so widely as to render any guidelines impractical,[25] notable exceptions being tariff cases for drug-trafficking offences[26] and the sliding scale of sentence discounts for guilty pleas.

[22] Roberts, 'The evolution of sentencing guidelines'.

[23] In *Chan Chi-ming* v. *R* [1979] HKLR 491; [1979] HKCU 60, the Hong Kong Court of Appeal concluded that it was their duty to give guidance to the lower courts regarding sentencing, as well as to ensure consistency to minimise extreme variations between the decisions of sentencing judges and magistrates.

[24] G. Cross and P. S. W. Cheung, *Sentencing in Hong Kong*, 8th ed. (Hong Kong: LexisNexis, 2018), p. 341.

[25] Ibid.

[26] In *Seabrook* v. *HKSAR* [1999] 1 HKLRD 853 at 860–1; [1999] 1 HKC 567, the Hong Kong Court of Final Appeal remarked:

> Sentencing guidelines come about in a number of ways . . . In the course of hearing appeals against sentence and reviews of sentence, the Court of Appeal will, over a period, detect a general level of sentence in respect of a particular offence. There will however be a number of strays-some on the high side and some on the low side. In such circumstances, the Court of Appeal will very properly consider it appropriate to assist sentencing judges by laying down a set of guidelines for that offence . . . If the offence is trafficking in a dangerous drug, then the guidelines will naturally lend themselves to something in the nature of a table with each band defined by quantity. And different types of drugs will attract different sets of guidelines appropriate to the harm which they do. If a new type of drug appears on the scene, sentencing judges will tend to sentence in respect of them by reference to existing guidelines for some other type of drug, making such adjustments as seem appropriate. Over a period, more and more becomes known about the new drug and eventually, it receives a set of guidelines of its own.

Sentencing guidelines for drug trafficking are based on the type and quantity of the drug (in grammes), which correspond to a sentence range (length of imprisonment). Guidelines for the trafficking of heroin/cocaine were first established in *R* v. *Lam Tak-ming and Others* [1990] 2 HKLR 370; [1990] HKCU 399, and modified in *HKSAR* v. *Abdallah Anwar Abbas* [2009] 2 HKLRD 437; [2009] 2 HKC 197. Guidelines for the trafficking of ketamine were established in *Secretary for Justice* v. *Hii Siew-cheng* [2009] 1 HKLRD 1; [2008] 3 HKC 323.

Nevertheless, scholars have emphasised that sentencing guidelines are not meant to be 'straitjackets' or 'prescriptive'.[27] Likewise, the Hong Kong Court of Appeal has stated, 'Guidelines are meant only to guide. They are not intended to place lower courts in straight jacket. There may well be cases where circumstances do warrant a lesser sentence and humanitarian considerations must always be respected. On occasions they may even so strong that suspension of the sentence would be appropriate.'[28] Sentencing judges are free to depart from existing guidelines provided that they give justification. Yet the Court of Appeal has also cautioned that while it is up to individual judges to determine sentences, a measure of consistency in sentencing should still exist: 'We must of course respect the discretion of each sentencing judge. But at the same time, justice and even-handedness requires that we bring a measure of uniformity to sentencing.'[29] Although certain organisations, such as the Democratic Alliance for the Betterment and Progress of Hong Kong (DAB),[30] have pushed for establishing a sentencing council like that for England and Wales, Chief Justice Andrew Cheung has rebuffed these suggestions.[31] Consequently, there appears to be more room in Hong Kong for exercising judicial discretion to depart from sentencing guidelines compared to England and Wales.

Empirical Studies Measuring Consistency of Adhering to Sentencing Guidelines

Empirical studies have generally found that the English courts consistently abide by the sentencing guidelines set out by the Sentencing Council. For instance, using 2011 Crown Court Sentencing Survey (CCSS) data for assault cases, Pina-Sánchez and Linacre found that the prescribed factors in the relevant guidelines were consistently applied across different courts and that the factors demonstrated an expected influence on sentence lengths.[32] This is consistent with the findings of

27 Cross and Cheung, *Sentencing in Hong Kong*, p. 345.

28 *Attorney General* v. *Lam Ping-chun* [1989] 1 HKLR 161 at 162; [1989] HKCU 358.

29 *Attorney General* v. *Lo Ching-fai* [1996] 2 HKCLR 19 at 21.

30 The DAB is the largest pro-establishment political party in Hong Kong. Their call for a sentencing commission came as a result of perceived leniency in sentencing over cases relating to the 2019 anti-extradition movement.

31 RTHK, 'New chief justice rules out sentencing review panel' (11 January 2021), available at https://news.rthk.hk/rthk/en/component/k2/1569836-20210111.htm.

32 J. Pina-Sánchez and R. Linacre, 'Sentence consistency in England and Wales: evidence from the Crown Court Sentencing Survey' (2013) 53 *British Journal of Criminology*,

Irwin-Rogers and Perry, who examined CCSS data for 2012, focusing exclusively on domestic burglary cases. They found that most sentencing factors listed in the relevant sentencing guidelines demonstrated expected associations with the final sentence; specifically, aggravating factors increased sentence severity and mitigating factors reduced it. An exceptional factor was previous convictions, which were found to have a strongly significant effect on the severity of the final sentence.[33]

Nevertheless, certain indications have pointed to the English courts deviating from the sentencing guidelines, particularly when pertaining to sentence reductions for guilty pleas. Despite the guidelines explicitly stating that the level of sentence discount should only reflect the timing of when the guilty plea was entered and whether the prosecution's case is overwhelming – and no other mitigating factors or assistance to authorities – to ensure 'no double counting',[34] evidence suggests that the English courts do not always abide by this. For instance, when assessing CCSS data for assault cases in 2011, Pina-Sánchez and colleagues found other factors to be significant in the courts' determination of the level of sentence reduction for guilty pleas. Defendants deemed to be of good character and those who demonstrated genuine remorse were given more substantial sentence discounts for their guilty pleas, even when such factors should only apply in determining the seriousness level of the offence. Likewise, where the assault was committed in the presence of others or where the defendant was under the influence of drugs or alcohol, the likelihood of a lower sentence discount increased.[35] In their analysis of CCSS data regarding judicial compliance with the definitive guidelines on sentence reductions for guilty pleas between 2011 and 2012, Roberts and Bradford found that English judges mostly complied with the guidelines for nearly all cases disposed through early guilty pleas, granting defendants a sentence discount of one-third or more. Yet they also found greater variation regarding compliance with

1118–38. The authors also found similar results when analysing burglary and robbery cases.

[33] K. Irwin-Rogers and T. W. Perry, 'Exploring the impact of sentencing factors on sentencing domestic burglary', in J. V. Roberts (ed.), *Exploring Sentencing Practice in England and Wales* (London: Palgrave MacMillan, 2015), pp. 212–13.

[34] Sentencing Guidelines Council, *Reduction in Sentence for Guilty Plea: Definitive Guideline* (London: Sentencing Guidelines Secretariat, 2007), paragraph 2.4.

[35] J. Pina-Sánchez, I. Brunton-Smith, and G. Li, 'Mind the step: a more insightful and robust analysis of the sentencing process in England and Wales under the new sentencing guidelines' (2020) 20 *Criminology & Criminal Justice*, 268–301.

guidelines for cases resolved through late pleas, with only 12 per cent of late plea cases resulting in a sentence discount of one-third or more.[36] Moreover, the authors discovered that significant variation existed among different types of offences in terms of the actual sentence discount given, which was also inconsistent with the timing of guilty pleas being the only relevant consideration as per the sentencing guidelines.[37]

In Hong Kong, few empirical studies have focused on measuring the courts' consistency in applying sentencing guidelines. One key exception is the study by Cheng and colleagues, who investigated judicial compliance with the tariff guidelines for trafficking in dangerous drugs cases. They found that judges demonstrated high compliance by sentencing within ranges stipulated in the guidelines. However, these sentence ranges, measured in duration of imprisonment, are based on the type and quantity of drugs measured in grammes, making it possible to calculate an 'arithmetic starting point of sentence' for each gramme of drug being trafficked. Using more fine-tuned calculations, inter-judge disparities in sentence outcomes were revealed; however, these disparities are masked by their general conformity with the sentencing guidelines' broader sentencing ranges.

Guilty Plea Stage and Sentence Discount

Following the analyses conducted by Roberts and Bradford,[38] the current study performed cross-tabulations for guilty plea stages and sentence discounts. In the CCSS dataset, sentence discounts are categorised into five ranges: one-third or more (≥33 per cent), 21–32 per cent, 11–20 per cent, 1–10 per cent, and no reduction. Table 7.1 presents the results for guilty plea stages and plea discounts as per the ranges given in the dataset and as in Chapters 1–6, guilty pleas are categorised as early, intermediate, or late pleas.[39] As the table shows, plea discounts closely aligned with the guidelines on sentence reductions for guilty pleas. Most early pleas (74.38 per cent) were given the recommended one-third sentence discount or more. Most intermediate pleas resulted in sentence discounts in the

[36] J. V. Roberts and B. Bradford, 'Sentence reductions for a guilty plea in England and Wales: exploring new empirical trends' (2015) 12 *Journal of Empirical Legal Studies*, 187–210, p. 197.

[37] Ibid., 201.

[38] Ibid.

[39] See Chapter 2, fn 49.

Table 7.1 *Cross-tabulation of guilty plea stage and plea discount: England and Wales*[a]

	Plea discount					
Plea stage	≥33%	21–32%	11–20%	1–10%	No reduction	Total
Early	12,808 (74.38%)	3,615 (20.99%)	709 (4.12%)	72 (0.42%)	16 (0.09%)	17,220
Intermediate	195 (15.37%)	328 (25.85%)	639 (50.35%)	104 (8.20%)	3 (0.23%)	1,269
Late	232 (9.01%)	154 (5.98%)	605 (23.49%)	1,563 (60.68%)	22 (0.84%)	2,576

[a] Only includes defendants whose cases resulted in immediate custody.

ranges of 11–20 per cent (50.35 per cent) and 21–32 per cent (25.85 per cent). Lastly, most late pleas resulted in sentence discounts in the lower range of 1–10 per cent (60.68 per cent).

However, as Chapters 1–6 have discussed, the stage when a guilty plea is entered may not reflect the first opportunity when a defendant can plead guilty. Consequently, another cross-tabulation was performed to compare whether the defendant pleaded guilty at 'the first reasonable opportunity' with the range of sentence discount awarded. Table 7.2 illustrates the results, which provide further evidence that the sentencing guidelines are closely adhered to. The majority of pleas made at the first opportunity resulted in a sentence discount of one-third or more (88.2 per cent), with very few defendants receiving a sentence discount of less than 10 per cent (0.5 per cent). Likewise, very few defendants entered a guilty plea after the first opportunity received a sentence discount of one-third or more (4.7 per cent).

A similar cross-tabulation was conducted for the Hong Kong District Court sample, for which the categories for guilty plea stages are early, late, and no plea (conviction after trial). The range categories for the sentence discount for guilty pleas are greater than one-third (≥33 per cent), one-third (33 per cent), 21–32 per cent, 11–20 per cent, 1–10 per cent, and no reduction. Table 7.3 illustrates the results, which demonstrate even greater compliance with the recommended sentencing guidelines compared with the CCSS sample. Virtually all defendants who pleaded guilty at the early stage were given a one-third sentence discount (98.9 per cent), with only a few cases receiving a higher or lower sentence discount. For late guilty pleas, most sentence discounts were in the ranges below the recommended one-third discount, with 46 per cent and 35 per cent of defendants receiving sentence discounts in the ranges of 21–32 per cent and 11–20 per cent, respectively. Lastly, almost all (95.6 per cent) defendants who did not plead guilty but were ultimately convicted post-trial did not receive any sentence discount. These results suggest that Hong Kong judges observe the sliding scale of sentence discounts even more closely than their English counterparts.

Despite the results shown in Table 7.3, Chapter 6 found no significant difference between early and late guilty pleas in terms of sentence outcomes, regardless of sentence length or whether the sentence imposes immediate imprisonment. A potential reason for this lack of contrast is that the difference between the recommended sentence discount ranges for early and late pleas in the Hong Kong sentencing guidelines is not that large. For instance, the Hong Kong guidelines state that for

Table 7.2 *Cross-tabulation of guilty plea timing and plea discount: England and Wales*[a]

	Plea discount					
Plea timing	≥33%	21–32%	11–20%	1–10%	No reduction	Total
At first opportunity	13,454 (88.2%)	1,198 (7.9%)	515 (3.4%)	69 (0.5%)	13 (0.0%)	15,249
Later plea	309 (4.7%)	2,990 (45.8%)	1,492 (22.9%)	1,701 (26.1%)	31 (0.5%)	6,523

[a] Only includes defendants whose cases resulted in immediate custody.

Table 7.3 *Cross-tabulation of guilty plea stage and plea discount: Hong Kong*[a]

	Plea discount						
Plea stage	≥33%	33%	21–32%	11–20%	1–10%	No reduction	Total
Early	6 (0.5%)	1,177 (98.9%)	5 (0.4%)	1 (0.1%)	0 (0.0%)	1 (0.1%)	1,190
Late	2 (2.0%)	16 (16.0%)	46 (46.0%)	35 (35.0%)	1 (1.0%)	0 (0.0%)	100
No plea	0 (0.0%)	7 (4.4%)	0 (0.0%)	0 (0.0%)	0 (0.0%)	151 (95.6%)	158

[a] Only includes defendants whose cases resulted in immediate custody.

defendants who plead guilty during trial, the sentence discount should be reduced to less than one-fifth,[40] whereas the 2007 definitive guidelines issued by the Sentencing Guidelines Council – which the CCSS is based on – recommend that pleas at the door of the court or during trial only be given a one-tenth(!) discount;[41] the Hong Kong guidelines are hence more lenient. Moreover, the Hong Kong guidelines for late guilty pleas stipulate a sentence discount range of 20–25 per cent for when a defendant pleads guilty between when a trial date has been fixed and the first day of trial.[42] As Table 7.3 shows, Hong Kong judges tend to be more lenient with late guilty pleas, with nearly half of late pleading defendants (46.0 per cent) receiving a sentence discount of 21–32 per cent; certain defendants who did not plead guilty at the first opportunity even received the one-third sentence discount (16.0 per cent), and two defendants even received more.

Factors Affecting Actual Sentence Discounts

Although both the English and Hong Kong courts predominantly follow their respective sentencing guidelines for guilty pleas, instances of departures can still occur. This section turns towards investigating what factors affect the actual sentence discount the courts grant to the defendant using multivariate regressions. In the CCSS, sentence discounts were reported in ranges as indicated in the previous section; an ordinal logistic regression was therefore performed, using the sentence discount granted as the outcome variable. The models also controlled for case variables, defendants' characteristics, and the stage when guilty pleas were entered. Table 7.4 presents the results of the model for the CCSS sample.

As expected, the variables for the timing of guilty pleas were significant. Defendants who did not plead guilty at the first opportunity were significantly more likely to receive a lower sentence discount compared to defendants who did. Similarly, defendants who pleaded guilty at an intermediate or late stage were also more likely to receive a lower sentence discount compared to defendants who pleaded guilty at an early stage. These results confirm that the stage when guilty pleas are entered has an important effect on sentence discounts. Nevertheless, Crown

[40] *HKSAR* v. *Ngo Van Nam and Abdou Maikido Abdoulkarim* [2016] 5 HKLRD 1; [2016] HKCA 397.

[41] Sentencing Guidelines Council, Reduction in Sentence for Guilty Plea.

[42] *Ngo Van Nam and Abdou Maikido Abdoulkarim.*

Table 7.4 *Regression results for actual sentence discount given: England and Wales*

Predictors	Odds ratio	95% CI
(Intercept)	3.86***	3.29–4.53
Guilty plea at first opportunity (ref.: yes)		
No	0.01***	0.01–0.01
Timing of guilty plea (ref.: early)		
Intermediate	0.42***	0.39–0.44
Late	0.26***	0.23–0.29
Offence type (ref.: drugs)		
Arson	1.58*	1.46–1.72
Assault	1.03	0.84–1.26
Burglary	0.66***	0.62–0.71
Death	1.15	0.91–1.45
Driving	1.03	0.92–1.15
Fraud	1.15	0.92–1.58
Indecent photography of children (IPC)	1.17	0.97–1.42
Other	1.01	0.93–1.09
Robbery	1.08	0.98–1.20
Sex	1.46***	1.31–1.63
Theft	1.12	1.04–1.20
Age group (ref.: 35–44)		
18–24	1.13*	1.06–1.20
25–34	1.03	0.97–1.09
45–54	0.99	0.91–1.07
≥54	1.05	0.94–1.17
Gender (ref.: male)		
Female	1.22**	1.14–1.31
Previous offences (ref.: no)		
Yes	1.00	0.96–1.04
Existing illness (ref.: no)		
Yes	1.01	0.93–1.09
Confession made (ref.: no)		
Yes	1.49***	1.42–1.57
Observations	15,848	
Nagelkerke's R^2	0.71	

$^{+}p < 0.1$, $^{*}p < 0.05$, $^{**}p < 0.01$, $^{***}p < 0.001$.

Court sentencers adhered overall to the sentencing guidelines establishing the sliding scale of sentence discounts.

Regarding the demographic characteristic of age, young adult defendants (aged 18–24) were more likely to receive a higher sentence discount for their guilty pleas compared with the reference group of defendants aged 35–44. Interestingly, female defendants were more likely to receive a higher sentence discount compared to male defendants. Echoing the finding of Chapter 6 that female defendants in the Crown Courts were more likely to receive more lenient sentences, the present finding also reveals that female defendants are also more likely to receive favourable sentence outcomes through receiving higher sentence discounts for their guilty pleas.

Confessions were also found to be significant. Defendants who had made a confession were more likely to receive a higher sentence discount compared with defendants who had not. This finding is interesting when considering that the 2007 sentencing guideline states, 'Whilst there is a presumption in favour of the full reduction being given where a plea has been indicated at the first reasonable opportunity, the fact that the prosecution case is overwhelming without relying on admissions from the defendant may be a reason justifying departure from the guideline.'[43] In this case, the departure is a reduced sentence discount of 20 per cent for the guilty plea.[44] However, the regression results show that the courts have considered defendants' admissions and are more lenient in giving greater sentence discounts for their subsequent guilty pleas.

Similar statistical analysis models were constructed for the Hong Kong District Court dataset, with the key exception that exact sentence discounts for guilty pleas as reported by the sentencing judge could be extracted from 'Reasons for Sentence' reports. Therefore, an ordinary least squares (OLS) regression was run instead, with the outcome variable being the sentence discount, controlling for case-related and demographic characteristics.[45] The timing of guilty pleas, including no plea, also served as an independent variable. Since 96.5 per cent of the defendants in the sample were given a guilty plea discount in accordance with Hong Kong sentencing guidelines, using the guilty plea stage as a control variable is an accurate proxy for the expected guilty plea discount. Table 7.5 presents the regression results.

43 Sentencing Guidelines Council, Reduction in Sentence for Guilty Plea, paragraph 5.3.

44 Ibid., paragraph 5.4.

45 A simple linear regression model was used, since when the regression was run using hierarchical linear modelling (HLM), the standard deviation for judges was 0, indicating no substantial difference among the sentence discounts that judges awarded.

Table 7.5 *Regression results for actual sentence discount given: Hong Kong*

	Defendants who pleaded guilty		**All defendants**	
Predictors	**B**	**SE**	**B**	**SE**
(Intercept)	32.61***	0.29	32.22***	0.39
Guilty plea stage (ref.: early)				
Late	−8.76***	0.26	−8.63***	0.37
No plea	–	–	−30.66***	0.36
Offence type (ref.: drugs)				
Assault	0.43+	0.25	−0.15	0.33
Burglary/robbery	−0.15	0.17	−0.53*	0.24
Driving	0.12	0.36	−0.73	0.44
Fraud	−0.69**	0.25	−1.33***	0.32
Other	0.20	0.21	−0.23	0.29
Theft	0.02	0.20	−0.41	0.29
No. of charges per defendant	0.01	0.00	0.03	0.00
Age group (years) (ref.: 35–44)				
18–24	0.00	0.20	−0.22	0.27
25–34	0.03+	0.16	0.08	0.23
45–54	0.08	0.18	−0.27	0.25
≥55	0.03	0.20	−0.09	0.27
Gender (ref.: male)				
Female	0.31	0.19	1.10***	0.26
Race/ethnicity (ref.: local Hong Kong)				
Foreigner	−0.30	0.21	−0.35	0.29
Mainland Chinese	0.00	0.25	0.18	0.35
Previous offences (ref.: no)				
Yes	0.00	0.14	0.17	0.19
Existing illness (ref.: no)				
Mental illness	−0.84**	0.28	−0.84*	0.38
Physical illness	0.00	0.22	0.04	0.31
Confession made (ref.: no)				
Yes	0.20	0.17	0.63**	0.23
Legal representative (ref.: private lawyer)				
Legal aid	0.12	0.20	0.32	0.26
Prosecution (ref.: on fiat)				
Public prosecutor	0.14	0.12	0.13	0.17
Observations	969		1,049	
R^2	0.81		0.71	

+$p < 0.1$, *$p < 0.05$, **$p < 0.01$, ***$p < 0.001$.

Unsurprisingly, both late guilty pleas and no pleas significantly affected the sentence discount. Consistent with the sentencing guidelines, compared to defendants who entered an early plea, defendants who entered a late plea were more likely to receive a lower sentence discount. Likewise, defendants who did not plead guilty and were convicted after trial were significantly more likely to receive a lower sentence discount compared to defendants who had made an early guilty plea. The findings support the overall observation that judges in Hong Kong adhere to the sentencing guidelines that determine sentence discounts based on the timing of guilty pleas.

In terms of defendants' characteristics, defendants with mental illnesses were more likely to receive lower sentence discounts. This is surprising given that the appellate courts have recognised that such defendants should be treated more leniently in sentencing, since their illnesses may reduce their moral culpability in the offence, thus calling into question whether a deterrent (heavier) sentence would be effective.[46] The Hong Kong Court of Appeal has noted, 'Care must always be taken in assessing assertions of personality disorders and, even if established, the degree to which such a disorder in a particular case is relevant to sentence.'[47] Furthermore, the Court has stated, 'In the case before us, the disorder appears to have been relevant to the offence . . . But the severity of the disorder does not, *of itself*, appear to us to negate considerations of general deterrence. In this case, it reduced rather than removed moral culpability, although we recognise that there were other cogent mitigating factors at play.'[48] Although mental illness may not always remove culpability, the expectation is that it leads to leniency. Yet regarding sentence discounts for guilty pleas, Hong Kong judges appear not only to have refrained from leniency for mentally ill defendants but also adopted more stringent attitudes towards them.

Lastly, akin to the CCSS results, both gender and confessions were significant predictors of a greater sentence discount for guilty pleas. In particular, the results show that like their English counterparts, Hong Kong judges are more likely to be favourable towards female defendants as demonstrated by the greater likelihood of granting them a higher sentence discount compared to male defendants. The results from both

[46] Cross and Cheung, *Sentencing in Hong Kong*, p. 458.

[47] *Secretary for Justice* v. *Yan Shen* [2012] 3 HKC 557; [2012] 3 HKLRD 652 at paragraph 41.

[48] Ibid., paragraph 44.

the CCSS and Hong Kong datasets offer evidence supporting the 'chivalry' and 'paternalism' hypotheses used in criminology to explain the preferential treatment in sentencing given to female defendants. The chivalry hypothesis posits that court actors, who are predominately male, treat female defendants more leniently, and that the protective stance that male legal authorities adopt prevents them from inflicting too much harm on female defendants. On the other hand, the notion of paternalism posits a stereotypical passive image of women who require protection.[49] Furthermore, defendants who had made a confession were also more likely to receive a higher sentence discount compared with defendants who had not. Echoing the finding of Chapter 6 that confessions were associated with the likelihood of a lighter sentence, the present finding also reveals confessions to be associated with a lighter sentence in terms of judicial decisions awarding greater sentence discounts for guilty pleas.

Sentencing Process

Consistency in sentencing should not only be viewed in terms of sentence outcomes. Consideration must also be given to consistency throughout the sentencing process, given that the courts must pass through several steps to arrive at a final sentence. For the courts in England and Wales, sentencing guidelines provided by the Sentencing Council (and previously the Sentencing Guidelines Council) list out such steps in the sentencing process, which are meant to be sequential and non-overlapping. A step-by-step sentencing process is illustrated using the definitive guidelines on inflicting grievous bodily harm or unlawful wounding, a misdemeanour under section 20 of the Offences against the Person Act 1861:[50]

- Step 1: determining the offence category by assessing the offender's culpability and the harm caused by the offence in question. The court determines these factors while referring to the factors listed in the guideline that comprise the factual elements of the offence. The

[49] B. K. Crew, 'Sex differences in criminal sentencing: chivalry or patriarchy?' (1991) 8 *Justice Quarterly*, 59–83; E. F. Mould, 'Chivalry and paternalism: disparities of treatment in the criminal justice system' (1978) 3 *The Western Political Quarterly*, 416–30; M. Farnworth and R. H. C. Teske, Jr, 'Gender differences in felony court processing: three hypotheses of disparity' (2008) 6 *Women & Criminal Justice*, 23–44.

[50] Sentencing Council, *Assault: Definitive Guideline* (London: Sentencing Council, 2011).

guideline stipulates that only listed factors should be referenced.[51] For instance, a factor indicating greater harm is 'victim is particularly vulnerable because of personal circumstances', while one indicating lesser harm is 'injury which is less serious in the context of the offence'. A factor indicating higher culpability is 'a significant degree of premeditation', while one indicating lesser culpability is 'excessive self-defence'.

- Step 2: determining the starting point for sentencing and the category range of the offence. For instance, if the offence is determined to be a Category 1 offence (highest harm level), depending on culpability, the starting point of sentence is recommended at two to four years' custody, with a category range of two years six months to four years' custody.[52] The guideline further provides non-exhaustive lists of aggravating and mitigating factors for the courts to determine whether to make any upward or downward adjustments to the starting point of sentence.[53]
- Step 3: considering any other factors that indicate a reduction of sentence, such as any assistance the defendant provides to the prosecution or investigator.
- Step 4: applying a sentence discount for the timing of guilty pleas. Specifically, the 2007 sentencing guidelines on sentence reductions for guilty pleas states, 'When deciding the most appropriate length of sentence, the sentencer should address separately the issue of remorse, together with any other mitigating features, *before* calculating the reduction for the guilty plea.'[54] The revised 2017 guidelines reiterate this point by stating, 'The guilty plea should be considered by the court to be independent of the offender's personal mitigation .... Factors such as admissions at interview, co-operation with the investigation and demonstrations of remorse ... should be considered separately and *prior* to any guilty plea reduction.'[55] (Emphasis added.)
- Step 5: considering extended sentences for dangerousness.
- Step 6: considering the totality principle; required for cases where the defendant is being sentenced for more than one offence.[56]

[51] Ibid., p. 8.
[52] Ibid.
[53] Ibid., p. 9.
[54] Sentencing Guidelines Council, Reduction in Sentence for Guilty Plea, paragraph 2.4.
[55] Ibid., paragraph B.
[56] For more on totality, see Sentencing Council, 'Totality' (2012), available at www.sentencingcouncil.org.uk/overarching-guides/magistrates-court/item/totality/.

- Step 7: considering whether to make compensation and/or ancillary orders.
- Step 8: giving reasons for and explaining the effects of the sentence.
- Step 9: considering giving credit for time that the defendant may have spent remanded in custody or on bail.

Although empirical assessments of the English courts have found that they adhere overall to the sentencing guidelines, studies have also observed notable deviations from the step-by-step approach as stipulated in this chapter. Besides the timing of guilty pleas, certain studies have found influences on sentence discounts from other factors. For instance, in their investigation of assault cases, Pina-Sánchez and colleagues found that the culpability and harm factors for Step 1 have significant effects on final sentence determinations, even when such factors should only apply to determining offence seriousness. Previous convictions were also found to be a significant factor for Step 1, Step 4 (applying the sentence discount for guilty pleas), and the final sentence outcome. Both observations point to judges deviating from the sentencing guidelines, which stipulate that sentencing considerations should be made sequentially, with the considerations relevant to individual steps not coinciding with each other.[57]

In Hong Kong, a step-by-step sentencing process is not neatly laid out in a specific guideline document. Nevertheless, the Court of Appeal presented such a process in *Islam Azharul*:

> [It] is a useful reminder of the importance for a sentencing court in following the discipline of taking the necessary steps when determining a just and appropriate sentence to be imposed upon an offender. In the case of a single offence, this usually involves in its basic form the sentencing court first adopting a starting point based on the blameworthiness of the offender and the harm caused by the offence. Secondly, the sentencing court should list the aggravating factors, explaining which factors have or have not been taken into account and specifying the amount of enhancement given for the factors that have been taken into account. Thirdly, the sentencing court should list the mitigating factors, explaining which factors have or have not been taken into account and specifying the amount of reduction given for the factors that have been taken into account. Having specified the enhancements given for the aggravating factors, it is important for the sentencing court to ensure that the aggregation of the enhancements does not result in an oppressive and

[57] Pina-Sánchez, Brunton-Smith, and Li, 'Mind the step', 281.

> overloaded sentence, and by the application of the totality principle this will require determining an appropriate effective total of the enhancements.[58]

The court did not mention where the sentence discount for a guilty plea should apply in the aforementioned sentencing process.

Moreover, as observed from the data extracted from the 'Reasons for Sentence' reports used for the Hong Kong District Court dataset, this study discovered that sentencing judges adopt different steps when sentencing. For instance, a case in the dataset regarding the theft of a large amount of money by a police officer, in the reasons for sentencing, the sentencing judge first referred to various mitigating factors to lower the starting point of sentence before applying the sentence discount for guilty pleas to arrive at the final sentence. Specifically, the judge first adopted a starting point of sentence based on 'an arithmetical application' of the sentencing guidelines for theft: 'The total amount stolen is around HK$861,290. An arithmetical application of the tariff would lead to a starting point of 34 months' imprisonment. This is the starting point I adopt.'[59] He then lowered this starting point based on mitigating factors, stating, 'The defendant had been an exceptional police officer and had contributed much to society over the years. I find that there should be a sentencing discount of 2 months on the starting point on this basis, leading to a sentence of 32 months' imprisonment.'[60] Thereafter, the judge reduced the sentence based on the defendant's early guilty plea: 'The defendant is, therefore, sentenced to 21 months' imprisonment *after* granting him the full one-third discount.'[61] (Emphasis added.)

In another case involving the burglary of a mobile phone store (Charge 1) and failure to surrender to lawful custody (Charge 2), the sentencing judge adopted different sentencing approaches for each charge. For Charge 1, the judge first adopted a starting point of sentence and increased it based on aggravating factors, but then reduced it based on a guilty plea and doing so even further based on mitigating factors. Specifically, the judge first stated, 'Adopting the customary starting point

[58] *HKSAR* v. *Islam Azharul* [2020] HKCA 29 at paragraph 20.

[59] *HKSAR* v. *Lau Wing Fai* [2019] HKDC 286 at paragraph 21. For the sentencing guidelines on theft, see *HKSAR* v. *Ng Kwok Wing* [2008] 4 HKLRD 1017.

[60] *Lau Wing Fai* at paragraph 25.

[61] Ibid. at paragraph 26.

of 30 months, I increase it by 4 months to take into account the joint enterprise with 3 others. The actual starting point is 34 months.'[62] Afterwards, he considered the defendant's late guilty plea and then made further reductions based on a mitigating factor: 'After a less than one-third discount for the late plea of guilty, the sentence for Charge 1 is 24 months. I deduct 3 months from it for no property was lost to the shop. The sentence is 21 months for Charge 1.'[63] Conversely, for Charge 2, the judge adopted a starting point of sentence and then considered the early guilty plea prior to further reductions based on mitigating factors: 'I take a starting point of 12 months for Charge 2. After a one-third discount for the plea of guilty, the sentence is 8 months. As he surrendered himself to be arrested, I give him 2 months' extra discount. The sentence for Charge 2 is 6 months.'[64] These differences in sentencing approach can profoundly affect the final sentence. Considering Charge 2, for instance, had the sentencing judge first adjusted the starting point of sentence for mitigating factors before applying the sentence discount for the guilty plea, the final sentence would have been around 6.7 months.[65] Whereas the extra half month does not seem like a sizeable difference in this case, if the sentence terms dealt instead with years, the hypothetical sentencing approach would result in an extra half year of imprisonment.

In certain cases, the court did not provide any adjustments for mitigating factors whatsoever, instead subsuming them under the sentence discount for guilty pleas.[66] For example, in a case of a street robbery by a young adult offender (aged 19 at the time of the offence),[67] the sentencing judge ordered a background report on the defendant before passing sentence. He found the defendant to be 'suffering from post-traumatic stress disorder'[68] after an industrial accident and his 'suspected Dyslexia and Attention Deficiency conditions were never properly dealt with'.[69] However, in his sentencing remarks, the judge stated that 'although I do

62 *HKSAR* v. *Fung Chung-keung* [2019] HKDC 704 at paragraph 19. For the customary sentence for burglary of non-domestic premises, see *R* v. *Wong Man* [1993] 1 HKC 80.

63 *Fung Chung-keung* at paragraph 19.

64 Ibid. at paragraph 20.

65 The starting point of sentence was 12 months. Mitigating factors reduced the starting point by 2 months to 10 months. Thereafter, subtracting one-third from 10 months is approximately 6.7 months.

66 For more on how mitigating factors may be subsumed under the sentence discount for guilty pleas, see the discussion in Chapter 2.

67 *HKSAR* v. *Chan Chun Nam* [2018] HKDC 429.

68 Ibid. at paragraph 18.

69 Ibid. at paragraph 17.

sympathize with the various difficulties the defendant had to face during his formative years as disclosed in the background report, and I do appreciate his work ethics, I find that these personal circumstances do not warrant any further reduction in the sentence that would not already be subsumed by the one-third discount granted to him for his plea of guilty.'[70] Under this sentencing approach, sentence reductions for mitigating factors are incorporated under the sentence discount for guilty pleas rather than considered separately, leading to a higher final sentence.

Actual Sentence Discounts on Sentence Lengths

Two additional statistical models, one for the CCSS dataset and another for the Hong Kong District Court dataset, were run to determine potential effects of the actual sentence discount given by the courts on the final sentence length imposed on the defendant. Table 7.6 presents regression results for the CCSS dataset, with sentence length as the outcome and the actual sentence discount replacing the guilty plea stage as the primary factor; all other independent variables were identical to those in previous models. Given how the CCSS presents sentence length using ranges, an ordinal logistic regression was performed. As expected, the greater the sentence discount that sentencing judges said they awarded, the lower the final sentence length. Guilty plea discounts, including those less than one-third and those equal to one-third or more, correlated with more lenient sentences compared to no sentence discount. This result shows that the sentence discount for guilty pleas has a significantly large effect on the final sentence, even when controlling for case and defendant characteristics.

Table 7.7 presents regression results for the Hong Kong dataset. Because the actual sentence length could be determined from the 'Reasons for Sentence' transcripts, a linear regression with Heckman's correction was conducted, with logged sentence length as the outcome. The actual sentence discounts stated by sentencing judges replaced the guilty plea stage as the primary factor, with all other variables being identical to previous models. Unsurprisingly, as in the CCSS data, the actual sentence discount for guilty pleas was found to be significant. The greater the sentence discount the judge pronounced for the defendant's guilty plea, the lower the sentence length that the defendant eventually

[70] Ibid. at paragraph 51.

Table 7.6 *Regression results for actual sentence discount on sentence length: England and Wales*

Predictors	Odds ratio	95% CI
(Intercept)	4.10***	3.71–4.53
Guilty plea discount: (ref.: none)		
Less than one-third	0.16***	0.11–0.22
One-third or more	0.10***	0.08–0.15
Offence type (ref.: drugs)		
Arson	0.81	0.72–0.91
Assault	0.30***	0.29–0.32
Burglary	0.70***	0.67–0.73
Death	3.25***	2.80–3.78
Driving	0.16***	0.15–0.18
Fraud	0.20***	0.17–0.24
IPC	0.30***	0.20–0.41
Other	0.13***	0.12–0.14
Robbery	2.23***	2.10–2.36
Sex	1.46***	1.36–1.57
Theft	0.16***	0.15–0.16
Age group (years) (ref.: 35–44)		
18–24	0.77***	0.74–0.80
25–34	0.92*	0.89–0.92
45–54	1.15**	1.09–1.21
≥54	1.26**	1.16–1.36
Gender (ref.: male)		
Female	0.84***	0.79–0.88
Previous offences (ref.: none)		
Yes	0.86***	0.84–0.88
Existing illness (ref.: no)		
Yes	0.99	0.93–1.05
Confession made (ref.: no)		
Yes	0.68***	0.67–0.69
Observations	16,983	
Nagelkerke's R^2	0.24	

$+p < 0.1$, $^{*}p < 0.05$, $^{**}p < 0.01$, $^{***}p < 0.001$.

Table 7.7 *Regression results for actual sentence discount on logged sentence length: Hong Kong*

Predictors	B	SE
(Intercept)	3.66***	0.01
Guilty plea discount	−0.70***	0.17
Offence type (ref.: drugs)		
Assault	−0.44***	0.05
Burglary/robbery	−0.31***	0.03
Driving	−1.04***	0.06
Fraud	−0.29***	0.05
Other	−0.44***	0.04
Theft	−0.49***	0.04
No. of charges per defendant	0.04***	0.00
Age group (years) (ref.: 35–44)		
18–24	0.08	0.09
25–34	−0.03	0.03
45–54	−0.02	0.04
≥55	−0.03	0.04
Gender (ref.: male)		
Female	0.00	0.04
Race/ethnicity (ref.: local Hong Kong)		
Foreigner	−0.05	0.07
Mainland Chinese	0.03	0.07
Previous offences (ref.: no)		
Yes	0.04	0.05
Existing illness (ref.: no)		
Mental illness	−0.11*	0.05
Physical illness	−0.08$^+$	0.04
Confession made (ref.: no)		
Yes	0.00	0.03
Legal representative (ref.: private lawyer)		
Legal aid	0.03	0.03
Prosecution (ref.: on fiat)		
Public prosecutor	0.07**	0.02
Model statistics		
Inverse Mills Ratio (IMR)	−0.31	0.34
Sigma	0.43	
Rho	−0.72	
Observations	1,435	
Nagelkerke's R^2	0.31	

$^+p < 0.1$, $^*p < 0.05$, $^{**}p < 0.01$, $^{***}p < 0.001$.

received. This finding again demonstrates that the sentence discount for guilty pleas has a significant effect on the final sentence. Interestingly, gender and confessions were not found to be significant in this model, even though female defendants and defendants who had confessed were given greater sentence discounts for their guilty pleas compared with their male and non-confessing counterparts, respectively. This particular finding shows that leniency in the final sentence can be influenced by the sentence discount. The differences found in this model may be attributed to how Hong Kong judges go about the sentencing process. As discussed earlier, certain judges subsume mitigating factors under the sentence starting point, whereas others adjust for such factors after determining the starting point or incorporating them into the sentence discount for guilty pleas.

Conclusion

This chapter examined judges' observance of the sentencing guidelines for sentence discounts for guilty pleas. Despite both the English and Hong Kong courts having the discretion to depart from guidelines, judges in both jurisdictions mostly followed the recommended ranges established in their respective sliding scale of sentence discounts closely when making their sentencing decisions. As with the findings of Chapter 6, this phenomenon reveals that the timing of guilty pleas matters in sentence outcomes; *when* the defendant enters a guilty plea influences the sentence discount, consequently profoundly affecting the sentence outcome. Interestingly, other factors besides guilty plea timing were discovered to affect the sentence discount. In England and Wales and in Hong Kong, female defendants and defendants who had previously confessed were found to receive higher sentence discounts for their guilty pleas even after controlling for plea timing. This finding shows that judges are more lenient towards both groups, demonstrating this lenience by adjusting the sentence discount.

Another issue that may cause inconsistency is the sentencing process itself – the steps for deriving sentences. Such inconsistencies are a more acute problem in Hong Kong, where the procedural stages for deriving a sentence are not as well defined as the steps set out by the Sentencing Council of England and Wales. When aggravating and mitigating factors are applied during the sentencing process (e.g. adjusting the starting point of sentence or simply being subsumed into the sentence discount for guilty pleas), it can also significantly affect the final sentence. If the goal of the courts is to have consistency in sentencing, then sentencing guidelines should not just specify the sentence discount with respect to the stage when the guilty plea is entered, but also how to calculate the starting point of sentence, when to adjust for aggravating and mitigating factors, and when judges can depart from recommended sentences.

8

Public Opinion and Sentence Discounts

A justification given for the sliding scale of sentence discounts for guilty pleas is that encouraging early guilty pleas is in the public interest. The sliding scale supposedly promotes efficient justice that saves public resources and shows justice being done, thus enhancing public confidence in the criminal justice system. Both governments and the courts have pointed to the importance of public opinion in their decision-making regarding sentences. Yet extant research on public confidence in the courts and attitudes towards sentencing reveal that the public frequently perceives sentences as being 'too lenient'. Consequently, while the aim of sentence discounts for guilty pleas is bolstering efficiency and promoting public confidence, they may actually have the adverse effect of reducing sentences that the public already considers too lenient. This chapter examines the issue of public attitudes towards sentence discounts for guilty pleas by placing it in the wider context of the relationship between public opinion and sentencing. It begins by examining the role that public opinion plays in sentencing before reviewing existing literature on public confidence in the courts and attitudes towards sentencing. The chapter also reviews the limited literature on public attitudes towards plea bargaining and sentence discounts. It then shows that the public is not supportive of sentence discounts for guilty pleas, especially large sentence reductions. If achieving public confidence in sentencing is indeed their goal, politicians and judges should proceed with caution in their pursuit of efficiency through the sliding scale of sentence discounts.

Public Influence on Sentencing

The public plays a role in influencing sentencing policy. For instance, when formulating sentencing guidelines, the Sentencing Council for England and Wales conducts public consultation during the process, including when they prepare their definitive guidelines on sentence reductions for guilty pleas.[1] The courts themselves have authoritatively underscored the importance of public opinion when deciding sentences. In the often-quoted case of *Sargeant*, Lawson LJ stated,

> The Old Testament concept of an eye for an eye and tooth for tooth no longer plays any part in our criminal law. There is, however, another aspect of retribution which is frequently overlooked: it is that society, through the courts, must show its abhorrence of particular types of crime, and the only way in which the courts can show this is by the sentences they pass. The courts do not have to reflect public opinion. On the other hand courts must not disregard it. Perhaps the main duty of the court is to lead public opinion.[2]

In the subsequent case of *Broady*, the English Court of Appeal reiterated the notion of how judges should take public opinion into account during sentencing. As Watkins LJ stated,

Judges are not here to gain approval or avoid disapproval from the public, and thus decide their sentences perhaps on the basis of the lowest common denominator of public opinion. But at the same time, public abhorrence of behaviour like the defendant's should not be, and must not be, disregarded by the courts, who have a duty to the public to pass judgment in a way which is generally acceptable amongst right-thinking, well-informed persons.[3]

Although perceptions of public opinion should not drive sentences, these two cases clearly illustrate that public opinion is something that sentencing courts should consider.

The United Kingdom Government's 2001 review of the English sentencing framework, commonly known as the Halliday Review, placed at the forefront the need for sentences to attract public confidence and for sentencers to understand public opinion. The review emphasised that '[s]entencing, and the framework within it operates, need to earn and merit public confidence, but this is a complex relationship, and not one in which sentencers can simply be "driven before the wind" of apparent public mood ... More can and should be done to improve public understanding of sentencing, and sentencers' understanding of public

[1] See for example Sentencing Council, *Reduction in Sentence for a Guilty Plea: Response to Consultation* (London: Sentencing Council, 2017).

[2] *R* v. *Sargeant* (1974) 60 Cr App R 74 at 77.

[3] *R* v. *Broady* (1988) 10 Cr App R (S) 495 at 498.

opinion'.[4] Likewise, the recent 2020 government white paper titled *A Smarter Approach to Sentencing* explicitly states that '[t]he paper sets out plans to deliver . . . and go further with wider sentencing reform, to improve public safety and public confidence'.[5] It is clear then that for both sentencing decisions the courts make and for sentencing policies the government sets, public opinion matters, particularly the need for public confidence.

Public Confidence in the Courts

One function of the Sentencing Council is 'the need to promote public confidence in the criminal justice system',[6] illustrating the importance of positive public opinion towards the criminal justice process, particularly sentencing. Public confidence in the criminal justice system is considered important because the system needs the cooperation of the public to function effectively.[7] The police rely on members of the public to report crimes and provide evidence, while the courts rely on individuals to act as witnesses and serve as jurors.[8]

However, various polls have revealed the public to have lower confidence in the courts compared with other criminal justice agencies. Surveys conducted in Britain found that the public had the most confidence in the police but the least confidence in the courts. An early study conducted in 2003 found that the public expressed the most confidence in their local police force, giving a 'very or fairly confident' rating (76 per cent), followed by the police forces in England and Wales (73 per cent). The level of confidence towards the judiciary was lower overall, with

[4] J. Halliday, *Making Punishments Work: Report of a Review of the Sentencing Framework for England and Wales (The Halliday Review)* (London: Home Office, 2001).

[5] Ministry of Justice, *A Smarter Approach to Sentencing* (London: Ministry of Justice, 2020).

[6] Section 120(11) of the Corners and Justice Act 2009.

[7] Bradford and colleagues posit that public confidence is akin to a 'job rating' for the various agencies in the criminal justice system. Confidence is an abstract assessment of the efficiency and fairness of an agency, in addition to how well it represents public interests. See B. Bradford, J. Jackson, M. Hough, and S. Farrall, 'Trust and confidence in criminal justice: a review of the British research literature', in A. Jokinen, E. Ruuskanen, M. Yordanova, D. Markov, and M. Ilcheva (eds.), *Review of Need: Indicators of Public Confidence in Criminal Justice* (Helsinki: European Institute for Crime Prevention and Control, 2009), pp. 1–20, p. 2.

[8] J. Wood, 'Why public opinion of the criminal justice system is important', in J. Wood and T. A. Gannon (eds.), *Public Opinion and Criminal Justice* (Abingdon, Oxon: Routledge, 2009), pp. 33–48.

confidence in magistrates at 55 per cent, judges at 54 per cent, the courts overall at 51 per cent, and youth courts at 46 per cent. The judiciary overall was also rated lower in confidence than both the Probation Service (59 per cent) and Crown Prosecution Service (57 per cent).[9]

In a more recent report commissioned by the Sentencing Council, Marsh and colleagues conducted research on public confidence in sentencing and the criminal justice system in England and Wales. They elicited online surveys from 2,000 adults in March 2018 and conducted qualitative interviews.[10] Respondents were asked if they had ever been in contact with criminal justice agencies, including the police, witness support, victim support, probation services, and the criminal courts (the Magistrates' Courts or the Crown Court). Most respondents (64 per cent) stated that their contact with victim support had been very or mostly positive, while only 6 per cent stated that they had a very or mostly negative contact experience. A similar response was observed for witness support, with 62 per cent of respondents stating they had a positive contact experience. As for the police, 60 per cent of respondents stated they had a positive contact experience, while 17 per cent held negative views of their contact with the police. Crucially, respondents' views were less positive regarding the criminal courts, with only 47 per cent rating their contact with the courts as very or mostly positive, and 18 per cent rating their contact as very or mostly negative. Similar results were found for probation services.[11] This issue is not limited to England and Wales; surveys in Australia also found the courts and legal system to have lower confidence ratings in the public eye compared to other institutions such as the police, defence forces, universities, charities, major companies, and the Federal Parliament.[12] Likewise, in Canada, the justice

[9] M. Hough and J. V. Roberts, *Confidence in Justice: An International Review (Findings No. 234)* (London: Home Office, 2004).

[10] N. Marsh, E. McKay, C. Pelly, and S. Cereda, *Public Knowledge of and Confidence in the Criminal Justice System and Sentencing: A Report for the Sentencing Council* (London: Sentencing Council, 2019).

[11] Ibid., p. 14. Among the respondents, 200 had contact with victim support, 140 had contact with witness support, 933 had contact with the police, 473 had contact with the criminal courts, and 144 had contact with probation services.

[12] C. Bean, 'Is there a crisis of trust in Australia?', in S. Wilson, G. Meagher, R. Gibson, D. Denemark, and M. Western (eds.), *Australian Social Attitudes: The First Report* (Sydney: UNSW Press, 2005), chapter 8, pp. 122–40.

system has been found to have a lower public confidence rating than banks, the health care system, and the school system.[13]

Notably, the criminal trial itself serves as a vehicle for promoting public confidence in the justice system. Goldstein acutely points out,

> In its very detail and drama – in examination and cross-examination of witnesses and the adversarial sifting of facts and legal issues – the trial becomes a morality play which impresses upon the public that the law is being enforced and that justice is being fairly administered ... Guilty pleas drive a gaping hole through these assumptions. If too few contested trials occur, there is a real risk that the larger public will not be taught the moral lessons on which a system of criminal law depends.[14]

The public display of a trial, where evidence is tested and legal arguments are heard, is a display of the criminal justice system at work and a demonstration that it is working. Conversely, plea arraignments are quick by design; guilty pleas, as well as the rationale for why a defendant pleads guilty, are hidden from public view. The moral lessons that can be learned from a trial, including the subsequent written trial judgment where legal principles can be advanced, are absent from guilty plea cases. Viewed in this way, not having a public trial is a lost opportunity for enhancing public confidence in the justice system.

Another area in the criminal process that likely affects public confidence is sentencing. After all, sentences capture the public imagination. In one survey that asked the public about the functions of the courts, the majority considered 'passing the right sentence' as an essential function. However, when asked about the confidence that they have in these various functions, respondents ranked 'passing the right sentence' the lowest, lower than other court functions such as respecting the rights of

[13] J. V. Roberts, 'Public confidence in criminal justice in Canada: comparative and contextual analysis' (2007) 49(2) *Canadian Journal of Criminology and Criminal Justice*, 153–84. Roberts posits that the justice system is rated lower than other institutions because it has conflicting mandates. As he states at p. 162:

> [We] should not lose sight of the fact that the health care or educational systems have quite different mandates from that ascribed to the justice system. The health care system exists for the benefit of the health consumer: the patient. In contrast, the justice system has a more complex mandate to fulfil and must respond to the interests of multiple parties. Offenders, victims, and the families of both groups have rights and needs that sometimes come into conflict.

[14] A. S. Goldstein, 'Converging criminal justice systems: guilty pleas and the public interest' (1996) 49 *SMU Law Review*, 567–77, p. 569.

defendants, supporting victims and witnesses, making the right decision about whether to grant bail, and ensuring that the guilty are convicted while the innocent are acquitted.[15] Ultimately, sentences send a message to the public like criminal trials do; each sentencing decision has the potential to bolster (or erode) public confidence. However, sentencing appears to be the court function that garners least public confidence. So what does the public really think about sentencing?

Public Attitudes towards Sentencing

As mentioned in the previous section, a wealth of literature on public opinion and sentences exists. In general, the public tends to find the sentences that courts in various jurisdictions impose to be 'too lenient'.[16] For instance, the Sentencing Council's 2019 public survey found that when asked about general attitudes towards sentencing, around 70 per cent of respondents thought that sentencing in England and Wales was too lenient, whereas only about 17 per cent believed that the sentences given were about right.[17] When asked further about their views towards sentencing for specific criminal offences such as rape, death by dangerous driving, manslaughter, assault, robbery, and theft, the public continued to feel that sentences were too lenient.[18] The same public sentiments have been found for the United States, Canada, and Australia.[19]

Despite the public's punitive attitudes, politicians' reliance on referring to them as justification for increasingly harsher sentences, such as the implementation of mandatory minimums or the three-strikes laws in the United States, have resulted in what has been coined as 'penal populism'

[15] J. V. Roberts and M. Hough, *Understanding Public Attitudes to Criminal Justice* (Maidenhead, Berkshire: Open University Press, 2005), pp. 70–1.

[16] Ibid. See also F. T. Cullen, B. S. Fisher, and B. K. Applegate, 'Public opinion about punishment and corrections' (2000) 27 *Crime and Justice*, 1–79. Nevertheless, the authors criticise that general polling questions asking respondents on views about sentencing are typically punishment-oriented with no follow-up questions. These polls therefore cannot capture progressive opinions or complex opinions; see pp. 7–8.

[17] Marsh *et al.*, Public Knowledge and Confidence, p. 24.

[18] Ibid., p. 25.

[19] See for example Cullen *et al.*, 'Public opinion about punishment'; G. MacKenzie *et al.*, 'Sentencing and public confidence: results from a national Australian survey on public opinions towards sentencing' (2012) 45 *Australian & New Zealand Journal of Criminology*, 45–65; J. V. Roberts, N. Crutcher, and P. Verbrugge, 'Public attitudes to sentencing in Canada: exploring recent findings' (2007) 49(1) *Canadian Journal of Criminology & Criminal Justice*, 75–108.

or 'popular punitiveness'.[20] These harsh sentencing policies are promoted when politicians attempt to exploit the public's general anxiety towards crime, resentment towards offenders, and general punitive attitudes, as illustrated earlier. In particular, this exploitation occurs when such punitive attitudes are taken only at face value. Consequently, the shift towards harsher sentences is based on perceived public sentiments and not on sentences' overall effectiveness in responding to crime. Roberts and colleagues hence define sentencing policies as populist if 'they are advanced to win votes without much regard for their effects'.[21] In essence, 'penal populism consists of the pursuit of a set of penal policies to win votes rather than to reduce crime rates or to promote justice'.[22]

Yet penal populism is not limited to Western liberal democracies; it can be observed in Asian societies as well.[23] Going beyond Roberts and colleagues, Pratt defines penal populism not just as a way of getting votes, instead contending that '[i]t feeds on expressions of anger, disenchantment and disillusionment with the *criminal justice* establishment. It hold this responsible for what seems to have been the insidious inversion of commonsensical priorities: protecting the well-being and security of law-abiding "ordinary people", punishing those whose crimes jeopardize this'.[24] Penal populism taps into not just public opinion per se, but public feelings, in particular public resentment.

The exploitation of public resentment relates to the finding that the public is generally ill informed about the criminal justice system and lacks knowledge about sentencing. For instance, Hough and Roberts analysed public *attitudes* and *knowledge* of sentencing using data from the 1996 British Crime Survey,[25] exploring a sample of over 8,000 respondents across England and Wales.[26] Once again, most respondents (79 per cent) thought that sentences were too lenient overall. But why

[20] See T. Newburn, '"Tough on crime": penal policy in England and Wales' (2007) 36 *Crime and Justice*, 425–70.

[21] J. V. Roberts, L. J. Stalans, D. Indermaur, and M. Hough, *Penal Populism and Public Opinion: Lessons from Five Countries* (Oxford: Oxford University Press, 2003), p. 5.

[22] Ibid.

[23] See for example J. Pratt and M. Miao, 'Penal populism: the end of reason' (2017) 9 *Nova Criminis*, 71–105.

[24] J. Pratt, *Penal Populism* (Abington, Oxon: Routledge, 2007), p. 12.

[25] Now known as the Crime Survey for England and Wales.

[26] M. Hough and J. V. Roberts, 'Sentencing trends in Britain: public knowledge and public opinion' (1999) 1 *Punishment & Society*, 11–26.

does the public feel that way? One potential reason is that the public is unaware of alternative sentences, namely non-custodial sentences. Only about 35 per cent of respondents in Hough and Robert's study identified probation as a sentencing option.[27] Moreover, multivariate regressions revealed that misconceptions about crime rates, changes in the use of imprisonment, and the proportion of recorded crimes involving violence were factors that affected public attitudes towards sentence leniency.[28] However, when respondents were presented with a real case involving a specific crime and a particular offender, along with a list of sentencing options, the public chose options that were more lenient than the actual sentence handed down by the courts.[29] Hough and Roberts suggested that when responding to generic questions about their views on sentencing, members of the public likely have the worst offenders in mind, recall media reports of lenient sentences, and fail to consider non-custodial sentences,[30] hence leading to the (false) image that the public is punitive.

Furthermore, sentencing research has pointed out that when the public is given more information about sentencing, rather than just general questions about their thoughts on sentences, their responses are more nuanced and less punitive.[31] For example, Applegate and colleagues sampled 400 respondents in the United States about their views on 'three-strikes-and-you're-out laws'[32] in 1995. When asked a general polling question, nearly 90 per cent of respondents supported the implementation of the law. Yet when given a specific case scenario, only a small minority supported imposing a life sentence for the repeat offender in question, with most choosing a prison sentence of 5–15 years instead.[33] Other research also shows that although the public does hold punitive attitudes, they would like to see offenders be both punished and

27 Ibid., 15.
28 Ibid., 18.
29 Ibid., 19.
30 Ibid., 13.
31 This phenomenon illustrates the contrast between measurements of global and specific attitudes. Global attitudes are general views towards a sentencing policy, whereas specific attitudes are particular views expressed when a policy is applied to a case with attributes.
32 'Three-strikes-and-you're-out' laws mandate that a life sentence be imposed for a crime if the defendant has two prior convictions defined as serious or violent.
33 B. K. Applegate, F. T. Cullen, M. G. Turner, and J. L. Sundt, 'Assessing public support for three-strikes-and-you're-out laws: global versus specific attitudes' (1996) 42 *Crime & Delinquency*, 517–34, p. 525.

rehabilitated. In short, both punitive and progressive responses to crime have public support.[34]

Public Attitudes towards Plea Bargaining

Some limited empirical studies on public attitudes towards plea bargaining have been conducted throughout the years. In particular, a dated but widely cited Canadian study by Cohen and Doob found that the public generally disapproves of plea bargaining.[35] The authors administered a public survey to the Canadian public in February 1988. Respondents were given one of five different hypothetical scenarios that portrayed a criminal case. The scenarios depicted: (1) a case resulting in the charge being withdrawn with no plea bargain, (2) a standard plea bargain, (3) a plea bargain with explanation from the defence counsel in open court, (4) a plea bargain taking place in the judge's office, and (5) a plea bargain rejected by the judge. Each scenario was presented to about 200 respondents, yielding 1,049 respondents in total.[36] The survey observed general disapproval towards plea bargaining (almost 70 per cent), with reading the various scenarios doing little to affect this.[37] Moreover, only small differences were observed in attitudes between different demographic groups.[38] However, the authors found a relationship between respondents who felt that sentences were too lenient and their disapproval of plea bargaining, as they perceived plea bargaining to be a way for defendants to receive a lower sentence than what they deserved.[39]

Another study conducted in Israel by Herzog, focusing on the manipulation of crime seriousness, also used hypothetical crime vignettes to assess public opinion towards plea bargaining. A random sample of 606 Israeli adults participated in the study from February to March

[34] Cullen *et al.*, 'Public opinion about punishment'; M. Hough, J. V. Roberts, and J. Jacobson, *Public Attitudes to the Principles of Sentencing* (London: Sentencing Advisory Panel, 2009).

[35] S. Cohen and A. N. Doob, 'Public attitudes to plea bargaining' (1989) 32 *Criminal Law Quarterly*, 85–109.

[36] Ibid., 95. This study defined a plea bargain as 'the practice whereby an accused person agrees to plead guilty on return for the promise of some benefit such as agreement that certain charges be dropped and/or certain recommendations be made to the judge on what the sentence should be'.

[37] Ibid., 96.

[38] Ibid. There was no difference in terms of geographic region, age, gender, education level, income levels, mother tongue, and community size.

[39] Ibid., 97.

2002.[40] Respondents were asked about their subjective evaluations of the seriousness of the crimes depicted in the vignettes, as well as their support for the plea bargain in each case. Herzog found that the two most serious offences, namely murder and rape, were associated with the lowest support for plea bargaining. Conversely, the least serious offence of tax evasion was associated with the highest support for a plea bargain.[41] Even after controlling for other variables, such as the demographic characteristics of respondents, a negative correlation was observed between perceived crime seriousness and public support for plea bargaining.[42]

A subsequent study by Herzog used hypothetical scenarios manipulating greater participation and transparency in the plea-bargaining process to determine whether such factors would elicit greater support for plea bargaining from the Israeli public. He sampled 731 adults in December 2002.[43] In this study, respondents were given three scenarios, each depicting a criminal case and the plea bargain, that manipulated variables relevant to judicial intervention, victim participation, and public disclosure of the prosecutor's considerations.[44] In terms of judicial intervention, certain scenarios had the judge encouraging the parties to reach a plea bargain, while others had the judge acting as an arbitrator. Regarding victim participation, the various options presented to respondents included the victim being informed by the prosecutor of an offer for a plea negotiation, the victim being informed of the details of a finalised plea bargain, and the victim expressing their opinion about the plea bargain to the judge.[45] Herzog discovered that increased participation and transparency in the plea-bargaining process was associated with higher public support for plea bargaining overall.[46] His study suggests that making plea bargaining less covert, as well as expanding its

[40] S. Herzog, 'The relationship between public perceptions of crime seriousness and support for plea-bargaining practices in Israel: a factorial survey approach' (2003) 94 *Criminology*, 103–32.

[41] Ibid., 118.

[42] Ibid., 123.

[43] S. Herzog, 'Plea bargaining practices: less covert, more public support?' (2004) 50 *Crime & Delinquency*, 590–614.

[44] Ibid., 599.

[45] Ibid., 600.

[46] Ibid., 603. This positive association remained significant even after controlling for other variables, including the perceived seriousness of the crime in the scenarios and the respondents' demographic characteristics.

participants to include victims and judges, would help generate public approval of the practice.

In Hong Kong, Cheng has investigated the effects of defendants' personal characteristics on public approval of plea bargaining. His study recruited a random sample of 374 respondents via a telephone survey in July 2014. As in the previous studies, respondents were presented with hypothetical crime scenarios. However, this study differed from others by focusing on manipulations of defendant characteristics, including defendants' gender, age, socioeconomic status, criminal record, and attitudes.[47] The study found greater support for plea bargaining when cases involved elderly defendants over 70 years old compared to the reference group of defendants in their forties. Respondents also expressed more support for plea bargaining for defendants who had a clean criminal record compared to those who had previous criminal convictions, as well as for defendants who displayed remorse. However, they expressed less support for defendants who came from high-income backgrounds.[48] Lastly, regarding variables in the bargaining process itself, the study found less support for fact bargaining compared to sentence bargaining, in addition to greater public support for plea bargains made in the presence of a judge.[49]

Public Attitudes towards Sentence Discounts

In 2011, a research team commissioned by the Sentencing Council for England and Wales conducted a rare study that directly investigated public attitudes towards sentence reductions for guilty pleas.[50] This study

[47] K. K. Cheng, 'Public approval of plea bargaining in Hong Kong: the effects of offender characteristics' (2016) 26 *International Criminal Justice Review*, 31–48.

[48] Ibid., 39–40. These associations remained significant even after controlling for other variables, including the type of crime in the scenarios, as well as the respondents' demographic characteristics and experiences of victimisation.

[49] Ibid., 39.

[50] This study was part of the Sentencing Council for England and Wales' four stages of research for developing their definitive guideline on sentence reductions for guilty pleas. The first stage, discussed here, included a quantitative study of public attitudes towards sentence discounts, as well as qualitative interviews with crime, victims, crime witnesses, and a small sample of defendants. The second stage included qualitative interviews with magistrates and judges that focused on their practices while giving sentence discounts for guilty pleas. The third stage also included qualitative interviews with magistrates and judges, but focused instead on their views regarding sentence guidelines for guilty pleas. The fourth stage included qualitative interviews with defence representatives. See

surveyed 987 members of the public aged 15 and above across England and Wales, collecting data between October and December 2010. The study also conducted qualitative interviews with victims of crime, witnesses, and defendants, focusing less about spontaneously elicited, general attitudes towards sentence discounts for guilty pleas and more about their experiences in their particular cases. Here, this book focuses on discussing the quantitative results.[51]

The survey results revealed that, consistent with other studies, the public in England and Wales had little confidence in the criminal justice system and rarely agreed with sentences imposed by the courts. Only one-quarter of respondents replied that sentences were about right, whereas a majority (65 per cent) thought that sentences were too lenient, and only 3 per cent believed that sentences were too tough.[52] Sentences were thought to not reflect the severity of crimes nor provide enough compensation to victims of crime. The survey also found a positive correlation between respondents' feelings that sentencing is about right and their confidence in the criminal justice system.[53] Regarding sentence discounts for guilty pleas more specifically, while members of the public did not have broad knowledge about sentencing, most were aware of the fact that defendants who plead guilty most likely receive a lower sentence than defendants convicted after trial.[54]

However, the public in England and Wales did not entirely agree with this principle. Twenty-nine per cent of respondents stated that an offender pleading guilty to a criminal offence should never be given a more lenient sentence. Forty-five per cent stated that such an offender should receive a more lenient sentence only in some cases. Only 16 per cent stated that such an offender should receive a more lenient sentence in certain cases, and only a small minority of 5 per cent stated that a more lenient sentence should be given in all cases.[55] Breaking down the data into different demographic groups revealed additional differences in attitudes. Women felt more negatively about offering a more lenient

Sentencing Council, *Research to Support the Development of a Guideline for Reduction in Sentence for a Guilty Plea* (London: Sentencing Council, 2017).

51 W. Dawes, P. Harvey, B. McIntosh, F. Nunney, and A. Phillips, *Attitudes to Guilty Plea Reductions (Sentencing Council Research Series 02/11)* (London: Sentencing Council, 2011).

52 Ibid., p. 13.

53 Ibid.

54 Ibid., p. 16.

55 Ibid., p. 17.

sentence to defendants who pleaded guilty compared to men. On the other hand, people with higher educational attainment of at least the degree level, people who read broadsheet newspapers, and people who were more knowledgeable about sentencing were all more supportive of more lenient sentences for defendants who plead guilty.[56]

Regarding the level of sentence discounts, 20 per cent of respondents replied that the courts should give 'no reduction' even after being told that defendants who plead guilty save the courts' time and resources.[57] Twenty-nine per cent replied that the reduction should be about 10 per cent, while a further 21 per cent stated that the reduction should be about one-quarter. Thus, a majority of 70 per cent of respondents thought that a sentence discount for a guilty plea should be one-quarter at most, or even zero, despite being told its supposedly utilitarian benefits.[58] Only 22 per cent of respondents felt that the level of sentence reductions should be one-third or more.[59] Concerning the timing of guilty pleas, respondents were asked whether a sentence discount should be increased from one-third if the defendant pleads guilty at the earliest opportunity. Fifty-eight per cent of respondents disagreed, while only 22 per cent agreed.[60] Furthermore, the public was mixed about how to scale sentence discounts with respect to the stage when the defendant enters a guilty plea. Forty per cent of respondents strongly or somewhat agreed that defendants who plead guilty at the first opportunity should receive a larger sentence discount, whereas 28 per cent disagreed, and 9 per cent still felt that the courts should give no reduction.[61] Unsurprisingly, the public showed greater support for sentence discounts for minor offences and not for more serious offences, especially where crimes included a strong human element, such as a victim who experienced harm.[62]

The results also revealed an apparent disconnect between what the public thought the courts' rationale for sentence discounts for guilty pleas is and what they felt the rationale should be. Around one-third of

56 Ibid.

57 Ibid., p. 25. The survey question was preceded by a statement stating that offenders who plead guilty save the justice system from the costs of conducting a trial. The question itself then asked the respondent what level of sentence reduction, if any, was appropriate for offenders who plead guilty.

58 Ibid.

59 Ibid. Eight per cent of respondents replied 'don't know' to this question; the proportions of respondents thus do not add up to 100 per cent.

60 Ibid.

61 Ibid., p. 26. Four per cent of respondents replied 'don't know' to this question.

62 Ibid., p. 29.

respondents said that they believed that the courts gave lower sentences to defendants who pleaded guilty to save time, including the court's time and the police's time, and a further one-third of respondents believed that the courts' rationale was to save money in the criminal justice system. Only 2 per cent of respondents felt that sentence discounts were given to spare victims and witnesses from having to testify in court. Nevertheless, 40 per cent of respondents felt that sparing victims and witnesses from giving testimony was a justification that the courts should consider when giving sentence discounts for guilty pleas.[63]

Although the study by Marsh and colleagues for the Sentencing Council did not focus on sentence discounts and guilty pleas, the team also surveyed respondents about the issue and reported results that were consistent with previous findings.[64] Respondents were asked about the relative importance of various sentencing factors that are important for a judge when sentencing, as well as which factors should be important. In both cases, a defendant's guilty plea ranked second last, only ahead of personal circumstances. Other sentencing factors all ranked higher than the defendant's guilty plea included the seriousness of the offence, the harm the defendant caused to the victim, the protection that a sentence would offer the public, what sentence would most likely punish the offender adequately, and what sentence would most likely change the defendant's behaviour.[65] These results show that the public believe judges give greater weight – and should do so – to sentencing principles such as public protection, retribution, and rehabilitation than to guilty pleas.

Yet another demonstration of the English public's attitudes towards sentencing can be found in response to the Ministry of Justice's 2010 green paper *Breaking the Cycle*, which considered a proposal to increasing the sentence reduction for guilty pleas entered at the first opportunity from one-third to up to one-half.[66] Most responses to public consultation on the green paper opposed the proposal, with negative responses raising concerns that such a high reduction would damage the public's confidence in sentencing.[67] Then Prime Minister David Cameron would eventually scrap the proposal in June 2011, saying that

[63] Ibid., p. 23.

[64] Marsh *et al.*, *Public Knowledge and Confidence.*

[65] Ibid., p. 30.

[66] Ministry of Justice, *Breaking the Cycle: Effective Punishment, Rehabilitation and Sentencing of Offenders* (London: HMSO, 2010), p. 63.

[67] J. Beard, *Briefing Paper: Reduction in Sentence for a Guilty Plea (No. 5974)* (London: House of Commons Library, 2017), p. 9.

> In the Green Paper we consulted on a proposal to increase the current discount available for an early guilty plea at the earliest possible stage to 50%. For the most serious crimes we have concluded this would certainly not be right. The sentence served would depart far too much from the sentence handed down by the judge and this is simply not acceptable. We also looked at whether the 50% discount could only be applied to less serious crimes, but again we reached the same conclusion: the sentence would be too lenient, the wrong message would be sent out to the criminal and it would erode public confidence in the system. What's more, in reaching our conclusions we considered the strong views expressed by serious people working in the criminal justice system that 50% was just too high and that we needed to find better ways of speeding up the process for victims and witnesses and for the police and the courts. So there will be no change to the current position on early guilty pleas for any category of case.[68]

Studies from other jurisdictions also found the public to be unsupportive of sentence discounts for guilty pleas. For instance, in Scotland, Black and colleagues submitted a report to the Scottish Sentencing Council about public perceptions of sentencing in the Scottish courts and sentence discounts for guilty pleas, surveying 1,000 Scottish adults by telephone between March and April 2019.[69] They found that 54 per cent of respondents believed that a guilty plea should make no difference in the sentence imposed on the defendant, whereas only 26 per cent felt that a defendant who pleaded guilty should be given a more lenient sentence. Somewhat surprisingly, 17 per cent of respondents said that a defendant who pleaded guilty should be given a tougher sentence.[70] Breaking down the results by age, the study discovered that respondents in the oldest age bracket of 55 years and above were more supportive of more lenient sentences for defendants who plead guilty compared to younger respondents. Within specific age brackets, 33 per cent of respondents aged 55 and above supported more lenient sentences for guilty pleas, compared with only 25 per cent of respondents aged 35–54 and 17 per cent of respondents aged 18–34.[71]

[68] Prime Minister's Office, 'PM's press conference on sentencing reforms', 21 June 2011, available at www.gov.uk/government/speeches/pms-press-conference-on-sentencing-reforms.

[69] C. Black, R. Warren, R. Ormston, and C. Tata, *Public Perceptions of Sentencing by Scottish Courts* (Edinburgh: Scottish Sentencing Council, 2019).

[70] Ibid., p, 16. Three per cent of respondents replied 'don't know' to this question.

[71] Ibid., p. 17.

In a study conducted in Australia, Warner and colleagues investigated public attitudes towards sentence discounts for guilty pleas while focusing particularly on jurors and sex offences.[72] Their study recruited 989 jurors in trials for sex offences and other violent offences between 2014 and 2016, who were surveyed after trial about their views on sentences and sentence discounts for guilty pleas. The study also recruited two groups of non-jurors for the overall sample. Four hundred and fifty respondents were 'unempanelled jurors', members of the public who had responded to jury service but were ultimately not selected to serve on a jury. An additional 306 respondents were recruited through an online survey.[73] Warner and colleagues found that only around 34 per cent of all respondents supported giving the defendant a sentence discount if they had entered a guilty plea. Among the three respondent groups, jurors were the most supportive of a sentence discount for guilty pleas, with 36.5 per cent responding in favour, whereas unempanelled jurors and online survey respondents were less supportive (32 and 25 per cent, respectively).[74] Among respondents in favour of sentence discounts, while nearly all replied that they would reduce the custodial sentence length if the defendant had pleaded guilty, very few would shift from a custodial sentence to a non-custodial one.[75] Offence type also mattered, as the results found less support for a sentence discount for guilty pleas in sex offence cases compared with other violent offences. Unsurprisingly, there was less of an appetite for giving a sentence discount in a sex offence case involving a child than one involving an adult.[76]

In addition, a 2019 review of the sentence discounts for guilty pleas scheme in South Australia found that the public was not supportive of sentence discounts for defendants who plead guilty. The public felt that such a scheme was created for practical reasons to the neglect of victims and their families, the justice system should not be seen as a 'supermarket' where sentences are bargained over, a high sentence discount is 'offensive' to victims and should be capped at 10 per cent, and large sentence discounts for serious offences are detached from public opinion

[72] K. Warner, C. Spiranovic, L. Bartels, L. Roberts, and K. Gelb, 'Juror and community views of the guilty plea sentencing discount: findings from a national Australian study' (2022) 22 *Criminology & Criminal Justice*, 78–96.

[73] Ibid., 6.

[74] Ibid., 7.

[75] Ibid.

[76] Ibid., 9.

and expectations.[77] Consequently, based on the recommendations of the review, the Government of South Australia in 2020 reduced the sentence discounts for serious indictable offences, including manslaughter, causing death by dangerous driving, rape, and unlawful sexual intercourse. The reforms for such offences were as follows:

- Where an early guilty plea is entered within four weeks after the defendant's first court appearance, the maximum sentence discount can only be one-quarter, reduced from 40 per cent.
- Where the guilty plea is entered after the first four weeks of the defendant's first court appearance, but on or before the day of their committal appearance, the maximum sentence discount can only be 15 per cent, half of the previous 30 per cent.
- Where the guilty plea is entered from the day after the committal appearance until the defendant is committed to stand trial, the maximum sentence discount can only be 10 per cent, half of the previous 20 per cent.
- Where the guilty plea is entered between when the defendant has been committed to stand trial and immediately after the first arraignment date, the maximum sentence discount can only be 5 per cent, one-third of the previous 15 per cent.
- Finally, where the guilty plea is entered after the first arraignment date but prior to the start of trial, the maximum sentence discount can only be 5 per cent, half of the previous 10 per cent.[78]

Attorney-General Vickie Chapman stated that the reason for lowering sentence discounts for guilty pleas at different stages was based on the public's negative reactions, explaining that '[c]learly, a 40 per cent reduction was seen as far too lenient, and this new regime should give the community greater faith in the sentences handed down in these serious matters'.[79]

Finally, in Hong Kong, Cheng surveyed a random sample of 818 members of the public by telephone to elicit their views about sentencing and sentence discounts for guilty pleas between April and

[77] B. R. Martin, *Review of the Sentence Reduction Scheme* (Adelaide: South Australia Attorney-General's Department, 2019), p. 31.

[78] South Australia Attorney-General's Department, 'Sentence discount legislation to pass today', 13 October 2020, available at www.agd.sa.gov.au/newsroom/sentence-discount-legislation-pass-today.

[79] Ibid.

June 2017.[80] Respondents were asked whether they thought that the sentences the courts handed down were generally appropriate. Unlike the English public, most respondents in Hong Kong (73 per cent) felt that courts sentences were about right; nearly 20 per cent thought that sentences were too lenient, and very few (about 1.5 per cent) thought that sentences were too tough.[81] When asked about whether defendants pleading guilty should receive a more lenient sentence, 56 per cent of respondents stated that defendants who plead guilty should be given a more lenient sentence only in certain cases. Around one-quarter of respondents said that such defendants should receive lenient sentences in most cases. Conversely, 11 per cent stated that this should never be the case. Lastly, respondents were asked about the level of sentence reduction, if any, appropriate for a defendant who pleads guilty. Thirty-eight per cent stated that the sentence discount should only be about 10 per cent. Thirty-six per cent stated that it should be about one-third, which is consistent with the usual practice of a one-third sentence discount for guilty pleas made at the first opportunity. Nearly 6 per cent of respondents said that the sentence discount should be about half or more than half.

Conclusion

Although sentencing policy should not blindly follow public opinion, it nonetheless serves as an important indicator, especially if the state aims to bolster public confidence in the criminal justice system.[82] Sentencing research has demonstrated that, when asked about sentences generally, the public perceives them as being too lenient. Unsurprisingly, when subsequently asked about plea bargaining or sentence discounts for guilty pleas, the public does not support the notion that defendants who plead guilty should receive a lower sentence than they would otherwise get after trial. The public is especially against large sentence discounts for guilty pleas. However, the justification for the sliding scale of sentence discounts for guilty pleas is that it encourages earlier pleas, thus making the

[80] The results of this survey were previously unpublished until now.

[81] Around 6.4 per cent of respondents did not give a definitive answer to this question.

[82] See J. V. Roberts, 'Clarifying the significance of public opinion for sentencing policy and practice', in J. Ryberg and J. V. Roberts (eds.), *Popular Punishment: On the Normative Significance of Public Opinion* (Oxford: Oxford University Press, 2014), pp. 228–52.

criminal process more efficient, which is ultimately in the public interest. Yet while the public would most likely want an efficient justice system, it also wants other objectives to be met. Studies where the public supports both punitive and progressive responses to crime show that while the public recognises that saving time and resources is a primary rationale for sentence discounts for guilty pleas, they would also like to see that the sentencing regime protects victims and witnesses, as well as that sentences reflect the seriousness of offences.

9

Conclusion

Guilty pleas have become the predominant mode of criminal cases dispositions. While guilty pleas themselves are nothing new, the increased focus on not just *whether* defendants plead guilty but *when* they do so is a recent development. The end goal of the criminal process today is not just a guilty plea, but an *early* guilty plea. This change is most vividly expressed in the implementation of the sliding scale of sentence discounts for guilty pleas. The sliding scale of sentence discounts was introduced based on assumptions that tactical defendants who 'play the system' cause cracked trials, in addition to realising the utilitarian benefits of a more efficient criminal justice system. These assumptions and the sliding scale of sentence discounts originated in England and Wales have since been adopted by other legal jurisdictions such as Hong Kong.

This book challenges such assumptions about tactical defendants that different legal jurisdictions have consistently cross-referenced and made into the predominant narrative about criminal justice. Yet even if defendants want to 'play the system', the criminal process as currently designed makes it difficult to do so, even for experienced defendants.[1] Instead, as this book has argued throughout, the criminal process should not be seen as a process that defendants can easily manipulate; instead, the process itself pushes defendants into pleading guilty. Consequently, the sliding scale of sentence discounts for guilty pleas should not just be taken as an isolated strategy to encourage early guilty pleas, but must be considered as part of the broader criminal process that has become increasingly geared towards guilty pleas as the preferred method of case disposition over the past decades. Other strategies that the process includes to encourage early guilty pleas are advanced sentence indications, explicit communications of sentence discounts by the courts and defence lawyers, the acceptance of plea bargaining – including informal and implicit

[1] See Chapter 4.

forms, and various costs associated with going through the criminal process.[2] The sliding scale of sentence discounts differs from these other strategies in its focus on the timing of guilty pleas as it seeks to promote an *accelerated guilty plea process.*

In a sentencing regime where the timing of guilty pleas plays such a prevailing role, defendants who are considered more vulnerable, such as younger adult defendants and indigent defendants who rely on legal aid, are more likely to plead earlier rather than pleading later or taking their chances at trial. The pressures of going through the criminal process can also impel individuals to enter earlier guilty pleas. Such pressures can come from having already made a confession to the police, or being denied bail and having to serve time in pretrial detention.[3] More importantly, failure to plead guilty and do so earlier may incur a 'trial penalty' or a 'late-plea penalty'.[4] The reality that failure to plead guilty or enter a guilty plea at the first opportunity most likely leads to a more severe punishment is made explicitly clear to defendants by sentencing judges through their consistent adherence to sentencing guidelines for guilty pleas.[5]

Despite disagreement about whether to implement a quantified sliding scale of sentence discounts for guilty pleas, there is agreement across different legal jurisdictions that sentencing discounts should account for the timing of guilty pleas (if one is made), their utilitarian justification of efficiency, and, by extension, the public's interest. However, public opinion seems to suggest otherwise, with the public in several jurisdictions disapproving of large sentence reductions for guilty pleas.[6]

Thinking About Efficiency More Holistically

Of course, this is not to say that the criminal justice system should not pursue efficiency. An inefficient criminal process would cause difficulties for the courts and other legal personnel, be unfair to defendants, and not receive public confidence. As Gormley and Tata acutely observe,

> [It] is important to note that the efficiency argument, properly made, is not necessarily amoral. The justice system runs on public money, and

[2] See Chapter 3.
[3] See Chapter 5.
[4] See Chapter 6.
[5] See Chapter 7.
[6] See Chapter 8.

> there is a moral duty to ensure it is spent wisely. Thus, the efficiency rationale can be made in such a way to provide it with a moral (utilitarian) foundation.[7]

The issue in modern criminal justice is a narrow focus on efficiency as measured by case dispositions. In other words, the criminal process has focused on getting through the daily court list.[8] Brown refers to this as 'production efficiency' in criminal adjudication, that is, 'the production of more criminal court judgments at a lower per-unit cost'.[9] These judgments can refer to those regarding guilty pleas in place of contested trials, or regarding an early guilty plea in place of a cracked trial. Even so, as previously discussed, the introduction of the sliding scale of sentence discounts for guilty pleas has made little difference in terms of overall guilty plea rates, cracked trial rates, and average wait times for trial.

The other supposedly utilitarian benefit of early guilty pleas is cost savings. The assumption is that more defendants pleading earlier leads to a more efficient criminal process, specifically a more cost-efficient criminal process. Moreover, as previously noted, there is a moral duty to look at how the public purse is spent on criminal justice. For instance, in England and Wales, the Sentencing Council conducted a resource assessment of its definitive guidelines on sentence reductions for guilty pleas as they had done for other definitive sentencing guidelines.[10] However, unlike for other offence-specific guidelines, the Council discovered that their sentencing guidelines for guilty pleas affected both defendants' and defence lawyers' behaviours, therefore making it difficult to predict the various factors that would result in a guilty plea.[11] In response to their findings, the Sentencing Council considered two scenarios regarding guilty pleas: an optimistic one and a pessimistic one. The former assumes that more defendants plead guilty at the first stage of proceedings, whereas the latter assumes that more plead guilty at a later stage. In the

[7] C. Tata and J. Gormley, 'To plead or not to plead? "Guilt" is the question: rethinking sentencing and plea-decision making in Anglo American countries', in C. Spohn and P. K. Brennan (eds), *Handbook on Sentencing Policies and Practices in the 21st Century* (New York: Routledge, 2020), p. 20.

[8] For further reading, see K. Mack and S. Roach Anleu, '"Getting through the list": judgecraft and legitimacy in the lower courts' (2007) 16 *Social & Legal Studies*, 341–61.

[9] D. K. Brown, 'The perverse effects of efficiency in criminal process' (2014) 100 *Virginia Law Review*, 183–224, p. 186.

[10] Section 127 of the Coroners and Justice Act 2009.

[11] Sentencing Council, *Final Resource Assessment: Reduction in Sentence for a Guilty Plea* (London: Sentencing Council, 2017), paragraph 3.3.

optimistic scenario, the Council estimated that under the sliding scale of sentence discounts, additional prison places would still be required across England and Wales; in the pessimistic scenario, up to 1,500 additional prison places would be required annually, costing up to £30 million.[12] While the Council cautioned that 'considerable uncertainty around the exact resource implications' remains, they also stressed that additional prison places are likely still required, given that defendants are unlikely to receive a substantial sentence discount if they pleaded guilty late.[13]

The Sentencing Council's assessment underscores the need for looking at the criminal process more holistically. Just as the decision to plead guilty should not be considered in isolation, efficiency in the criminal process should not just be evaluated in terms of the number and length of court hearings. So how can this efficiency be looked at more holistically? From the defendants' perspective, the criminal process should ideally be just and fair, incentivising the defendant to refrain from re-offending. Tata observes, 'The output of a justice system must, by definition, be justice. Therefore, an approach which pits the quality of justice against case-volume throughput cannot be "efficient."'[14]

The vast literature on procedural justice theory offers some valuable insights into achieving such efficiency.[15] Procedural justice theory posits that how individuals perceive their treatment by authorities shapes how legitimate[16] they perceive such authorities to be. Furthermore, a greater sense of legitimacy produces utilitarian benefits, such as an individual's willingness to cooperate with authorities and compliance with the law.[17]

12 Ibid., paragraphs 4.5 and 4.6.

13 Ibid., paragraph 5.2.

14 C. Tata, *Sentencing: A Social Process* (Cham: Palgrave Macmillan, 2020), p. 154.

15 Interest in procedural justice theory has grown since the seminal work of Tyler. See T. Tyler, *Why People Obey the Law* (New Haven, CT: Yale University Press, 1990).

16 Legitimacy refers to 'people's beliefs about the right of justice institutions to hold power and influence'. See J. Jackson, M. Hough, B. Bradford, and J. Kuha, 'Empirical legitimacy as two connected psychological states', in G. Meško and J. Tankebe (eds.), *Trust and Legitimacy in Criminal Justice: European Perspectives* (New York: Springer, 2015), pp. 137–60.

17 See for example K. K. Cheng, 'Legitimacy in a postcolonial legal system: public perception of procedural justice and moral alignment toward the courts in Hong Kong' (2018) 43(1) *Law & Social Inquiry*, 212–28; J. Sunshine and T. Tyler, 'The role of procedural justice and legitimacy in shaping public support for policing' (2003) 37 *Law & Society Review*, 513–47; T. Tyler and J. Jackson, 'Popular legitimacy and the exercise of legal authority: motivating compliance, cooperation, and engagement' (2014) 20 *Psychology, Public Policy, and Law*, 78–95; T. Tyler and Y. J. Huo, *Trust in the Law: Encouraging Public Cooperation with the Police and Courts* (New York: Russell Sage Foundation, 2002).

Research has demonstrated that how fair people perceive their treatment under the court process to be has more influence than the outcome of their case.[18] This perception improves the people's internalisation of rules, norms, and laws,[19] indicating that evaluations of procedural justice are more important to individuals than their satisfaction with sentences.

Procedural justice comprises four key aspects. The first is voice, which refers to individuals being given the opportunity to tell their side of the story and feeling that their perspective has been considered. Evidently, if defendants are constantly being 'encouraged' to plead guilty without adequate consideration of their perspectives, or without the courts even asking why they choose to plead guilty, then their voices are diminished. The second aspect is neutrality, which refers to the notion that judges and other legal authorities make their decisions based on consistently applied rules and not personal opinions. Neutrality is bolstered when rules are transparent and decisions are explained. The opaque and informal nature of plea bargaining thus poses a particular challenge to neutrality. The third aspect is respect, which refers to individuals feeling that they have been treated courteously and politely. More importantly, respect also involves acknowledging individual legal rights. As previously discussed, encouraging guilty pleas and early guilty pleas ebbs important legal rights, such as the presumption of innocence and the right to a fair trial. The fourth aspect is trustworthiness, which refers to the notion that legal authorities are acting in the interests of everyone involved, and not in their personal interests – such as aiming to clear the daily court list as quickly as possible.

It must be emphasised that procedural justice is not just limited to the courts but involves everyone in the criminal process, whose interactions must also be treated holistically. This includes the public's encounters with and perceptions of the police, prosecutors,[20] lawyers, judges, and even court clerks and bailiffs. Procedural justice is also not limited to defendants, as Tyler points out:

> It is equally important to remember that everyone involved with the courts treats their experience as a 'civics lesson' about the legal system. This includes the parties to any case, but also is true for their families,

[18] T. Tyler, 'Procedural justice and the courts' (2007) 44 *Court Review*, 26–31.

[19] J. Fagan and T. Tyler, 'Legal socialization of children and adolescents' (2005) 18 *Social Justice Research*, 217–42.

[20] See K. K. Cheng, 'Prosecutorial procedural justice and public legitimacy in Hong Kong' (2017) 57(1) *British Journal of Criminology*, 94–111.

> friends, and other observers; witnesses; jurors; as well as all of those who hear stories about the courts from their friends, family, neighbors, or coworkers. And, of course, everyone is affected by the stories that appear in the mass media.[21]

However, the criminal process does not have to be long for procedural justice to be properly observed. Even in short encounters, such as street stops by police officers, legal authorities can act in procedurally just ways, leading individuals to feel that they have been treated in a procedurally just manner, as well as improving the authorities' perceived legitimacy.[22] Similarly, in the sentencing stage of the criminal process, the sentencing judge should be mindful of acting in procedurally just ways – explaining their decisions, considering the defendant's voice, and treating even convicted defendants with respect.[23] If the criminal process continues to be defined as a guilty plea process, then it will continue to be perceived as punitive.[24] Conversely, if everyone involved places greater emphasis on procedural justice, the process might become a positive experience and an important 'civic lesson'.

Informed Choice

Instead of solely focusing on reaching a guilty plea as early as possible, the criminal process should be recalibrated to ensure that the plea decision is indeed an informed and voluntary choice by the defendant. The pursuit of obtaining a guilty plea as early as possible means trade-offs in terms of due process, the supervision and scrutiny of pretrial decisions, and an increased risk of innocent defendants pleading guilty. The Supreme Court of New Zealand recognised such dangers in *Hessell* when it rejected a sliding scale of sentence discounts, observing that the

21 Tyler, 'Procedural justice', 30.

22 T. Tyler, J. Fagan, and A. Geller, 'Street stops and police legitimacy: teachable moments in young urban men's legal socialization' (2014) 11 *Journal of Empirical Legal Studies*, 751–85.

23 K. K. Cheng, N. Pushkarna, and R. Sayaka, 'Enhancing the legitimacy of sentences in the minds of the public: evidence from a public opinion survey in Hong Kong' (2020) 22 *Punishment & Society*, 617–36. Indeed, there have even been calls for the plea-bargaining process to adhere to procedural justice. See M. M. O'Hear, 'Plea bargaining and procedural justice' (2007) 42 *Georgia Law Review*, 407–70.

24 M. Feeley, *The Process Is the Punishment: Handling Cases in a Lower Criminal Court* (New York: Russell Sage Foundation, 1979).

pressure to enter a guilty plea in haste would lead to innocent defendants falsely pleading guilty.[25]

Moreover, the idea that defendants know they are guilty and do not require legal advice to make their plea decisions must be changed.[26] An inherent, incorrect belief in the modern criminal justice system is that all defendants are rational individuals who delay their pleas and seek legal advice merely for tactical reasons, such as assessing the strength of evidence against them. However, defendants may not actually know whether they are lawfully guilty of the crime they are charged with. Defendants should be able to assess the strength of evidence and their odds of conviction properly *before* they make a plea decision. This will ensure that their plea decision is an *informed* choice. Regrettably, in the current era focused on the timing of guilty pleas, defendants who do so are frowned upon.

More attention should also be given to different groups of defendants. The results of the current study have shown that young adult defendants are more likely to plead guilty earlier. While this does not necessarily call for establishing a separate justice system for young adults like current juvenile justice systems, at the very least, the current system should distinguish them from older adult defendants. For instance, young adult defendants may require further explanations from their lawyers and the courts to ensure that they fully understand their case and the consequences of any guilty plea decisions. The courts may also assist currently practising legal personnel in addressing the needs of young adult defendants by improving access to specialist training and support staff, or perhaps even legal aid.

Such assistance for young adult defendants should also be provided beyond the plea-decision stage. For instance, specialised staff should be available during police interviews to ensure that young adult suspects understand the consequences of a confession, which influences subsequent plea decisions. This not only ensures that their rights are protected but also helps improve the effectiveness of the criminal justice system. As the United Kingdom House of Commons Judicial Committee report, *The Treatment of Young Adults in the Criminal Justice System*, notes,

> Young adults offend the most but have the most potential to stop offending. They are resource intensive as they are challenging to manage.

[25] *Hessell* v. *R* [2010] NZSC 135 at 60. See also Chapter 2.

[26] *R* v. *Caley and Others* [2012] EWCA Crim 2821; Sentencing Council, *Reduction in Sentence for Guilty Plea: Definitive Guideline* (London: Sentencing Council, 2017), paragraph F1.

> A strong case could be made for recognising that expenditure to make the system more developmentally responsive would pay dividends in reduced costs to the system in reducing incidents of violence and to society in reducing offending and the creation of further victims.[27]

Paying more attention to the needs of young adult defendants throughout the criminal process may very well make the criminal process more efficient by reducing the overall number of young adults offending.

Lastly, the other 'costs' of the criminal process should be minimised. For instance, pretrial detention could be made less prison-like. Instead of detention centres, perhaps quarantine centres used during the COVID-19 pandemic could serve as a viable alternative for defendants who are denied bail. These changes can help to ensure that the guarantee of the defendant's freedom of choice in whether to plead guilty, as set out in *Turner*, is upheld.

Bringing Back the Adversarial Lawyer

As previously discussed, publicly funded lawyers have an image of being guilt presumptive, which has led to defendants not trusting that their legal advocates are truly advocating on their behalf. The extant literature on guilty pleas, especially in the English context, has long pointed to publicly funded defence lawyers as a source of pressure to plead guilty for defendants. Especially in England and Wales, cuts to legal aid and a shortage of criminal duty solicitors have also exacerbated the negative image of publicly funded lawyers.[28] As previously discussed, the professional codes of conduct for English and Hong Kong barristers and solicitors prescribe a duty to communicate sentence discounts for guilty pleas to clients. Given how the criminal process operates, defence lawyers should draw their clients' attention to the significant likelihood that a guilty plea, especially an early guilty plea, leads to a more lenient sentence. The issues lie in the manner of communication and whether it preserves the 'free choice' of the defendant in making their own plea decision. Moreover, defence lawyers have an additional overriding duty to the court to help ensure the efficiency of the criminal process.

[27] House of Commons Justice Committee, *The Treatment of Young Adults in the Criminal Justice System, Seventh Report of Session 2016–17* (London: House of Commons, 2016), paragraph 139.

[28] The Law Society, 'Criminal duty solicitors: a looming crisis' (7 July 2021), available at www.lawsociety.org.uk/campaigns/criminal-justice/criminal-duty-solicitors.

Blake and Ashworth correctly recommend that while the defence lawyer should recognise the structure of a guilty plea process, within this structure they should maximise their client's choice regarding plea decisions without being overly eager to persuade clients to plead guilty.[29] A defence lawyer ought to list out the costs and benefits of the plea decision neutrally. Blake and Ashworth further recommend that professional codes of conduct unequivocally state that it would be unethical for defence lawyers to recommend a guilty plea out of convenience or a desire to foster good working relationships with other legal actors, such as prosecutors or judges.[30] Another related change could be to clarify that the defence lawyer's overriding duty to the court to ensure efficiency does not entail reaching a guilty plea as early as possible, as this is neither in the client's best interests nor the public interest. Rather, efficiency should be defined more holistically – that the criminal process is efficient when it strives for a just outcome, which is in everyone's interests.

Furthermore, bringing back the image of the adversarial lawyer is vital to promoting public confidence in the criminal justice system. Advocacy should be the basis of the criminal process, not guilty pleas. Only by having strong advocates can the criminal justice system flourish. Such strong advocates emerge from experience, specifically from experiences of contesting evidence, examining legal issues, and appearing before court to question witnesses, and not simply from engaging in guilty pleas. In the case of *Crawley*, Sir Brian Leveson stated,

> The criminal justice system . . . requires the highest quality advocates both to prosecute and to defend those accused of crime: in addition, they are the potential judges of the future. The better the advocates, the easier it is to concentrate on the real issues in the case, the more expeditious the hearing and the better the prospect of true verdicts according to the evidence. Poor quality advocates fail to take points of potential significance, or take them badly, leading to confusion and, in turn, appeals and, even more serious, leading to potential miscarriages of justice. We have no doubt that it is critical that there remains a thriving cadre of advocates capable of undertaking all types of publicly funded work, developing their skills from the straightforward work until they are able to undertake the most complex.[31]

[29] M. Blake and A. Ashworth, 'Ethics and the criminal defence lawyer' (2004) 7 *Legal Ethics*, 167–89.

[30] Ibid., 182.

[31] *R* v. *Crawley* [2014] EWCA Crim 1028 at 57.

Returning focus to the adversarial lawyer, especially among publicly funded lawyers, not only bolsters the image of zealous defenders of justice but also ensures the professional development of lawyers, which then leads to better judges and the development of case law. After all, it is through submissions by legal advocates arguing on issues of law that common law continues to develop.

Further Research

The first area for further research is expanding comparative analyses across different legal jurisdictions. The current study only empirically examined two jurisdictions that have adopted a quantified sliding scale of sentence discounts for guilty pleas. Future research could compare findings from jurisdictions such as Scotland and New Zealand that consider the timing of guilty pleas to be important in sentencing, but have not adopted quantified sentence reductions based on the stage in the proceedings when the defendant pleads. If no official databases are available, future studies can adopt a methodology for compiling data similar to that used for creating the Hong Kong District Court dataset, which entails coding court cases and reasons for sentencing. Analyses can then be performed using the timing of guilty pleas as the dependent variable to investigate differences in sentences for defendants who plead guilty and plead not guilty, differences in when they plead guilty, as well as the consistency in how different sentencing judges apply sentence discounts for guilty pleas without strict quantified sentencing guidelines. Such analyses will enable further comparisons between sliding scales of sentence discounts across different jurisdictions and their effects on sentencing.

The second area for further study involves the use of qualitative research. Admittedly, the current study is limited by its greater emphasis on quantitative findings. While this book attempted to review past qualitative studies, future studies can focus more on defendant interviews and observations of defendants going through the criminal process in an era where the timing of guilty pleas is so vital. Moreover, *why* defendants plead guilty and why do they plead guilty *when* they do remain understudied questions. Is the sliding scale of sentence discount the deciding factor in decisions to plead guilty and when to plead guilty? If not, what other factors are more salient? Is it the odds of conviction, or some other extra-legal variables? Interviews and observational studies in future research should also focus on different groups of more vulnerable defendants, including young adults, individuals with metal health issues, and ethnic minorities. Better understandings of the experiences and perceptions of these defendant groups can pave the way for recommendations on how to better protect their rights as they pass through the criminal process. Qualitative data will also help us understand the propensity for false guilty pleas and the extent of innocent defendants pleading guilty.

Likewise, more qualitative studies should be conducted on legal personnel, including defence lawyers, prosecutors, and judges. Regarding defence lawyers, for instance, how does the timing of guilty pleas and the sliding scale of sentence discounts affect their legal advice to clients? Do they face any ethical dilemmas? Are there differences between the experiences of privately retained lawyers and publicly funded lawyers? Regarding judges, it would be useful to understand when and why they may depart from recommended sentencing guidelines for guilty pleas. Conversely, if judges do not make such departures, why do they consistently apply the recommended ranges in accordance with the sliding scale of sentence discounts? Within the recommended ranges for sentence discounts based on guilty plea stage (e.g., 20–25 per cent), how do judges decide upon the exact discount? And how do judges determine whether the defendant has a genuine need for legal advice, or that the defendant is merely delaying their plea in order to assess the strength of the case against them?[32]

The third area for future research is the understudied area of public opinion towards guilty pleas, sentence differentials between defendants who plead guilty and defendants who do not, and sentence differentials between defendants who plead early and defendants who plead late. While various studies have been done on public attitudes towards sentencing and public confidence, little research has addressed the topic of guilty pleas. If early guilty pleas are in the public interest, as many claim them to be, then more research should be devoted to measuring what the public thinks about them. What does the public think about the current sentencing guidelines? How does the sliding scale of sentence discounts for guilty pleas affect public confidence in the criminal justice system? Are there any differences between how the public imposes a sentence based on the timing of guilty pleas compared with professional judges? Hypothetical vignettes can help test this last question.

[32] Sentencing Council, *Reduction in Sentence for Guilty Plea: Definitive Guideline*, paragraph F1.

Concluding Remarks

We need to reconsider how we think about the criminal process. It is time to take a step back and reconsider how we can make the criminal process more efficient in a holistic sense, instead of doubling down on how to expedite the guilty plea process (as the more stringent sliding scale of sentence discounts for guilty pleas does in England and Wales). The early guilty plea as the outcome may not be the ideal outcome that realises all the utilitarian benefits it promises, as it can also very well lead to undesirable outcomes. We also need to reconsider the assumptions that have driven the discourse on cracked trials and late guilty pleas. The field should no longer regard the assumption of a manipulative defendant 'playing the system' through tactical plea decisions as the predominant image of defendants. Indeed, this very image of a cunning defendant playing the system starkly contrasts the image of individuals being presumed innocent until proven guilty beyond a reasonable doubt by a court of law. Here, it is worth quoting remarks made by the Supreme Court of Canada in the seminal case of *Oakes*:

> An individual charged with a criminal offence faces grave social and personal consequences, including potential loss of physical liberty, subjection to social stigma and ostracism from the community, as well as other social, psychological, and economic harms. In light of the gravity of these consequences, the presumption of innocence is crucial. It ensures that until the State proves an accused's guilt beyond all reasonable doubt, he or she is innocent. This is essential in a society committed to fairness and social justice. The presumption of innocence confirms our *faith in humankind*; it reflects our belief that individuals are decent and law-abiding members of the community until proven otherwise.[33] (Emphasis added)

The presumption that cunning defendants 'play the system' goes against the presumption of innocence, which is based on our faith in humankind and our belief that individuals are decent and law-abiding. Anything contrary should be proven and not presumed at the outset.

[33] *R* v. *Oakes* [1986] 1 SCR 103 at paragraph 29.

INDEX

www.ingramcontent.com/pod-product-compliance
Lightning Source LLC
LaVergne TN
LVHW011813200926
848484LV00005B/1176
* 9 7 8 1 0 0 9 1 5 8 6 0 2 *